DB2® For Windows® For Dummies®

Basic SQL Syntax

Note: Words written in uppercase are SQL reserved words (that is, they are actually part of the SQL syntax); the italicized words enclosed in angle brackets (< and >) are examples of table, column, or schema names that you supply.

SELECT * FROM *<schema name>.<table name>*;

Lists all of the rows in a table. The SELECT statement reads data from a database table. The asterisk (*) means that all of the rows are to be returned. The semicolon (;) marks the end of the SQL statement.

SELECT * FROM *<schema name>.<table name>*

ORDER BY *<column name>*;

Lists all of the rows in a table, putting the values in the *<column name>* column in alphabetical order. The ORDER BY clause sorts the rows using a column that you specify to be the sort key. Remember that the table data itself is not sorted; only the rows that are returned by the query are sorted!

SELECT *<schema name>.<table1>.<column1B>*, *<schema name>.<table2>.<column2B>*

FROM *<schema name>.<table1>*, *<schema name>.<table2>*, *<schema name>.<table3>*

WHERE *<schema name>.<table1>.<column1A>* = *<schema name>.<table3>.<column3A>*

AND *<schema name>.<table2>.<column2A>* = *<schema name>.<table3>.<column3B>*

ORDER BY *<schema name>.<table2>.<column2B>*;

Data from three different tables is used to answer the preceding query: The FROM clause references *<table1>*, *<table2>*, and *<table3>* (there could be any number of tables, this is just an example). The WHERE clause defines the search criteria for the query: For the rows that are returned, the value in *<column1A>* from the *<table1>* must match the value in *<column3A>* from *<table3>*, AND the value in *<column2A>* from *<table2>* must match the value in *<column3B>* from *<table3>*.

SELECT *<schema name>.<table1>.<column1A>*, *<schema name>.<table1>.<column1B>*

FROM *<schema name>.<table1>*

WHERE *<schema name>.<table1>.<column1A>* IN

(SELECT *<schema name>n.<table3>.<column3A>* FROM *<schema name>.<table3>*

GROUP BY *<schema name>.<table3>.<column3A>* HAVING COUNT(*) > 1);

The IN predicate compares a value with several other values; in this case, *<column1A>* values must match values from the set of values returned by the subquery (the second SELECT statement in this query). In the subquery, the GROUP BY clause returns the data in groups, or sets of rows, each with identical values in the GROUP BY column; in this example, the GROUP BY column is *<column3A>* in *<table3>*. Here, the subquery is asking for all of the values in *<column3A>* that appear in more than one row of *<table3>*, but the GROUP BY clause ensures that they only appear once in the results set. The condition (more than one appearance in *<table3>*) is specified through the HAVING clause.

For Dummies®: Bestselling Book Series for Beginners

DB2® For Windows® For Dummies®

DB2 Command	What It Does
`db2start`	Starts the default database instance
`db2stop`	Stops the default database instance
`db2icrt`	Creates an instance
`db2idrop`	Drops an instance
db2 create *<database name>*	Creates a database
db2 drop *<database name>*	Drops a database
`db2sampl`	Creates the sample database that is supplied with DB2

Shortcut Command	What It Does
`db2cc`	Launches the Control Center
`db2cca`	Launches the Client Configuration Assistant
`db2cmd`	Launches the DB2 Command window where you can enter in DB2 command and SQL statements
`db`	Can be used for the word "database" in a command
`cfg`	Can be used for the word "configuration" in a command

DB2 Authority	Who It Is
SYSADM	Any user that belongs to the Administrators group on your Windows NT workstation. This user has the authority to perform any DB2 administration operations, access all database objects, and update the Database Manager Configuration parameters
SYSCTRL	Any user that has the authority to perform administration commands but cannot see database objects or update the Database Manager Configuration parameters
SYSMAINT	Any user that has the authority to perform most but not all administration commands on all databases in an instance. This user cannot access database objects nor update the Database Manager Configuration parameters
DBADM	Any user that has the authority to perform most but not all administration commands on a particular database, and can access all database objects for that database

Cheat Sheet $2.95 value. Item 0696-X.
For more information about IDG Books, call 1-800-762-2974.

For Dummies®: Bestselling Book Series for Beginners

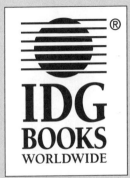

DB2® For Windows®

FOR DUMMIES®

by Paul Zikopoulos, Lily Lugomirski, and Roman B. Melnyk

Foreword by Brett MacIntyre
Director of Database Technology, IBM Canada

IDG Books Worldwide, Inc.
An International Data Group Company

Foster City, CA ◆ Chicago, IL ◆ Indianapolis, IN ◆ New York, NY

DB2® For Windows® For Dummies®

Published by
IDG Books Worldwide, Inc.
An International Data Group Company
919 E. Hillsdale Blvd.
Suite 400
Foster City, CA 94404
www.idgbooks.com (IDG Books Worldwide Web Site)
www.dummies.com (Dummies Press Web Site)

Library of Congress Control Number: 00-103393

ISBN: 0-7645-0696-X

Printed in the United States of America

10 9 8 7 6 5 4 3 2 1

1O/RU/QZ/QQ/IN

Distributed in the United States by IDG Books Worldwide, Inc.

Distributed by CDG Books Canada Inc. for Canada; by Transworld Publishers Limited in the United Kingdom; by IDG Norge Books for Norway; by IDG Sweden Books for Sweden; by IDG Books Australia Publishing Corporation Pty. Ltd. for Australia and New Zealand; by TransQuest Publishers Pte Ltd. for Singapore, Malaysia, Thailand, Indonesia, and Hong Kong; by Gotop Information Inc. for Taiwan; by ICG Muse, Inc. for Japan; by Intersoft for South Africa; by Eyrolles for France; by International Thomson Publishing for Germany, Austria and Switzerland; by Distribuidora Cuspide for Argentina; by LR International for Brazil; by Galileo Libros for Chile; by Ediciones ZETA S.C.R. Ltda. for Peru; by WS Computer Publishing Corporation, Inc., for the Philippines; by Contemporanea de Ediciones for Venezuela; by Express Computer Distributors for the Caribbean and West Indies; by Micronesia Media Distributor, Inc. for Micronesia; by Chips Computadoras S.A. de C.V. for Mexico; by Editorial Norma de Panama S.A. for Panama; by American Bookshops for Finland.

For general information on IDG Books Worldwide's books in the U.S., please call our Consumer Customer Service department at 800-762-2974. For reseller information, including discounts and premium sales, please call our Reseller Customer Service department at 800-434-3422.

For information on where to purchase IDG Books Worldwide's books outside the U.S., please contact our International Sales department at 317-572-3993 or fax 317-572-4002.

For consumer information on foreign language translations, please contact our Customer Service department at 1-800-434-3422, fax 317-572-4002, or e-mail rights@idgbooks.com.

For information on licensing foreign or domestic rights, please phone +1-650-653-7098.

For sales inquiries and special prices for bulk quantities, please contact our Order Services department at 800-434-3422 or write to the address above.

For information on using IDG Books Worldwide's books in the classroom or for ordering examination copies, please contact our Educational Sales department at 800-434-2086 or fax 317-572-4005.

For press review copies, author interviews, or other publicity information, please contact our Public Relations department at 650-653-7000 or fax 650-653-7500.

For authorization to photocopy items for corporate, personal, or educational use, please contact Copyright Clearance Center, 222 Rosewood Drive, Danvers, MA 01923, or fax 978-750-4470.

About the Authors

Paul Zikopoulos is a Database Specialist at IBM with more than five years experience with DB2, and has written numerous magazine articles and books about DB2. Paul is a DB2 Certified Advanced Technical Expert (DRDAb and Cluster/EEE) and a DB2 Certified Solutions Expert (Business Intelligence and Database Administration). You can reach him at paulz_ibm@yahoo.com.

Lily Lugomirski is a member of the DB2 development team at the IBM Toronto Laboratory. She currently provides technical support for the worldwide community of DB2 UDB users. This support includes system testing, problem determination, performance tuning, data recovery, and migration plans. In her support role, Lily has traveled extensively to visit DB2 customers and to speak at DB2 UDB Technical Conferences. You can reach her at llugomirski@yahoo.com

Roman B. Melnyk, PhD, is a senior member of the DB2 Information Development team, specializing in database administration and DB2 utilities. During more than five years at IBM, Roman has written numerous DB2 books and other related materials. You can reach him at roman_b_melnyk@hotmail.com.

ABOUT IDG BOOKS WORLDWIDE

Welcome to the world of IDG Books Worldwide.

IDG Books Worldwide, Inc., is a subsidiary of International Data Group, the world's largest publisher of computer-related information and the leading global provider of information services on information technology. IDG was founded more than 30 years ago by Patrick J. McGovern and now employs more than 9,000 people worldwide. IDG publishes more than 290 computer publications in over 75 countries. More than 90 million people read one or more IDG publications each month.

Launched in 1990, IDG Books Worldwide is today the #1 publisher of best-selling computer books in the United States. We are proud to have received eight awards from the Computer Press Association in recognition of editorial excellence and three from Computer Currents' First Annual Readers' Choice Awards. Our best-selling *...For Dummies®* series has more than 50 million copies in print with translations in 31 languages. IDG Books Worldwide, through a joint venture with IDG's Hi-Tech Beijing, became the first U.S. publisher to publish a computer book in the People's Republic of China. In record time, IDG Books Worldwide has become the first choice for millions of readers around the world who want to learn how to better manage their businesses.

Our mission is simple: Every one of our books is designed to bring extra value and skill-building instructions to the reader. Our books are written by experts who understand and care about our readers. The knowledge base of our editorial staff comes from years of experience in publishing, education, and journalism — experience we use to produce books to carry us into the new millennium. In short, we care about books, so we attract the best people. We devote special attention to details such as audience, interior design, use of icons, and illustrations. And because we use an efficient process of authoring, editing, and desktop publishing our books electronically, we can spend more time ensuring superior content and less time on the technicalities of making books.

You can count on our commitment to deliver high-quality books at competitive prices on topics you want to read about. At IDG Books Worldwide, we continue in the IDG tradition of delivering quality for more than 30 years. You'll find no better book on a subject than one from IDG Books Worldwide.

John Kilcullen
Chairman and CEO
IDG Books Worldwide, Inc.

Eighth Annual Computer Press Awards 1992

Ninth Annual Computer Press Awards 1993

X
WINNER

Tenth Annual Computer Press Awards 1994

Eleventh Annual Computer Press Awards 1995

IDG is the world's leading IT media, research and exposition company. Founded in 1964, IDG had 1997 revenues of $2.05 billion and has more than 9,000 employees worldwide. IDG offers the widest range of media options that reach IT buyers in 75 countries representing 95% of worldwide IT spending. IDG's diverse product and services portfolio spans six key areas including print publishing, online publishing, expositions and conferences, market research, education and training, and global marketing services. More than 90 million people read one or more of IDG's 290 magazines and newspapers, including IDG's leading global brands — Computerworld, PC World, Network World, Macworld and the Channel World family of publications. IDG Books Worldwide is one of the fastest-growing computer book publishers in the world, with more than 700 titles in 36 languages. The "...For Dummies®" series alone has more than 50 million copies in print. IDG offers online users the largest network of technology-specific Web sites around the world through IDG.net (http://www.idg.net), which comprises more than 225 targeted Web sites in 55 countries worldwide. International Data Corporation (IDC) is the world's largest provider of information technology data, analysis and consulting, with research centers in over 41 countries and more than 400 research analysts worldwide. IDG World Expo is a leading producer of more than 168 globally branded conferences and expositions in 35 countries including E3 (Electronic Entertainment Expo), Macworld Expo, ComNet, Windows World Expo, ICE (Internet Commerce Expo), Agenda, DEMO, and Spotlight. IDG's training subsidiary, ExecuTrain, is the world's largest computer training company, with more than 230 locations worldwide and 785 training courses. IDG Marketing Services helps industry-leading IT companies build international brand recognition by developing global integrated marketing programs via IDG's print, online and exposition products worldwide. Further information about the company can be found at www.idg.com.

1/26/00

Dedications

Paul Zikopoulos: This book is dedicated to the memory of Dennis Kritzer, a teacher at Moira Secondary School in Belleville Ontario, Canada. Mr. Kritzer was the kind of person for whom the 4:00 bell never rang so long as a kid was willing to learn. I have fond memories of Dennis, his son Andrew, and myself peeking and poking at a serial port on a Commodore 64 to get it to control a robotic arm that we built. I should have known then that I was doomed to this life of computer-geekdom. Unfortunately, Dennis suddenly passed away three years ago and I never got a chance to personally tell Mr. Kritzer how much of an influence he had on me and my life and how much respect I have for him. Thanks, Mr. Kritzer.

Lily Lugomirski: I would like to dedicate this book to my mother, father, and my brother Peter.

Roman B. Melnyk: For Professor Joseph Shortt, a most remarkable teacher, who long ago ignited my interest in relational database technology. The spark is still burning, Joe!

Authors' Acknowledgements

Before you start to write a book, you sit back and reflect on how you got to this position. Though hard work and dedication are two factors, I didn't get here alone. Professionally, I want to thank Sheila Richardson and Carole McClendon for their support of this project. Without them, this project may not have finished as the book in your hands. Thanks also to Ray Saunders for helping us get through the maze of contracts.

From IDG Books, Greg Croy and James Russell are terrific to work with and I want to thank them for believing in my idea and their help overcoming the hurdles.

Within IBM, I cannot thank the following people enough for helping me along the way: Chris Eaton, Jay Lennox, Kelly Schlamb, Jerome Colaco, Pamela Burnside, Susan Williams, Karl Rempel, Emad Boctor, Blair Adamache, Andrew Hilden, Juliana Hsu, Peter Kohlman, Scott Bailey, and Keri Romanufa. Oh yeah, and thanks to Roman and Lily for helping turn this idea into a book!

I would not have even been able to achieve the goal of writing this book without certain people in my life. I want to thank my mother and father for instilling in me the value of endless learning and a thirst for knowledge (by the way, I think that it's about quenched after this — at least for now). I wish that every kid had such dedicated parents, I love you both.

There are many fine educators that have had a huge affect on me, my choices, and my life. I have never taken the time to let them know. I would like to thank the following for being such great teachers: Dr. Bill Jacobs (not a great teacher of golf however), Dave Snedden, Claude Cairns, Harold Hildebrant, Ralph Gorcy, and Louise McKenzie. I would *especially* like to thank John Boultpee, Steven Wise, Ken Smith, and Arnold Frenzel — you have affected me in ways that you will never know. I wonder if other students are lucky enough to get teachers like this?

Finally, thanks to my fiancée Kelly, for calling me at 3:30 a.m. on a weeknight to remind me that it's okay to sleep five hours before going to work the next morning! You're the greatest!

There wasn't enough room to thank everyone, so if I missed you, I will get you in the next book! — *Paul Zikopoulos*

I would like to thank my wonderful mother who is a constant inspiration in all aspects of life. A special thanks to my brother Peter who brings constant joy and laughter into my days.

There are many good friends that I must also thank for being understanding when I had to cancel plans in order to work late nights and weekends on this book. Thanks — I owe you one!

I would also like to thank the following people for their time and patience through this project and always: Steve Raspudic, Rohan Omrow and Doug Doole. — *Lily Lugomirski*

Many thanks to my wife, Teresa, and to my children, Rosemary and Joanna, for their wonderful support, and for not minding the many lost evenings and weekends during the preparation of this book.

Thanks also to Miro Flasza and Kelly Rodger at IBM for carefully reviewing my chapters. — *Roman B. Melnyk*

Publisher's Acknowledgments

We're proud of this book; please register your comments through our IDG Books Worldwide Online Registration Form located at `http://my2cents.dummies.com`.

Some of the people who helped bring this book to market include the following:

Acquisitions, Editorial, and Media Development

Project Editor: James Russell, Pat O'Brien

Acquisitions Editor: Greg Croy

Copy Editor: Jeremy Zucker, Tim Borek

Proof Editor: Teresa Artman

Technical Editor: Robert Stanley

Permissions Editor: Carmen Krikorian

Associate Media Development Specialist: Megan Decraene

Editorial Manager: Kyle Looper

Media Development Manager: Heather Heath Dismore, Laura Carpenter

Editorial Assistant: Sarah Shupert

Production

Project Coordinator: Emily Wichlinski

Layout and Graphics: Amy Adrain, Karl Brandt Barry Offringa, Kristin Pickett, Jill Piscitelli, Jacque Schneider

Proofreaders: Corey Bowen, Charles Spencer, York Production Services, Inc.

Indexer: York Production Services, Inc.

Special Help

IBM Corp.

General and Administrative

IDG Books Worldwide, Inc.: John Kilcullen, CEO

IDG Books Technology Publishing Group: Richard Swadley, Senior Vice President and Publisher; Walter R. Bruce III, Vice President and Publisher; Joseph Wikert, Vice President and Publisher; Mary Bednarek, Vice President and Director, Product Development; Andy Cummings, Publishing Director, General User Group; Mary C. Corder, Editorial Director; Barry Pruett, Publishing Director

IDG Books Consumer Publishing Group: Roland Elgey, Senior Vice President and Publisher; Kathleen A. Welton, Vice President and Publisher; Kevin Thornton, Acquisitions Manager; Kristin A. Cocks, Editorial Director

IDG Books Internet Publishing Group: Brenda McLaughlin, Senior Vice President and Publisher; Sofia Marchant, Online Marketing Manager

IDG Books Production for Branded Press: Debbie Stailey, Director of Production; Cindy L. Phipps, Manager of Project Coordination, Production Proofreading, and Indexing; Tony Augsburger, Manager of Prepress, Reprints, and Systems; Shelley Lea, Supervisor of Graphics and Design; Debbie J. Gates, Production Systems Specialist; Steve Arany, Associate Automation Supervisor; Robert Springer, Supervisor of Proofreading; Trudy Coler, Page Layout Manager; Kathie Schutte, Senior Page Layout Supervisor; Janet Seib, Associate Page Layout Supervisor; Michael Sullivan, Production Supervisor

Packaging and Book Design: Patty Page, Manager, Promotions Marketing

◆

The publisher would like to give special thanks to Patrick J. McGovern, without whom this book would not have been possible.

◆

Contents at a Glance

Cartoons at a Glance

By Rich Tennant

The 5th Wave
By Rich Tennant

"TELL THE BOSS HE'S GOT MORE FLAME MAIL FROM YOU-KNOW-WHO."

page 271

The 5th Wave
By Rich Tennant
SETTING UP AN INTRANET HAS REALLY HELPED OUR BUSINESS.
MUSTARD
HOT DOGS
RELISH
BUNS

page 47

The 5th Wave
By Rich Tennant
Bill and Irwin discover The Land of Lost Files
MY GOD! THIS IS A BUDGET AND ANALYSIS REPORT FOR THE MARKETING DEPT. OF A FORTUNE 500 COMPANY. MUST HAVE KILLED THE POOR FOOL TO LOSE THIS.

page 191

The 5th Wave
By Rich Tennant

"WELL, SHOOT! THIS EGGPLANT CHART IS JUST AS CONFUSING AS THE BUTTERNUT SQUASH CHART AND THE GOURD CHART. CAN'T YOU JUST MAKE A PIE CHART LIKE EVERYONE ELSE?"

page 103

The 5th Wave
By Rich Tennant
IT'S REALLY QUITE SIMPLE. WITH THE REVISED MAINFRAME PRICING POLICY, YOU'LL BE CHARGED ONE-QUARTER OF THE PREVIOUS PRICE PER CPU BASED ON A 3-TIERED SITE LICENSING AGREEMENT FOR UP TO 12 USERS, AFTER WHICH A 5-TIERED SYSTEM IS EMPLOYED FOR UP TO 64 USERS WITHIN THE ORIGINAL 4-TIERED SYSTEM FOR NEW CUSTOMERS USING OLD SOFTWARE OR OLD CUSTOMERS USING NEW SOFTWARE ON EACH OF THREE CPUs RUNNING A NEW OLD OPERATING SYSTEMS SITE LICENSED UNDER THE OLD NEW AGREEMENT BUT ONLY ON THURSDAYS WITH LESS THAN 10 PEOPLE IN THE ROOM,...

page 7

Fax: 978-546-7747

E-mail: richtennant@the5thwave.com

World Wide Web: www.the5thwave.com

Table of Contents

Letter from Brett MacIntyre, Director of Database Technology

Relational database technology was invented at IBM Research over two decades ago, and IBM delivered the first commercially available relational database, DB2, in the early 1980s. The power and promise of relational technology was the ability to represent data in a simple tabular form, access it through the powerful SQL query language, and put it in the hands of business analysts and other decision makers. Over the last twenty years, many businesses have realized this promise. Today, tens of thousands of businesses all over the world, large and small, rely on DB2 databases to store their key corporate data assets and run their business both traditionally and over the Web.

As companies move into an Internet age of broadband communications, databases must be able to store and serve huge multimedia files, manage ever-increasing volumes of data, handle the tremendous growth in the number of users, deliver steadily improved performance, and support the next generation of applications. With its virtually unlimited ability to scale, its multimedia extensibility, its industry-leading performance and reliability, and its platform openness, DB2 Universal Database has helped lead this evolution. DB2 Universal Database is the first multimedia, Web-ready relational database management system strong enough to meet the demands of large corporations and flexible enough to serve medium-sized and small businesses.

DB2 For Windows For Dummies was written to allow you to harness the power of DB2. It introduces the concept of relational databases and DB2's implementation of the relational model. It looks at the features and functions of the database — the rich and strong SQL, the powerful administration tools, the easy-to-use replication and data handling facilities. *DB2 For Windows For Dummies* provides valuable, hands-on information about how to install and set up DB2, and how to perform common administration tasks such as creating tables and analyzing performance. Finally it concludes with a wealth of hints and tips that will enhance your experience with DB2.

The next millennium will bring tremendous opportunity and challenge to database professionals charged with the task of database administration and database application development. There is a growing demand for skilled people who can deal with the ever-increasing requirements for DB2 in modern business applications. *DB2 For Windows For Dummies* will help you develop these skills.

Introduction

You have a personal goal, to become your office's top geek. So you scramble around trying to figure out ways to impress your boss. You come across some impressive-looking DB2 documentation on a coworker's desk.

"What's DB2?" you ask, feeling not just a little timid.

"It's a RDBMS," your coworker answers cryptically. Seeing the dumb look on your face (you know, it's the same one that gripped your face during that economics test back in college), the coworker elaborates: "It stands for Relational Database Management System — it's the thing that *runs* our business," in a not-quite condescending tone.

"Is it better than DB1?" you respond. Your coworker looks at you and starts laughing raucously, and you walk away blushing furiously and making it your new personal goal to become the all-knowledgeable DB2 geek. Well, if you're a new or intermediate user to DB2, you've come to the right place! Oh, one more thing, there's no such thing as an all-knowledgeable DB2 person. Every time you think you are that person, you meet someone that makes you realize you're not. So enjoy the journey!

About This Book

This book introduces you to the basics of DB2, how it works, and what you can use it for. This book gives you a good start on what we call "DB2-speak," which has been developed over the years by the geekiest of geeks, so that you can talk DB2 at water coolers around the globe, all from the people at IBM that live, breathe, and sweat DB2.

Who Should Read This Book

Everyone should read this book! Okay, so that's a little extreme — this book just doesn't have the same readability value as, say, *War and Peace.* But if you've never heard of DB2 before and you want to check it out and not be bombarded with condescending tones and text so thick you need to be a math professor to sort through it then this book is for you. If you've used other databases (like Oracle or SQL Server) and want to learn about DB2, you should read this book. Did we mention that if you're in pursuit of eternal happiness that you should read this book?

Note that, while DB2 is pretty much the same regardless of the platform you're running it on, this book comes with a 60-day trial version of DB2 for Windows NT 4.0 (with Service Pack 3 or higher installed; Windows 2000 also works) and so that platform is the focus of this book. If you're using DB2 for Linux or another platform, Parts I and II won't do you an awful lot of good, although most of Parts III and IV are pretty much universal when it comes to DB2 (except for Chapter 7 and parts of Chapter 9).

Conventions Used in This Book

Now, we know your first thought when we say "conventions" is of hordes of people getting together in a big hotel and chattering about something that (presumably) interests the whole slew of them. So, to clear this up right away, there are no geeky DB2 conventions lurking within the pages of this book (lucky for you!). What we mean by conventions in this case is to clue you in to how we do things with the text in this book to make your life easier.

Putting stuff in bold

For example, when we want you to type something, we'll say "type **this**" and put the text that we want you to type in **bold** font so that you know you exactly what you have to type. Note that we also put steps in numbered lists in bold, and if the step tells you to type something then in that case the word that you type in won't be bold so that it stands out from the rest of the step. For example:

9. **Type** greeneggsandham **at the command prompt and press Enter.**

Code and monofont

For commands, filenames, directory names, URLs, and text that appears onscreen (such as the results of entering a command at a command prompt), we use what *For Dummies* editors call `monofont` to set it apart from other text, which we think makes this stuff easier to find for you. For example, if we tell you to go to `www.ibm.com`, that URL is in monofont. If we refer to the `set` command, the command is in monofont, and so on. When monofont stuff (again, code, URLs, and so on) appear on their own line, they look like the following command:

```
db2set DB2INSTDEF=<instance_name>
```

Generic commands (this is important!)

When we show you a command (this book has a lot of SQL commands, for example) we put it in what we call "generic" form. Now, this doesn't mean that the command is cheaper than the name brand and infinitely more stale, it means that we write our commands such that you can easily identify those parts of the command you have to replace and what you have to replace them with. To do this, we use italics within angle brackets in commands to indicate that you should replace whatever the command requires for the angle brackets and the italic text within. Confused? Don't be. Here's an example:

If we give you the following command:

```
set DB2INSTANCE=<instance name>
```

that means you need to replace <*instance name*> with the name of the instance that you want DB2 to set as your system's default instance. Don't worry about instances and all that jargon for now, just know that when you typed in the command, you would replace the <*instance name*> with an instance name. For example, in this case you may type in **set DB2INSTANCE=DB2TEST** if DB2TEST was the name of the instance you wanted set. Remember: Do not type in the angle brackets! They're just to clue you in that what's between them needs to be replaced, they aren't a part of the command.

Keystrokes and command arrows

When you see us tell you things such as "press Ctrl+Alt+Del" that means we want you to press the Ctrl, Alt, and Del keys at the same time. If you see a menu path with arrows in the middle of it, where we tell you to "click the Start button and choose Programs⇨Accessories⇨Notepad" or something like that with funny arrows in between, we mean that you should click the Start button with your mouse pointer and then choose the Programs menu, the Accessories menu, and then the Notepad item. Basically we use shortcuts such as these to keep the book heavy on content rather than endlessly repeating how to do simple things like choose a menu path or press keys simultaneously, and that should make you (and your pocketbook) quite happy.

Foolish Assumptions

Much as we know the whole "ass you me" bit (har de har, har), we have to assume a few things about you so that the content of this book can focus on the topic at hand: DB2. So, following are the assumptions that we make about you:

- You have a Pentium-class computer running Windows NT 4.0 with Service Pack 3 or later, or Windows 2000 (see the CD Appendix for more info on hardware requirements).
- You know how to use Windows. For example, when we say "click the Start button" you know that we're referring to the Start button on your taskbar and not the Start button on your VCR.
- You know what the Windows command prompt is and how to open it (by clicking the Start button and choosing Programs⇨Command Prompt.
- You know what a database is, at least vaguely.
- You want to check out DB2. If this last isn't true, we hope you didn't pay money for this book!
- You don't want to become a DB2 guru, at least not yet.

How This Book is Organized

Knowing how this book is organized will help you work through the book more efficiently, and enable you to jump directly to parts that interest you the most. We broke this book down into five parts, each of which we describe briefly in the following five sections.

Part I: Getting to Know DB2

If you're new to DB2 you should probably check out this part; this is where we get into the basics of DB2 introducing the software, packaging options, and the different things you can do with DB2. We also give you some basic database concepts and other technical goodies, and show you how to design your first database!

Part II: Installing and Setting Up DB2

Enough of the theory. Here you get some hands-on experience with DB2 by first installing a DB2 server and then a DB2 client to make that server useful! Then of course we show you how to get your DB2 client to talk to your DB2 server. You also get a sneak preview at the DB2 graphical tools and see how to create the oh-so-creatively titled SAMPLE database.

Part III: Working with DB2

This part introduces you to the major components of DB2, including information on how to create and manage DB2 instances, the heart of a DB2 database, as well as how to create a database from scratch. We also describe the concept of table spaces and how they can be used to store and retrieve data more efficiently, we show you how to create the actual tables that are going to hold your data, and then we finish up describing some other odds and ends, such as indexes, buffer pools, views, and schemas.

Part IV: DB2 Tasks That Every Good Geek (err . . . Administrator) Should Know

The day to day operations of a DB2 administrator that are key to getting the job done. Obviously you need to put data into your database, and at some point you may need to take data from a DB2 database and put it somewhere else. We also discuss some real nastiness, such Murphy's law and its potential effects on your DB2 enterprise, and some backup and restore capabilities to DB2. We also spend some time discussing data replication when you want to keep things in sync and about performance and how to make DB2 run faster (exercise won't work by the way), and then finish up with some helpful troubleshooting tips.

Part V: The Part of Tens

Last, but certainly not least, is this *For Dummies* prerequisite. A *Dummies* book just isn't a book without the Part of Tens! This part of the book has five short chapters chock-full of useful information or pointers to more information about DB2, including some important terms, tips, and common mistakes, and some places to find out more info about DB2.

What You're Not to Read

The cool thing about *For Dummies* titles is that they filter out nonsense that the average user doesn't want to know. Sometimes, though, we include some of this information if we think you may in fact find it useful or interesting, but when we do so we call it out obviously. Basically, sidebars in this book are extra info you don't need but may want to check out — it's up to you. Feel free to skip them; you won't hurt our feelings.

Also, the Technical Stuff icons (you can see what the icon looks like in the next section) calls out information only the geekiest of the geeky may want to know. Again, if this isn't you, feel free to avoid info under these icons like the plague.

Icons in This Book

Various eye-catching icons with bombs, geeky cartoon characters, bull's eyes, and so on appear throughout this book, but they're not just for show, they actually help you find certain types of important (or avoid not-so-important) info. You can see and read the descriptions of them below:

This icon represents something that can really help you get things done or avoid hassles. Remember these, you can share them with your friends and make it look like you knew what were you doing all along!

This icon warns you about things you may not like if you don't follow the instructions in this book. Don't skip over these — they're here because we fell for this stuff, or see other people fall into these traps all the time, and we want you to avoid them.

See that geek in the circle? Well, he really likes the ins and outs of everything. That guy wants to know it all, even when it's more information than he needs to know. If you look in the mirror, and you resemble this guy, read these sections. This stuff isn't crucial, but it may help you out in the future.

If you see this icon, read the text next to it twice. We use this icon to drive home a key point or to remind you of something that you may have been exposed to elsewhere in the book, and need to remember it again now.

Part I

Getting to Know DB2

The 5th Wave **By Rich Tennant**

©RICHTENNANT
IT'S REALLY QUITE SIMPLE. WITH THE REVISED MAINFRAME PRICING POLICY, YOU'LL BE CHARGED ONE-QUARTER OF THE PREVIOUS PRICE PER CPU BASED ON A 3-TIERED SITE LICENSING AGREEMENT FOR UP TO 12 USERS, AFTER WHICH A 5-TIERED SYSTEM IS EMPLOYED FOR UP TO 64 USERS WITHIN THE ORIGINAL 4-TIERED SYSTEM FOR NEW CUSTOMERS USING OLD SOFTWARE OR OLD CUSTOMERS USING NEW SOFTWARE ON EACH OF THREE CPUs RUNNING A NEW OLD OPERATING SYSTEMS SITE LICENSED UNDER THE OLD NEW AGREEMENT BUT ONLY ON THURSDAYS WITH LESS THAN 10 PEOPLE IN THE ROOM,...

In this part . . .

In this first part you pretty much sign up to become fluent in DB2-speak, learn to wear four-inch pop-bottle glasses and to secretly carry a pocket protector, and to just generally be the envy of friends and colleagues alike. Well, that's a *little* extreme, really the main purpose of this part is to introduce you to DB2; as in: "Hey user, this is your friend DB2; DB2, this is a user." (Don't worry, DB2 has met lots of users around the world.) Database theory isn't exactly the most exciting thing in the world, but it is important to understand if you're going to use DB2, so we packed it all into one part. You can also see what you can do with DB2, and here also we briefly touch on the technical ins-and-outs of DB2, including instances, data types, authorities, and other stuff you probably never knew existed (or cared), and finally you can check out the basics of database design.

Chapter 1

Introducing DB2

In This Chapter

- Getting going with DB2
- Administering databases made easy
- Checking out DB2 version 6.1 enhancements
- Introducing the DB2 product family

Say the following out loud (if no one's around to glare at you, that is): "DB2 Universal Database version 6.1 Workgroup Edition for Windows NT." A bit of a mouthful, no? Lucky for you, most people just call it DB2 UDB, or just DB2. Now that you know how to say it, you're probably wondering what exactly this DB2 thing is good for. Good question! Well, the short answer is that DB2 is a database creation and management product that lets you store large amounts of data, retrieve it with speed and ease, and look at data in many different ways by slicing and dicing your data to fit your needs!

This chapter introduces you to the wonderful world of DB2 and gets you up to speed on all the different flavors of DB2 that you may see or hear about. We also briefly introduce you to the cool graphical tools that come with DB2, just so you know what they do and how they look. We discuss these tools in greater detail later in the book.

Getting a Grip on DB2

As the full name of DB2 is "DB2 Universal Database," you may see this and think to yourself, "What's so universal about DB2?" Well, the answer is that DB2 has:

- **Universal access:** Access database information from different platforms in the same way.
- **Universal management:** Manage your database with the same set of administration tools, no matter what platform you are on.

- **Universal scalability:** Scale the size and performance of your database no matter what platform you are using.
- **Universal application interface:** DB2 uses the same APIs and SQL to retrieve information from the database no matter what platform you are using.

Also, it's important to know that all the DB2 products on the different platforms share the majority of their design and architecture. Over 90 percent of the code that makes up DB2 is common to all platforms and packages, meaning that the function and commands are the same regardless of the machine on which you install DB2.

The 10 percent of the code that is not common to all platforms is used to leverage more performance from each particular platform. So, for example, in the case of Windows NT/2000, DB2 uses threads to provide excellent performance. Also, there is specific Windows code there to take advantage of the Windows security implementation, the operating system services, and the Windows performance monitor.

This book focuses on the Windows NT/2000 version of DB2. If you have DB2 for another platform, you can still get some use out of this book, but then again some of it (such as the installation procedure) is utterly useless to you.

Integrating with Windows

The beauty of this version of DB2 for Windows is that it not only supports the Windows NT/2000 native thread model and NTFS native file system, but was developed to be integrated with NT/2000. Here are some cool ways that DB2 integrates with Windows:

- DB2 diagnostic messages are written to the Windows Event Log, for easy one stop shopping for event viewing.
- DB2 participates in the Windows Software Registry.
- DB2 is integrated with Windows NT/2000 domain security, allowing for a secure single logon environment: you log on to one place securely and have only one password to remember! DB2 also supports trusted relationships between domains, and works with a backup domain controller in place.

Scaling your system with DB2

One of DB2's greatest design features is its incredible potential for scalability on any platform, allowing your database and number of users to grow at the same rate as your throughput — no matter the rate. As your data storage requirements grow and more users are added to the system, you can continue to manage the database with the same tools and commands, but still increase your throughput and speed up the queries.

Whether you are running DB2 on mobile devices (for example, a Palm Pilot), a small laptop, a desktop PC, or on a large server or a cluster of servers, DB2 is able to handle growth in data and take advantage of the extra processing power. If you are using a PC with multiple processors, your transactions can use all the processors in the computer to perform the work at the same time! You can also move your data to a cluster of Windows NT/2000 machines that are networked together, again letting DB2 divide your transactions and run them simultaneously to make it faster.

Making Administration Easy with DB2

The administration tools that come with DB2 can make you look good in front of the big bosses. Picture this — no fancy DB2 commands to remember, no figuring out what types of indexes to create and no techie mumbo jumbo . . . just a simple set of graphical panels that lead you through what you need to get done.

The graphical tools that come with DB2 are based in the Control Center, which is shown in Figure 1-1. You can use the Control Center to manage databases and all the other goodies that make up a database, including tables, views, indexes and so on. This is all you ever need for the day-to-day tasks of administrating DB2. You may even want to call it the Mission Control Center!

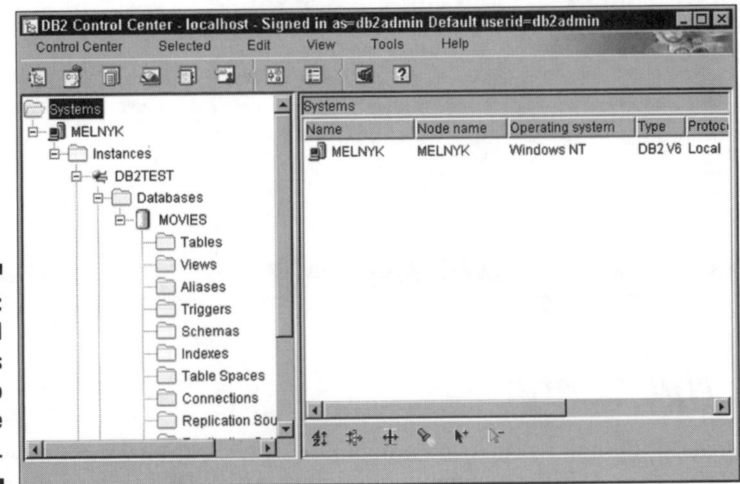

Figure 1-1: The Control Center is used to manage databases.

If the Control Center doesn't provide you with everything you need, you can extend its functions. The Control Center includes a set of Java interfaces that enable you to add additional items to the menu list or add buttons to the Control Center toolbar.

With the Control Center as your starting point (refer to Figure 1-1), you can access other DB2 graphical tools such as the Command Center, the Script Center, the Alert Center, the Journal, the License Center, and the Information Center. The following sections briefly describe each of these tools.

Command Center

The Command Center is used for running DB2 commands through a graphical interface rather than using a DB2 command line processor window or command prompt, giving you the freedom to:

- Run, see, and save the results of one or many SQL statements, DB2 commands, and operating system commands.
- Create scripts that you can later run in the Script Center.
- See the access plan (the method DB2 uses to retrieve data) and statistics associated with an SQL statement before you run it.

The Command Center interface is shown in Figure 1-2.

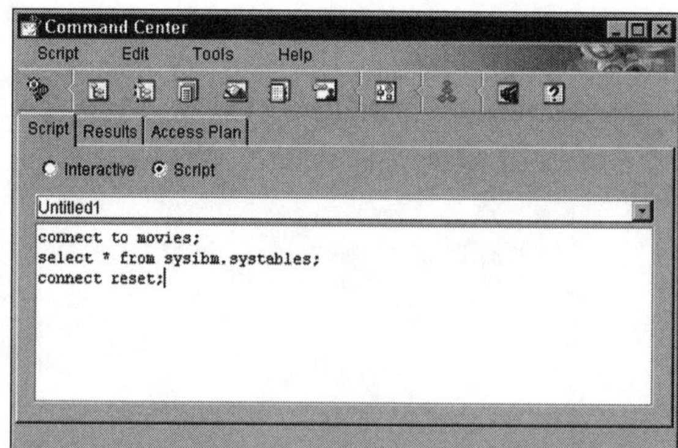

Figure 1-2: The Command Center is used for running DB2 commands in a graphical environment.

Script Center

The Script Center, working in conjunction with the Command Center, lets you create scripts of SQL statements or administrative DB2 commands so that you can automate tasks you do often. Figure 1-3 shows how the Script Center looks when you have several scripts saved and ready to go.

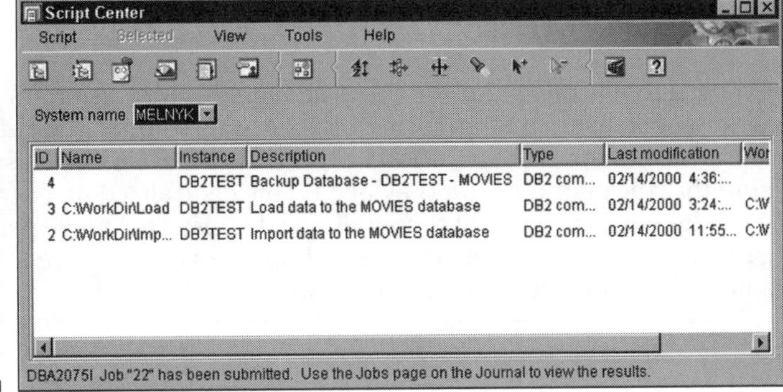

Figure 1-3: The Script Center lets you automate repetitive tasks.

License Center

The License Center displays what DB2 products are installed as well as their license status (for example, it may show that you are in trial mode for a particular product) and lets you add and remove registered users and show graph usage statistics.

You can bring the License Center up by selecting Tools from the Control Center menu bar. Figure 1-4 shows a typical License Center interface.

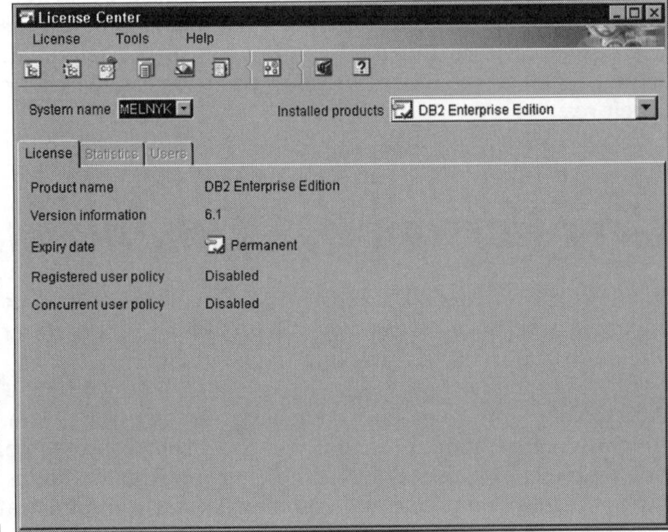

Figure 1-4: The License Center allows you to see the DB2 products installed.

Satellite Administration Center

This graphical tool is meant for database administrators (DBAs) that need to administer mobile users that are using DB2 Satellite Edition. The Satellite Administration Center enables you to keep track of these remote users and make sure that they get the data they need. This centralized place for administration reduces the amount of time that an administrator may spend maintaining those mobile users because the mobile users do not have to be maintained and administered on a one by one basis.

Alert Center

The Alert Center's function is kind of intuitive — it monitors your system and warns you of predefined conditions and any potential problems based on information you give the Alert Center beforehand. For example, the Alert Center can notify you that a particular server is suffering from unreasonably high memory usage or high buffer pool usage.

Journal

The Journal is similar to a database diary — it allows you to monitor any jobs you have submitted and look at their results. *Jobs* are generally repetitive tasks that involve one or several steps. For example, creating a database backup can be a job. By creating a job in the Journal and scheduling it, you have a running log of all the repetitive tasks you have run, when they were run, and their results.

Drooling Over Version 6.1 Enhancements

In version 6.1 of DB2 Universal Database, IBM concentrated on delivering improvements in several key areas over the previous version. Descriptions of three of the more important of these improvements follow:

- **Usability:** These improvements are clearly visible through some of the graphical administration tools that you see through the examples in the rest of the book. IBM also added some really cool SmartGuides that help you with the more mundane and complex database administration tasks. Our favorite is the Index Smart Guide (see Figure 1-5).

  You fill in your SQL workload through a series of panels. DB2 then tells you what indexes you need to create to make the SQL work better.

  SmartGuides for creating a database, creating a table, creating a table space, backing up a database, and restoring a database also exist.

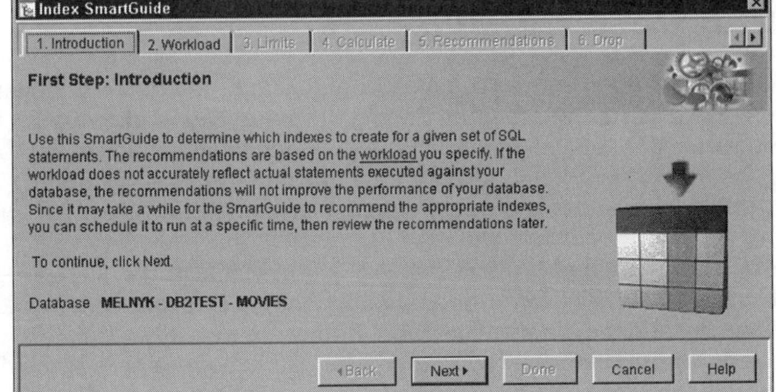

Figure 1-5: The Index Smart Guide helps you create indexes on your tables.

- **Administration**: Several key features are made available, with our favorite being enhancements to the load utility. The load utility was improved in several ways, including allowing indexes to be automatically rebuilt, allowing automatic restart for failed load operations, and the ability to roll back an interrupted load with the `terminate` command. More information on load can be found in Chapter 12.
- **Performance**: Here, techie-type features, such as forward and reverse index scans and optimized use of star join, are implemented. Because some of this performance stuff gets pretty technical, the best option is to go to some of the sources of information mentioned in Chapter 19.

Meeting the DB2 Family

DB2 is packaged in various configurations. These offerings, when grouped together, are often referred to as the DB2 Family. DB2 can work on almost any type of operating system. Following are some brief descriptions of each of the major DB2 editions.

Workgroup Edition

Workgroup Edition is particularly useful for a client-server environment running on Windows, OS/2, and Linux platforms. All functionality that comes with DB2 (creating databases, storing information, and retrieving information) comes with Workgroup Edition.

We only discuss Workgroup Edition (the Windows NT/2000 version) in this book, which is the version that comes on the CD.

Enterprise Edition

Enterprise Edition is the package meant for large and mid-size departmental servers. In addition to the functionality provided by Workgroup Edition, Enterprise Edition also includes DB2 Connect, which enables you to connect to host databases. (Look out for more information on DB2 Connect in the "Checking out add-on products" section later on in this chapter.)

Enterprise Edition also offers numerous optional features, such as Data Links Manager. Data Links is a cool technology that allows management of files that reside outside the database as though they are logically within the database. So, any files that exist on your computer can become a part of the database through the Data Links Manager.

Enterprise-Extended Edition

This package has the same features as Enterprise Edition, but it also gives you the ability to partition your database across multiple computers (which have to be all running the same operating system). This means that your database can grow to sizes limited only by the number of computers you have! The Enterprise-Extended Edition is meant for large data warehouses, online analytical processing workloads (OLAP), or high performance online transaction processing (OLTP) requirements. Enterprise-Extended Edition also allows databases on AIX, Solaris, HP-UX, and Windows NT/2000 machines to be clustered together under a single database image for very large-scale volumes.

Satellite Edition

Satellite Edition is meant for mobile database users — you know the ones I mean, always strutting around with their laptops, scurrying from airport to airport. Satellite Edition lets these nomadic types connect to a main database every once in a while, download to their laptop whatever information they need from the database, and go.

For those administrators that have to manage the Satellite Edition users, this package also offers a central location for keeping track of all satellite activity — from who's connecting from where to what information they're gathering and taking with them. This way, if you're administrating Satellite Edition users, you can quickly gather information and statistics about the information that is being downloaded from the main database to the mobile users.

Personal Edition

The Personal Edition is DB2 for a single user on a desktop PC. Personal Edition is available on OS/2, Windows 9*x* and NT/2000, and Linux. DB2 Personal Edition has all the features of Workgroup Edition (described earlier in this chapter), but remote clients cannot connect to databases that are running this package. As such, Personal Edition is useful for PCs that are not connected on a network. For example, you may want to install Personal Edition on your computer at home to keep track of information such as addresses of all your friends or just to learn the different functionalities of DB2. However, lots of people that develop applications for DB2 use Personal Edition and they are on networks. For this reason, Administrators can remotely administer Personal Edition workstations from the Control Center.

DB2 Everyplace

Remember those hotshots with the laptops? Well, now they are starting to carry around mobile devices. You know, like a PalmPilot or Desktop PC device. DB2 Everyplace provides access to your enterprise data from a variety of mobile or embedded devices. DB2 Everyplace is designed for mobile workers who need portable handheld devices for database applications in inventory, shipping, healthcare, and other industries. DB2 Everyplace is a relational database and enterprise synchronization architecture for mobile devices.

Checking out add-on products for DB2

Some nifty DB2 add-ons can also be purchased for specific business needs that perhaps the regular suite of DB2 offerings doesn't meet. Following are descriptions of a few of these add-ons:

DB2 Connect

The DB2 Connect product acts as a gateway that lets clients connect to databases on host systems, such as OS/390, MVS, VM/VSE, and AS/400. The clients can be on any supported DB2 platform. The DB2 Connect product has to be installed on a workstation that is running AIX, Linux, Solaris, HP-UX, OS/2, or Windows NT/2000. This is a useful product to have if most of the business information is on a host system, but most of the users of the information are running from their PCs. DB2 Connect can be installed on its own, or as a part of DB2 Enterprise Edition.

DB2 Data Links Manager

The Data Links Manager is an optional feature that you can install on top of DB2 Enterprise Edition that enables you to manage data files not normally found in a database, such as image files stored on a file system. The Data Links Manager lets you make such files a part of your database and even manage them with the same administration tools and commands as the rest of your data.

DB2 Query Patroller

You can install the Query Patroller with DB2 Extended-Enterprise Edition. The Query Patroller enables you to capture queries being sent to the database and then analyze them. Based on the information Query Patroller collects, you can manage resources or prioritize and schedule workloads across DB2 nodes.

Special packaging options geared towards application development also exist — what DB2 folks call Developer Editions, which we discuss in the next section.

Getting down and dirty with developer editions

IBM also offers two types of DB2 packages for application developers — DB2 Universal Developer's Edition and DB2 Personal Developer's Edition. Both of these come with tools for developing desktop business tools and applications for DB2. Both packages include the Software Developer Kit (SDK), which is made up of APIs, the Stored Procedure Builder (see Chapter 18), documentation, and so on.

DB2 Universal Developer's Edition is meant for building applications on any DB2 platform, and DB2 Personal Developer's Edition is meant for developing applications that run only on DB2 Personal Edition. So, DB2 Personal Developer's Edition can only be installed on machines running OS/2, Windows 9*x* and NT/2000, and Linux.

The Personal Developer's Edition is available as a free time-limited evaluation version (with the restriction that it not be used in a production environment) from the following URL:

```
www.ibm.com/software/data/db2/udb/downloads.html
```

Chapter 2

Getting Up to Speed with DB2 Basics

In This Chapter

- Checking out the different types of database objects
- Understanding data types: a data structure for all shapes and sizes
- Haggling with authorities

Just so you know, and we have no bones about telling you (drum roll): This chapter is full of database concepts and terminology! Ack! No, really, you can consider this chapter something of an initiation to DB2 and its main concepts. The first part of the chapter discusses database objects, the building blocks that make up DB2. And because databases are all about storing and retrieving data, the rest of the chapter describes all the various built-in data types that you can use with DB2, as well as some brief discussion of authorities and how to deal with them.

Checking Out Database Objects

DB2 is organized around a hierarchy of database *objects*. The following sections describe each of the major objects in order of hierarchy, as shown in Figure 2-1.

System

As you can see from Figure 2-1, at the top of the hierarchy is the *system*, which can be one or more computers. You can have one or more DB2 instances on your system, each of which can manage one or more databases. The databases may be partitioned among several nodegroups, where table spaces are stored. The table spaces in turn store table data.

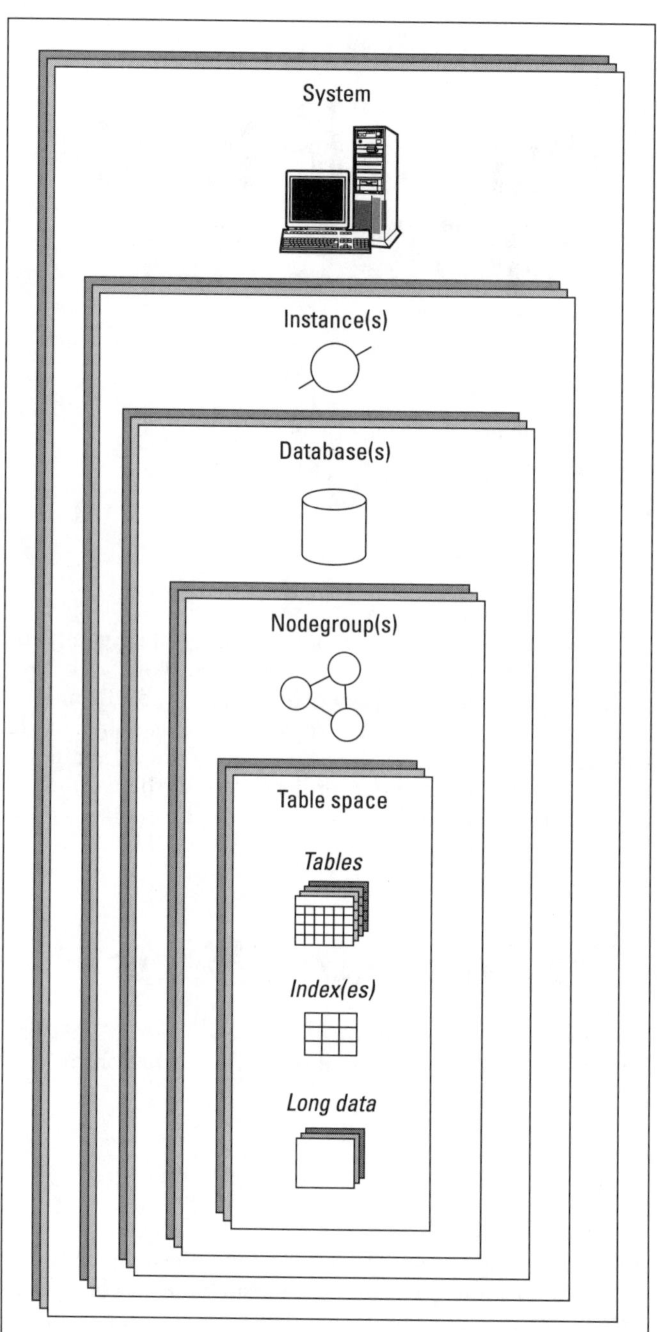

Figure 2-1: The DB2 hierarchy of database objects.

Instance

An *instance* (sometimes called a *database manager*) is a term for DB2 code that manages your databases. Instances are discussed in detail in Chapter 7, but following are a few of the main traits of an instance:

- Each instance controls what you can do to the data.
- Each instance manages system resources assigned to it.
- Each instance is a complete and separate environment.
- Each instance has its own databases that other instances cannot control.
- Each instance has separate security from other instances on the same machine (or system).

Database

A *relational database* presents data as a collection of tables. A *table* consists of a defined number of columns and any number of rows. Databases are discussed in detail in Chapter 8, but here is a summary of what each database includes:

- *System catalog tables* that describe the logical and physical structure of the data.
- A *configuration file* containing the parameter values allocated for the database.
- *Recovery logs* with ongoing transactions and transactions that can be archived.

Nodegroup

A *nodegroup* is a set of one or more database *partitions.* A partitioned database stores its data in different locations. In this book, we only discuss single-partitioned databases. When you want to create tables for a partitioned database, you first create the nodegroup where the *table spaces* are stored, and then you create the table space where the tables are stored. In single-partitioned databases (such as the ones that you are learning about in this book), the nodegroup is automatically created for you each time you create a database, so you don't have to worry about it.

Table space

A database is organized into parts called *table spaces.* A table space is quite simply a space to store tables. An allocation of physical storage (such as a file or a device) associated with a table space is called a container. Table spaces reside in nodegroups. When creating a table, you can have objects, such as indexes and large object (or LOB) data, kept separately from the rest of the table data. Such objects are sometimes kept in separate table spaces. A table space can also be spread over one or more physical storage devices.

The diagram in Figure 2-2 shows some of the flexibility you have in spreading data over table spaces. Table space 1 contains Table 1 data and an index. Table space 2 contains the system catalog tables. Table space 3 contains two tables (Table 2 and Table 3), but the large object (LOB) data in Table 2 is stored in Table space 5, and the indexes for these tables are contained in Table space 4. Table space 6 contains space for temporary tables.

A table space can be either one of the following types:

- **System-managed space (SMS):** Each container is a directory in the file space of the operating system, and the operating system's file manager controls the storage space.
- **Database-managed space (DMS):** Each container is either a fixed-size preallocated file or a physical device, such as a hard drive or disk, and the database manager controls the storage space.

Table spaces are covered in detail in Chapter 9.

Container

A *container* is a physical storage device that can be identified by a filename, directory name, or a device name. A container is assigned to a table space.

A single table space can span many containers, but each container belongs to only one table space.

Figure 2-3 illustrates the relationship between tables, a table space within a database, and the associated containers and disks. The EMPLOYEE, DEPARTMENT, and PROJECT tables are in the HUMANRES table space, which spans containers 0, 1, 2, 3, and 4. This example shows each container existing on a separate drive.

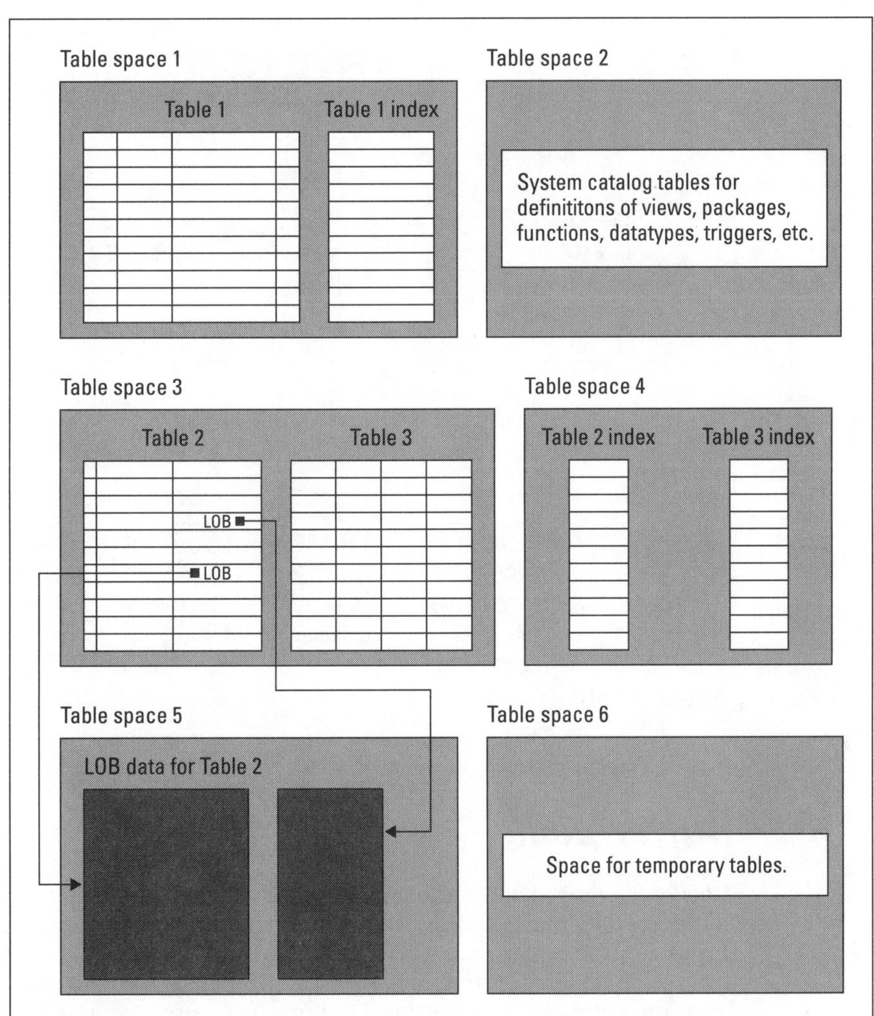

Figure 2-2: Various table spaces being used in different ways.

Data for a given table is stored on all the containers in its table space and the data is distributed as evenly as possible across the containers. The number of pages that the database manager writes to one container before using a different one is called the *extent size*.

Containers are covered in detail in Chapter 9.

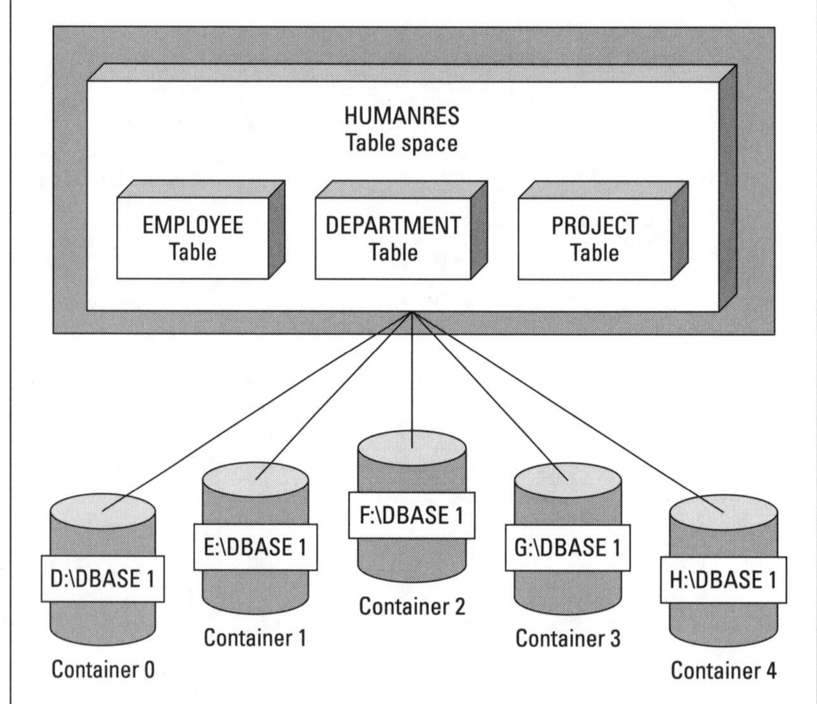

Figure 2-3: A HUMANRES table space with five containers.

Buffer pool

A *buffer pool* is the amount of main memory that is allocated to cache table and index data pages as they are being read from disk or being modified. The purpose of the buffer pool is to improve system performance. Data can be accessed much faster from memory than from disk; therefore, the fewer times the database manager needs to read from or write to a disk (I/O), the better the performance.

The configuration of the buffer pool is the single most important performance-tuning area, because you can reduce the delay caused by slow I/O.

Buffer pools are covered in detail in Chapter 11.

Table

A relational database presents data as a collection of tables. A *table* consists of data that is logically arranged in columns and rows. All database and table data is assigned to table spaces. The data in the table is logically related, and relationships are defined between tables. Data can be viewed and manipulated based on mathematical principles and operations called *relational algebra.*

Table data is accessed through *Structured Query Language* (SQL), a standardized language for defining and manipulating data in a relational database. A *query* is used in applications or by users to retrieve data from a database. The query uses SQL to create a statement like this:

```
SELECT <data_name> FROM <table_name>
```

Tables are covered in detail in Chapter 10.

View

A *view* is sort of a virtual table containing columns from one or more actual tables, and can include all or some of the columns or rows contained in the tables on which it is based. For example, you can join a department table and an employee table in a view, so that you can list all employees in a particular department. A view is an efficient way of representing data without having to maintain it. Views are often used as a way of controlling what data employees see when they try to access a table. For example, say that you had a table that contained all the information about each employee in your company. This table is called EMPLOYEES and contains information such as name, serial number, phone number, e-mail address, salary, and so on. You wouldn't want everyone to be able to see everyone else's salary, so you could create a view (let's call it EMPLOYEE) that does not include the salary column.

Views are covered in detail in Chapter 11.

Index

An *index* is a set of keys, each pointing to rows in a table. An index enables more efficient access to rows in a table by creating a direct path to the data through pointers record IDs (RIDs).

The DB2 *optimizer* automatically chooses the most efficient way to access data in tables. The optimizer takes indexes into consideration when determining the fastest access path to data.

Unique indexes are created to ensure uniqueness of the index key. An *index key* is a column or a collection of columns on which an index is defined. Using a unique index ensures that the value of each index key in the indexed column or columns is unique.

Indexes are covered in detail in Chapter 11.

Schema

A *schema* is an object identifier, such as a user ID, that helps group tables and other database objects. A schema can be owned by an individual, and the owner can control access to the data and the objects within it.

A schema is also an object in the database that can be created automatically when the first object in a schema is created. Such an object is anything that can be qualified by a schema name, such as a table, index, or view.

A schema name is used as the first part of a two-part object name. When an object is created, you can assign it to a specific schema. If you do not specify a schema, it is assigned to the default schema, which is usually the user ID of the person who created the object. The second part of the name is the name of the object. For example, a user named Smith might have a table named SMITH.PAYROLL.

Schemas are covered in detail in Chapter 11.

System catalog table

Each database includes a set of *system catalog tables* that describe the logical and physical structure of the data. DB2 creates and maintains an extensive set of system catalog tables for each database. These tables contain definitions of database objects, such as user tables, views, and indexes and security information about the authority that users have on these objects.

Each system catalog table is created along with each database and is updated during the course of normal operation. You cannot explicitly create or drop them, but you can query and view their contents.

Recovery log file

Recovery log files are created automatically with each database. You cannot directly modify a recovery log file. Recovery logs are used by DB2 to recover from application or system errors. In combination with database backups, they are used to recover the consistency of the database up to a particular point in time.

Database recovery is covered in detail in Chapter 13.

Recovery history file

The *recovery history file* is created automatically with each database. You cannot directly modify the recovery history file. The history file contains a summary of the backup information that can be used if all or part of the database must be recovered up to a given point in time, and is used by DB2 to track recovery-related events such as backup, restore, and load operations.

Database recovery is covered in detail in Chapter 13.

Configuration parameters

Configuration files contain configuration parameters and their values. Many of these parameters define the resources that are to be allocated to DB2 instances or to individual databases. DB2 uses two types of configuration files: a database manager configuration file for each DB2 instance and a database configuration file for each individual database.

A *database manager configuration file* is created with each DB2 instance that is created. The parameters it contains affect system resources at the instance level, independent of any one database that is part of that instance. Values for many of these parameters can be changed from the system default values to improve performance or increase capacity.

A *database configuration file* is created when a database is created, and resides where that database resides. There is one configuration file per database. Its parameters specify, among other things, the amount of resource to be allocated to that database. Values for many of these parameters can also be changed by the user to improve performance or increase capacity.

Constraints

Data must often adhere to certain restrictions or rules. For example, an employee number in a company's human resources database must be unique. DB2 provides the following types of *constraints* to enforce such rules:

- NOT NULL constraint
- Unique constraint
- Primary key constraint
- Foreign key (referential integrity) constraint
- Check constraint

NOT NULL constraint

The *NOT NULL constraint* prevents null values from being entered into a column that should not have null values. A null value represents an unknown data value. If a column is defined as NOT NULL, each row in that column must have a value.

Unique constraint

The *unique constraint* ensures that the values in a set of columns are unique and not null for all rows in the table. DB2 enforces this constraint during insert and update operations, ensuring data integrity.

Primary key constraint

Each table can have one *primary key.* A primary key is a column or combination of columns that has the same properties as a unique constraint.

- Because the primary key is used to identify a row in a table, it must be unique.
- A table cannot have more than one primary key, but it can have multiple unique keys.
- Primary keys are optional, and can be defined when a table is created or altered.

Foreign key (referential integrity) constraint

DB2 maintains *referential integrity* (literally meaning "integrity of references") through foreign key constraints (also known as *referential integrity constraints*), which require that all values for a given attribute or table column also exist in some other table or column. For example, a foreign key constraint may require that every employee in the EMPLOYEE table be in a department that exists in the DEPARTMENT table. No employee can be in a department that does not exist.

To establish this relationship, you must define the department number in the EMPLOYEE table as the foreign key, and the department number in the DEPARTMENT table as the primary key. A *foreign key* is a column or a set of columns in a table that refers to a unique key or the primary key of another table. A foreign key establishes a relationship with a unique key or the primary key to enforce referential integrity among tables. The column WORKDEPT in the EMPLOYEE table is a foreign key because it refers to the primary key, DEPTNO, in the DEPARTMENT table. In this example, the DEPARTMENT table is referred to as a *parent table*, and the EMPLOYEE table is a *dependent table*.

You can *insert* a row into a parent table at any time. You cannot, however, insert a row into a dependent table, unless there is a row in the parent table with a primary key value equal to the foreign key value of the row that is being inserted.

You can *delete* a row from a dependent table at any time. But when you delete a row from a parent table, DB2 checks if there are any dependent rows in dependent tables with matching foreign key values. If any dependent rows are found, several actions are possible. You can determine which action is taken by specifying a *delete rule* when you create the dependent table (the table containing the foreign key). Specifying the CASCADE rule, for example, causes DB2 to automatically delete any related rows in a dependent table when a row is deleted from the parent table. If some of these dependent rows have dependents of their own, the delete rule for those relationships is applied as well. DB2 manages cascading deletions.

DB2 prevents the *update* of a unique key for a parent row. When you update a foreign key in a dependent table, it must match some value of the parent key for the parent table of the relationship. If any referential constraint is violated by an update operation, an error occurs and no rows are updated.

Check constraint

A table check constraint is a rule that specifies allowable values for one or more columns in a table. The constraint is automatically activated when an UPDATE or INSERT statement is applied against the table. For example, in an EMPLOYEE table, you can define a SEX column whose valid values are Male or Female. With this constraint, any record with a different value in the SEX column is rejected.

Triggers

Triggers define a set of actions that are performed in conjunction with an INSERT, UPDATE, or DELETE request against a specified table.

You can use triggers to support business rules. For example, a trigger can check a customer's account balance before a debit card purchase is approved.

Triggers are coded once, stored in the database, and automatically called by DB2 as required when an application uses the database. This ensures that the business rules related to the data are always enforced. If a business rule changes, only the triggers need to be modified.

Triggers are covered in detail in Chapter 11.

Dealing with Data Types

Data types are merely the types of data that you can store in a DB2 database. Data types are defined when you create a table that belongs to a database. The data type describes the information that is contained in a column of a table. Essentially, you can use two kinds of data types in DB2: built-in data types that are provided by DB2 and user-defined data types (UDTs) that you can code yourself.

DB2 basically contains the following three types of data:

- Numeric data
- String data
- Date and time data

Figure 2-4 shows a family tree of the data types that you can use in your DB2 databases.

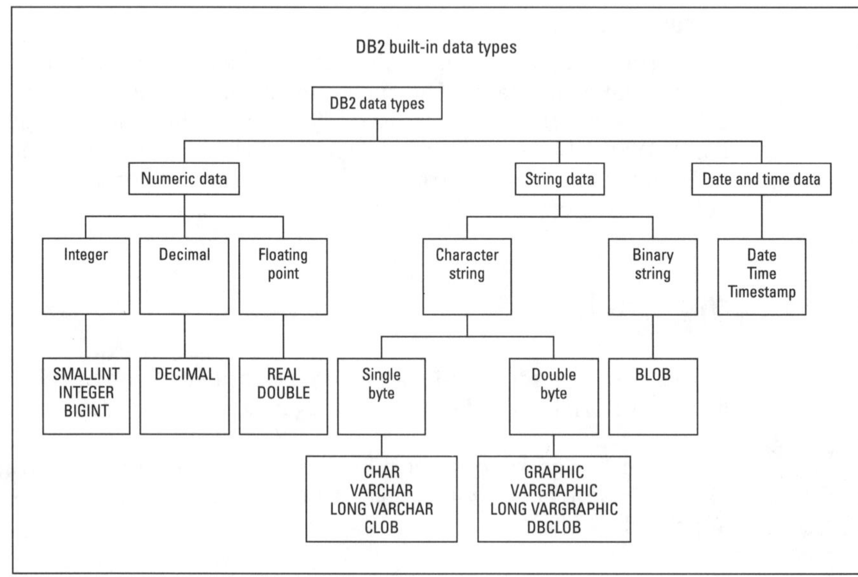

Figure 2-4: DB2's family tree of built-in data types.

Numeric data types

The numeric data type family consists of six types of data: SMALLINT, INTEGER, BIGINT, DECIMAL, REAL, and DOUBLE. The rest of this section explains each specific data type that belongs to this family.

This data type family is used to store different types of numeric data. Each data type is used for a different level or detail of numeric representation. In DB2 this is called *precision.* The precision of a numeric value is the number of decimal places used. Each data type in this family uses a fixed amount of storage.

The more precise a numeric value is, the more storage space it requires.

DB2 uses many numeric data types because these data types represent many different types of information. For example, you may use an INTEGER data type to represent the serial number of a product. Chances are that a product's serial number does not include a fraction in its value. However, if you were storing a test mark, 49.5 percent may be a valid score, in which case you choose a DECIMAL data type.

When you use a numeric data type, be careful not to enclose the data in quotation marks (" "). DB2 uses quotation marks to define character data (more on that later). So, if you are entering a number, enter it without quotation marks; otherwise, DB2 can't use it in arithmetic operations.

Small integer data (SMALLINT)

A SMALLINT can be used for any value between -32,778 and 32,767. Remember, integers are not allowed to have fractional values, so if you are using a SMALLINT data type, the value 5.25 isn't valid.

Because there can only be a maximum of 5 numbers in the SMALLINT data type, its precision is 5. This type of data uses the least amount of storage in a database: each SMALLINT entry in a column requires 2 bytes of storage.

Integer (INTEGER)

An INTEGER can be used for any value between -2,147,483,648 and 2,147,483,647. Again, integers cannot have fractional values, so the same restrictions apply as with the SMALLINT data type. You use this data type if you expect that the values in the column you are defining require entries greater than the 32,767 limit, or less than the -32,778 limit of the SMALLINT data type. (We hope that IDG Books Worldwide, Inc. uses an INTEGER data type when they define a NO_OF_BOOKS_SOLD column in their sales database for *DB2 For Windows for Dummies!*)

If you know that the values in a column will never exceed the limits for a data type, use the data type best suited for the limit. You don't want to use the INTEGER data type if you are not going to exceed the boundaries of the SMALLINT data type. What is the precision of an INTEGER? Right you are — 10. How much storage does an INTEGER require? Each INTEGER entry in a column requires 4 bytes of storage. Right again!

When you define an INTEGER data type, you can use the short form INT instead of specifying the full keyword INTEGER. When you see a reference to an INT data type, you can assume that it is an INTEGER data type.

Big integer (BIGINT)

BIGINT is the big daddy, the integer of all integers, the grandest of the grand. Use a BIGINT data type when you have to specify really large numbers that do not contain fractions. Are you ready for this? The range for the BIGINT data type is: -9,233,372,036,854,775,808 to 9,223,372,036,854,775,807. Each BIGINT entry in a column uses 8 bytes of storage, and its precision is 19.

As you get to know the rest of the built-in DB2 data types, you notice that you could use other data types to specify a number that could be represented by a BIGINT value. For example, you could use a DECIMAL, DOUBLE, or REAL value to represent a number that would be a valid BIGINT value. DB2, however, is more efficient at processing a BIGINT value than a DECIMAL value, and more precise when using a BIGINT value when compared to a DOUBLE or REAL value.

Decimal (DECIMAL)

A DECIMAL data type is used for those numbers that have fractional values as well as whole parts.

The precision of the DECIMAL data type is from 1 to 31. When you create a column that uses the DECIMAL data type, you specify the format of the data that is used for the column. By *format*, we are referring to the number of digits allowed in the numeral (precision) and the number of digits allowed to the right of the decimal place. In DB2-speak, the number of digits to the right of the decimal place (that is, the fractional component) is referred to as the *scale* of the numeral. So, if you are chatting data types with someone in the know and they ask you to create a DECIMAL data type, ask them what precision and scale they would like. That should impress them!

For example, say that you wanted to store someone's salary in a column. Salaries are usually measured in dollars and cents, with the limit of cents being 99, because 100 cents equals one dollar. So, if you wanted to define a column where you would store salary information, you would define it as DECIMAL(12,2). This specification would allow you the following range of values (including fractional values): -9,999,999,999.99 to 9,999,999,999.99.

The first entry is 12 because it represents the *total* number of digits in the numeral (its precision), while the second number specifies the scale of the numeric (those numbers to the right of the decimal place). Why would you need a DECIMAL(12,2) value in a salary column? You probably wouldn't, unless Bill Gates was working for you.

If you don't specify the precision and the scale of a DECIMAL data type, the default (5,0) is used, limiting you to the following range of values: -99,999 to 99,999. (Did you notice that there are no decimal places?)

Single-precision floating-point (REAL)

A single-precision floating-point number is a 32-bit approximation of a real number. The number can be zero, or can range from -3.402E+38 to -1.175E-37, or from 1.175E-37 to 3.402E+38.

Double-precision floating-point (DOUBLE or FLOAT)

A double-precision floating-point number is a 64-bit approximation of a real number. The number can be zero, or can range from -1.79769E+308 to -2.225E-307, or from 2.225E-307 to 1.79769E+308.

String data types

As you can see from Figure 2-4, the string data type family contains eight data types: CHAR, VARCHAR, LONG VARCHAR, CLOB, GRAPHIC, VARGRAPHIC, LONG VARGRAPHIC, and DBCLOB.

This data type family is used to store different types of character and multimedia data. There are many types of string data because you may want to store many different types of information in your database that do not fall into the numeric or the date and time data types.

If you are entering character-based data, you must surround that data with quotation marks (" ").

Character data (CHARACTER)

Character data, also called *fixed-length character strings,* is stored in a database using the entire amount of space allocated when the column using this data type is defined. When you use the CHARACTER data type, you specify the length in characters that any entry in the column using this data type uses. Any type of nonbinary data can be stored in a column defined with this data type.

When you define a CHARACTER data type, you can use the short form CHAR instead of specifying the full keyword CHARACTER. When you see reference to a CHAR data type, you can assume that it is a CHARACTER data type.

A good example of a CHAR data type is an employee's serial number. Perhaps at your company all of the serial numbers are five characters long. If you were using a CHAR for this column, you would define it as CHAR(5). In this case, each entry in this column would take up 5 bytes of storage.

Assume that your company's serial number is composed only of numbers. Would the CHAR data type still be the best choice for this type of data? Yes! Why? Generally, you don't use an employee's serial number in any sort of arithmetic calculations. If you are storing numbers that are not used in calculations, and are not date or time data, you should use a string-based data type.

A character value can contain 1 to 254 characters. If you do not specify a length for this data type, the default is 1.

Because the amount of storage reserved for this data type is fixed, you don't choose it for data with varying lengths. For example, say that you wanted a column in your table that listed everyone's last name in your company. Because the character data type is fixed, you would have to find the person whose last name had the most number of characters. The person creating the table could define this column as CHAR(10). Sounds good, doesn't it? But if you stop to consider the wasted storage space for this column, you may reconsider. You see, every entry in the column is going to have 10 characters assigned to it. If one of your employees is called Smith, five null (and unnecessary) characters are assigned to this value. You may want to consider using a varying length character (VARCHAR) instead. Generally, unless the data is of fixed length, you don't choose a CHAR data type.

Varying-length character data (VARCHAR)

Varying-length character data is stored in a database using only the amount of space required to store the data plus an additional byte for overhead. Any type of nonbinary data can be stored in a column defined with this data type. The maximum size of the VARCHAR data type is 32,672 bytes.

Some individuals fluent with DB2 also refer to VARCHAR data as CHAR VARYING or CHARACTER VARYING data.

If you define a column for someone's last name and use the VARCHAR data type, you might define it as VARCHAR(30). This would permit any name of 30 characters or less to be inserted into the column. If there is an entry that is only five characters long, only five characters of storage (plus one for overhead) would be allocated.

Varying-length long character data (LONG VARCHAR)

This data type is used for varying-length character strings up to 32,700 bytes in length. The LONG VARCHAR data type will most likely be dropped in future releases of DB2, because the VARCHAR data type was extended to handle 32,672 bytes in DB2 Version 6.

Character large object data (CLOB)

Character large objects are objects in a database that contain large amounts of character data. A good example of a CLOB is a resume, or a book. The maximum size of the CLOB data type is 2 gigabytes (GB).

Double-byte graphic string data (GRAPHIC)

Double-byte graphic string data, also called GRAPHIC data, is stored in a database using two bytes for each character. The maximum length of the GRAPHIC data type is 127 characters. The GRAPHIC data type is similar to the CHAR data type.

Typically, GRAPHIC data types (including VARGRAPHIC and LONG VARGRAPHIC) are used when it takes more than one byte of storage to represent a character. For example, any double-byte character set (DBCS) would have to use the GRAPHIC data type. An example of a DBCS is the character set for the Japanese language.

Double-byte varying-length graphic string data (VARGRAPHIC)

Double-byte varying-length graphic string data, or VARGRAPHIC data, is stored the same way that GRAPHIC data is stored; however, the maximum length of this data type is 16,336 characters. The VARGRAPHIC data type is similar to the VARCHAR data type, but uses a DBCS. Varying-length graphic data is stored in a database using only the amount of space required to store the data, plus an additional byte for overhead.

Double-byte varying-length long graphic string data (LONG VARGRAPHIC)

This data type is used for double-byte varying-length graphic strings up to 16,350 characters long. LONG VARGRAPHIC data is stored in a database the same way that GRAPHIC data is stored. The LONG VARGRAPHIC data type will most likely be dropped in subsequent releases of DB2, because the VARGRAPHIC data type was extended to handle 16,336 characters of data in DB2 Version 6.

Double-byte character large objects data (DBCLOB)

This data type is just an extension of the CLOB data type for those character sets that require double-byte support. Because two bytes of storage are required for each character, the maximum size of the DBCLOB data type is 1 gigabyte.

Binary large object data (BLOB)

This data type is used to store varying-length binary data. A BLOB is stored in binary format in the database. The BLOB data type spawned the *Universal* movement in databases. Support for these data types started in the mid-1990s, and a database was considered to be universal if it could support BLOB data types. BLOB data includes video clips, audio clips, pictures, and so on. The maximum size of a BLOB in DB2 is 2 gigabytes.

Date and time data

As you can see from Figure 2-4, three data types belong to the date and time data type family: DATE, TIME, and TIMESTAMP. This data type family is used to store different types of date and time data. Each data type in this family uses a fixed amount of storage.

DB2 provides special SQL functions that enable you to manipulate the data types in this family. For example, you can extract the year, month, day, or time from any of these columns by using the appropriate SQL function. As a general rule, if you are interested in a single element of a date or time data string, use one of the SQL functions provided by DB2.

Date (DATE)

This data type stores a date value in a column. DB2 stores this data type internally, and packs (which is DB2-speak for compresses) it as 4 bytes. Externally (what we see), the DATE value has a fixed character length of 10 bytes and is represented as MM-DD-YYYY.

YYYY represents the year, MM represents the month, and DD represents the day.

The two separator characters (in this case, hyphens) in MM-DD-YYYY take up space as well, which is why the date string MM-DD-YYYY requires 10 bytes of storage.

The date format reflects the country code of the database, and can therefore look different than this example. Because different countries represent their dates in different formats, you and DB2 need to be aware of each country's standard format. The string that DB2 uses to represent a DATE data type varies depending on the country code used for the database.

European databases work on the IBM European Standard, which is of the format DD.MM.YYYY. That means months and days are transposed, so watch out!

The valid formats of the DATE data type are presented in Table 2-1.

Table 2-1: Valid formats of the DATE data type

Format Name	*DATE Format*	*Short Form if you Want to Sound Smart*
International Standards Organization (ISO)	YYYY-MM-DD	ISO
IBM USA Standard	MM-DD-YYYY	USA
IBM European Standard	DD.MM.YYYY	EUR
Japanese Industrial Standard	YYYY-MM-DD	JIS
Self-Defined	Depends on the database country code	LOC

Did you notice that we have a Y10K problem with this 10-digit limitation? Once the year 9999 rolls around, you'd better start getting ready!

Time (TIME)

This data type stores a time value in a column. DB2 stores this data type internally and packs it as 3 bytes. Externally, the TIME value has a fixed character length of 8 bytes and is represented as HH-MM-SS.

The time format also reflects the country code of the database, and therefore can look different than this example. Because different countries represent their time values in different formats, you and DB2 need to be aware of the standard for each country. The string that DB2 uses to represent a TIME data type varies depending on the country code used for the database. The valid formats of the TIME data type are presented in Table 2-2.

Table 2-2: Valid Formats for the TIME Data Type

Format Name	*TIME Format*	*Short Form if Your Want to Sound Smart*
International Standards Organization	HH.MM.SS	ISO
IBM USA Standard	HH:MM AM or PM	USA
IBM European Standard	HH.MM.SS	EUR
Japanese Industrial Standard	HH:MM:SS	JIS
Self-Defined	Depends on the database country code	LOC

Timestamp (TIMESTAMP)

This data type stores a date *and* time value in a column. DB2 stores this type of data internally and packs it as 10 bytes. Externally, the TIMESTAMP value has a fixed character length of 26 bytes and is represented as YYYY-MM-DD-HH-MM-SS-NNNNNN (Year-Month-Day-Hour-Minute-Second-Nanosecond). This data type has only one external format and is not affected by the code page of your database.

Controlling Authorities

In this section we discuss the different ways of controlling access to data in DB2. Access can be controlled at the instance level, the database level, or the database object level by grouping typical database users according to what they do. The method DB2 uses to control access is by giving different authorities to different users. These authorities provide a hierarchy of capabilities and are described briefly in the following sections.

SYSADM (System Administration Authority)

The SYSADM authority is given to any user that belongs to the Administrators group on your Windows NT/2000 workstation. This user has the authority to perform any DB2 administrative operations, access all database objects, and update the database manager configuration parameters.

To give a group of users SYSADM authority, you have to change the SYSADM_GROUP parameter in the database manager configuration file to the name of the Windows users group. This is done using the `update database manager configuration` command as follows:

```
db2 update dbm cfg using sysadm_group <group name>
```

where *<group name>* is the name of the Windows users group that will have SYSADM privileges.

SYSCTRL (System Control Authority)

Users with the SYSCTRL authority can perform administrative operations but cannot see database objects or update the database manager configuration parameters.

To give a group of users SYSCTRL authority, you have to change the SYSCTRL_GROUP parameter in the database manager configuration file to the name of the Windows users group. This is done using the `update database manager configuration` command as follows:

```
db2 update dbm cfg using sysctrl_group <group name>
```

where <*group name*> is the name of the Windows users group that will have SYSCTRL privileges.

SYSMAINT (System Maintenance Authority)

Users with SYSMAINT authority can perform most administrative operations on all databases in an instance. A user with this type of authority cannot create or drop a database, force applications, or restore to a new database. These users also cannot create, drop, or alter a table space, nor can they access database objects or update the database manager configuration parameters.

To give a group of users SYSMAINT authority, you have to change the SYSMAINT_GROUP parameter in the database manager configuration file to the name of the Windows users group. This is done using the `update database manager configuration` command as follows:

```
db2 update dbm cfg using sysmaint_group <group name>
```

where <*group name*> is the name of the Windows users group that will have SYSMAINT privileges.

DBADM (Database Administration Authority)

Users with DBADM authority can perform any administrative task on the database, such as loading data, creating objects, and monitoring activity on the database. DBADM can also query, drop or create tables. The creator of a database automatically has DBADM authority and can assign it to other users by using the following `grant` statement:

```
grant dbadm on <database name> to <user name>
```

where <*database name*> is the name of the database to which you're giving access and <*user name*> is the name of the user to whom you want to grant access.

Chapter 3

Designing a Database

In This Chapter

- Checking out a design example: The MOVIES database
- Deciding what data to record in the database
- Defining a table structure
- Comprehending the not-so-normal process of normalization

Although designing databases can be a complicated and involving task, the fundamental principles of database design can be illustrated in a straightforward example, such as the MOVIES database that we design in this chapter. We refer to this database throughout the book, and have included related material on the CD that will help you try it out yourself. The next section provides a general description of the MOVIES database design, and the rest of this chapter explains the basic steps that you can follow when designing your own database.

Checking out a Design Example: The MOVIES Database

When you design a database, what you're really trying to do is create a model of some objects about which you are interested in collecting data. In the relational database world, these objects are called *entities,* and the data that ou collect about an entity relates to the *attributes* of that entity. You are also interested in the relationships among entities. You may have many entities in your model, and those entities may interact in complex ways. Imagine the design complexity of a large corporate database used for tracking inventory, sales, and customer data! To help you understand the entities and their relationships to one another, you can map them out in entity-relationship diagrams, which simply show a box for each entity, and arrows connecting the boxes.

Say that you want to design a database called MOVIES that contains information about movies, directors, and actors. The MOVIES database we design in this section consists of five normalized tables (we discuss normalization later in this chapter). The attributes for each table are shown in parentheses:

- MOVIE (MOVIE_ID, TITLE, YR_RELEASED)
- DIRECTOR (DIRECTOR_ID, DIRECTOR_NAME, DIR_YR_OF_BIRTH)
- ACTOR (ACTOR_ID, ACTOR_NAME, ACT_YR_OF_BIRTH)
- APPEARS_IN (ACTOR_ID, MOVIE_ID)
- DIRECTS (DIRECTOR_ID, MOVIE_ID)

The entity relationships for the MOVIES database are defined as follows:

- One or more directors directs one or more movies. This is a many-to-many relationship. (We discuss relationships in the "Defining tables for each type of relationship" section later in this chapter.)
- One or more actors appears in one or more movies. This is also a many-to-many relationship.

The attributes of the MOVIE entity, the DIRECTOR entity, and those of the ACTOR entity are grouped such that there are no partial functional dependencies or transitive dependencies in the defined relations. The relations are therefore in the third normal form (we discuss normal forms and normalization in general in the "Comprehending the not-so-normal process of normalization" section later in this chapter).

Look at the `create table` statement for one of these tables, APPEARS_IN. (Don't worry, you can find out a lot more about creating tables in Chapter 10. Here we just want to show you an example of a composite key, the application of a referential integrity constraint, and a delete rule. If you don't remember what those are — and I wouldn't blame you! — take another look at Chapter 2.)

The APPEARS_IN table is defined as follows (watch for comments in italics):

```
create table db2admin.appears_in
 (ACTOR_ID char(5) not null,          -- Foreign key
                                      --    in relation to
                                      --    the ACTOR table.
  MOVIE_ID char(5) not null           -- Foreign key
                                      --    in relation to
                                      --    the MOVIE table.
  primary key (ACTOR_ID,MOVIE_ID),    -- Composite key.
  foreign key (ACTOR_ID)
     references actor on delete cascade,
  foreign key (MOVIE_ID)
     references movie on delete cascade
 );
```

The primary key for the APPEARS_IN table is the concatenation of the two foreign keys, ACTOR_ID and MOVIE_ID; it is a composite key. This table definition includes a referential integrity specification: When a record in the ACTOR table or the MOVIE table is deleted, all corresponding APPEARS_IN records are deleted automatically.

Basic Steps in Database Design

The following steps are part of logical database design:

1. **Decide what data you want to record.**
2. **Define tables that will contain your data.**
3. **Provide column definitions for your tables.**
4. **For each table, identify one or more columns as the primary key.**
5. **Normalize your tables.**

These steps are discussed in the sections that follow.

Deciding what data to record in the database

The first step in developing a database design is to decide what tables you're going to need. In a relational database, both entities and their relationships to one another are represented as tables. Within a table, each column represents an attribute that describes the entity.

In our MOVIES example, we're going to be interested in answering questions such as: "Who directed *Casablanca?*", "Which actors appear in *Citizen Kane?*", and "Which directors have directed more than one movie?". To answer such questions, we're going to need tables that describe movies, directors, and actors. But we also need tables that show how directors and movies are related, and how actors and movies are related.

Defining a table structure

The next step in developing a database design is to define a table structure for the database. This process consists of the following steps (which we discuss in the next three sections):

- Defining tables for each type of relationship.
- Providing column definitions for all tables.
- Identifying one or more columns as the primary key for each table.

Defining tables for each type of relationship

Because entities and their relationships to one another are represented as tables, we need to define tables for each entity and relationship in the database. Hey, that makes sense!

In our MOVIES example, the MOVIE table has three columns, called MOVIE_ID, TITLE, and YR_RELEASED, because a unique movie identifier, a movie's title, and the year in which a movie was released are the only attributes about movies that we have decided to record.

Two other tables, DIRECTOR and ACTOR, contain columns that represent attributes of these entities. The remaining two tables in this example, APPEARS_IN and DIRECTS, represent relationships between actors and movies (actors appear in movies), and directors and movies (directors direct movies), respectively. Both of these relationships are one-to-many relationships.

One-to-many relationships? Yup. Several types of relationships can be defined in a database, including the following:

- **One-to-one relationships:** An example of a one-to-one relationship is: "A manager manages one department, and a department has only one manager."
- **One-to-many and many-to-one relationships:** An example of a one-to-many relationship is: "A director directs several movies." An example of a many-to-one relationship is: "Several actors appear in a movie."
- **Many-to-many relationships:** An example of a many-to-many relationship is: "One or more directors directs one or more movies."

Providing column definitions for all tables

To define a column in a relational table:

1. **Choose a name for the column.**

   Each column in a table must have a name that is unique in that table.

2. **State what kind of data is valid for the column.**

   You can choose from among the data types provided by DB2, or you can create your own user-defined types. (See Chapter 2 for information about the data types provided by DB2.)

3. **State which columns must have a value.**

   Some columns cannot have a value in each row because:

   • A column value is not applicable to the row. For example, a column containing a director's date of death (not a column in our DIRECTOR table!) is not applicable to a director who is still alive.

   • A value is not available. For example, an actor's date of birth may be unknown.

   Some columns, such as primary key columns, *must* have a value for each row; in such cases, a null value (a special value indicating that the column value is unknown or not applicable) is not allowed.

Identifying one or more columns as the primary key

The *primary key* is the most important unique key defined on a table. A *unique key* is one or more columns that uniquely identifies a row in a table; no two of its values are equal. It follows that (are you still with me?) the primary key cannot contain null values. A social security number column makes a fine primary key, because each value in the column identifies only one person. No two people can have the same social security number.

There can be only one primary key in a table.

DB2 automatically creates a *primary index* for the primary key. The primary index is used to access data more efficiently.

If every column in a table contains duplicate values, you cannot define a primary key with only one column. A key with more than one column is called a *composite key*. If a composite key cannot be easily defined, you can consider creating a new column that has unique values.

A unique number column is often the best choice for the primary key. A unique number is assigned only once and is not updated. In our MOVIES example, the MOVIE, DIRECTOR, and ACTOR tables all have primary key columns whose values consist of unique identification numbers (MOVIE_ID, DIRECTOR_ID, and ACTOR_ID, respectively).

Comprehending the not-so-normal process of normalization

Before we get into the fun of creating some tables, you should understand some theory about tables. We couldn't consider this chapter to be complete unless we introduced you to the concept of *normalization;* nobody can be considered fluent in DB2-speak without being able to slip with ease into a conversation about normalization!

Normalizing data helps you to avoid data redundancies and inconsistencies, and helps to make the tables less complex. Usually normalization leads to more tables, so you may feel that normalizing your data impacts performance because DB2 must join these extra tables to satisfy your queries. But fear not: The benefits derived from removing the complexity from your tables actually increases performance!

The ultimate goal of normalization is to reduce the number of columns in your tables to the point where all the nonkey columns in each table have a dependency only on the primary key of the table. When you normalize your data, you apply a set of rules to your tables. In DB2, these rules are referred to quite appropriately as as the *rules of normalization.* The database community generally accepts five forms of normalization. In this book, I discuss the first, second, and third normal forms. The fourth and fifth normal forms are quite advanced topics and are typically not of concern to average DB2 users.

- A table is in *first normal form* if there is only one value — never a set of values — in each cell. This form is quite straightforward: You should never stuff more than one column value into one row. In our MOVIES database example, this means that we don't want to see *Rear Window Psycho* in a TITLE column of a DIRECTS table entry for Alfred Hitchcock!
- A table is in *second normal form* if each column that is not part of the primary key is dependent upon the entire key (that is, if there are no *partial functional dependencies*). In our MOVIES database example, this means that there shouldn't be a DIRECTOR_NAME column in the DIRECTS table. Remember that the DIRECTS table has only two columns, DIRECTOR_ID and MOVIE_ID, and that both of these columns make up the primary key for the DIRECTS table. If you creat a DIRECTOR_NAME column in this table, DIRECTOR_NAME is dependent on DIRECTOR_ID, not on MOVIE_ID. And if you change Alfred Hichcock to Alfred Hitchcock in the row that contains the unique identifier for *Rear Window,* you have to remember to change the row that contains the unique identifier for *Psycho.* If you didn't remember to do that, you would have to slap yourself in the face, because you would have introduced an inconsistency to your data! And you would have to slap yourself again for having a redundancy in the first place!
- A table is in *third normal form* if each nonkey column is independent of other nonkey columns, and is dependent only on the primary key (that is, if there are no *transitive dependencies*). In our MOVIES database example, this means that there shouldn't be a DIRECTOR_NAME column and a STUDIO column in the MOVIE table, because the STUDIO attribute is dependent on DIRECTOR_NAME; that is, if you know the director's name, you know the studio (assuming that each director is associated with only one studio). If a particular director appears more than once in the MOVIE table, the studio name also appears more than once. Once again, there are redundancies and the real potential for introducing inconsistencies to your data. This time, don't slap yourself; instead, normalize your tables!

Part II

Installing and Setting Up DB2

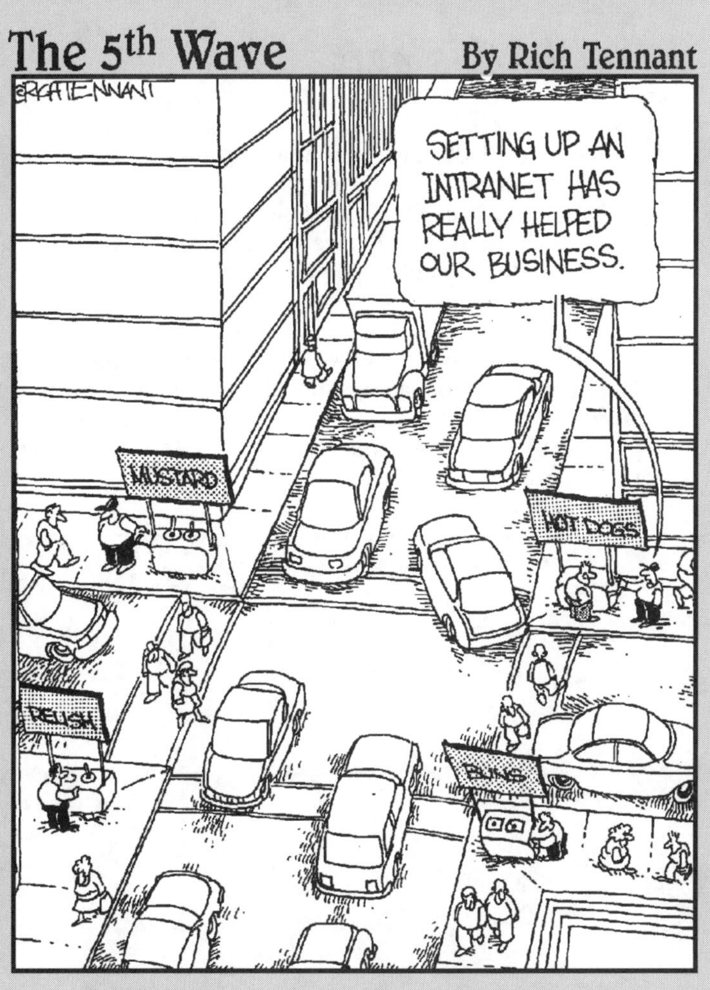

The 5th Wave
By Rich Tennant
©RICHTENNANT
SETTING UP AN INTRANET HAS REALLY HELPED OUR BUSINESS.
MUSTARD
HOT DOGS
RELISH
BUNS

In this part . . .

This part's lot in life is to show you how to install a DB2 server and a DB2 client and how to get a DB2 client to talk to a DB2 server (it's not too hard, though clients are kind of shy). Nerds call this client/server business a 'distributed' environment, which we also show you how to set up. This feat alone qualifies you for the esteemed pocket protector!

In these chapters we also show you some of the different tools that are used to manage your DB2 server and its environment through a demonstration tool called First Steps. This tool will even create a sample database for you that you can play around with.

Chapter 4

Installing a DB2 Server on a Windows NT/2000 Machine

In This Chapter

- Knowing what you need to install a DB2 server
- Installing a DB2 server
- Sampling databases
- Checking out First Steps

This chapter introduces you to the DB2 server, the software that handles all of the exciting things that DB2 can do for you. In this chapter you find out about what you need to install a DB2 Workgroup Edition server, and how to install it (you can read about the different editions of the DB2 servers in Chapter 1).

After we show you how to you install a DB2 server, we show you how to create the SAMPLE database and introduce you to some of the DB2 administration tools.

Knowing What You Need to Install a DB2 Server

Before you install a DB2 server, we should probably clue you in to what it is: The term *DB2 server* refers to the software on your computer that allows you to create and control your databases, and allows DB2 clients to connect to your computer and to retrieve data. Figure 4-1 shows a DB2 Server in a typical business environment.

To install the DB2 server that is provided on the CD-ROM in the back of the book, you definitely need a computer (duh!). It cannot be just any old computer — a VIC-20 is most definitely *not* going to cut it. The computer you have has to be an IBM-compatible PC with an Intel-compatible processor.

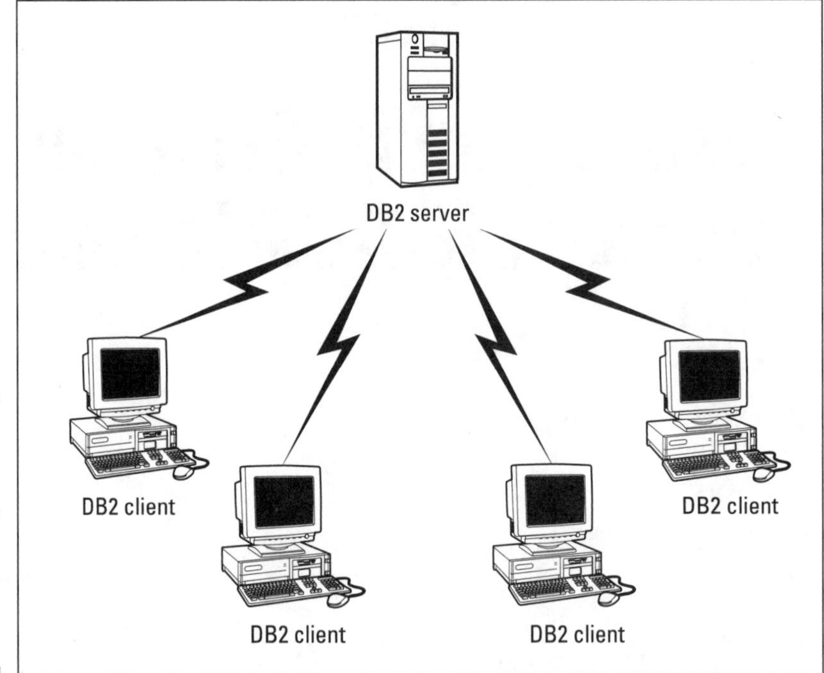

Figure 4-1: A typical implementation of DB2 in a business environment.

But the computer alone isn't the only consideration — you're also going to need hard drive space on that computer, some memory (RAM), and a processor with a certain amount of power (which is measured in MHz). If you want to get a DB2 client to talk to a DB2 server, you are also going to have communication software (or protocols), such as TCP/IP, installed and configured on your system. Table 4-1 shows the minimum, suggested, and optimal hardware configurations for installing a DB2 server, and the following sections also discuss each requirement briefly.

Table 4-1: Hardware Requirement for a DB2 Server

Requirement	*Minimum*	*Suggested*	*Optimal*
CPU	Pentium-class CPU	Pentium II or higher	Pentium III or higher
Free Hard Drive Space (for NTFS systems)	65MB	300MB	600MB
Memory (RAM)*	32MB	64MB	128MB

Requirement	*Minimum*	*Suggested*	*Optimal*
Windows NT version	Windows NT 4.0 with Service Pack 3 or higher (or Windows 2000)	—	Windows 2000
Communication Software (Protocol)	TCP/IP, NetBIOS, APPC, or IPX/SPX	TCP/IP	TCP/IP

** The amount of memory also depends on the number of concurrent DB2 client connections that you will have accessing this DB2 server. For more information, see the upcoming "Memory (RAM)" section.*

CPU

The CPU (central processing unit) is the heart of your computer, and its speed can make a big difference in how smoothly DB2 runs on your workstation. Make sure that your processor is Intel-compatible (meaning that Intel-compatible processors like AMD's Athlon or Transmeta's Crusoe are okay, too, but that you can't get the copy of DB2 in the back of this book to run on an RISC processor).

Free hard drive space

You can't install a DB2 server if you don't have the space for it. Sounds reasonable enough, doesn't it? In DB2-speak, the amount of space that DB2 takes on your computer is called the program's *footprint*. You need to have enough hard-drive space available to accommodate the size of the DB2 server's footprint. So, when your boss asks you at the water cooler whether you have enough hard drive space to handle the DB2 footprint, don't look down at his shoes!

Most Windows NT/2000-based computers use the NT File System (NTFS). Some computers may have drives formatted with the File Allocation Table (FAT) file system. If you are using a drive that was formatted as FAT, the footprint requirements may be signficantly (up to three times!) greater than the footprint requirements for an NTFS-formatted drive. The estimates in this chapter are for NTFS-formatted drives.

The footprint for a DB2 server is a tough thing to pinpoint with all the components and installation options that you have. Thankfully, the DB2 installation program helps you determine whether you have enough disk space to handle DB2.

To check the amount of space on a drive, double-click the My Computer icon on your desktop, right-click the icon representing your hard drive from the My Computer window that appears, and then select Properties. A Properties window similar to Figure 4-2 opens, informing you of the selected drive's free space.

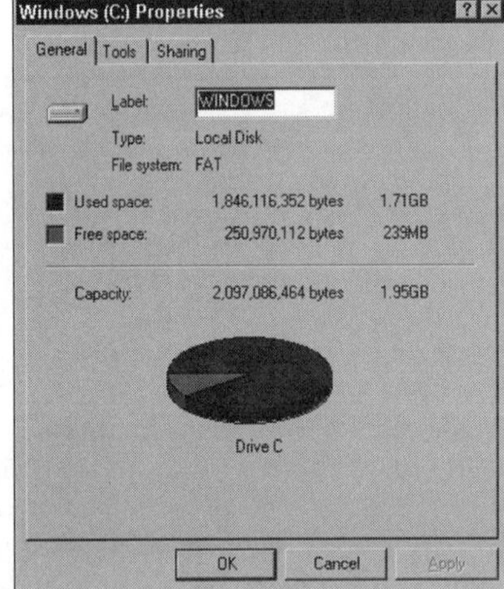

Figure 4-2: A pie chart showing the amount of available space on a computer's drive.

Memory (RAM)

You need memory to run a computer, (not yours, the computer's!). All applications use your computer's memory to reduce the amount of I/O on your machine's devices. The computer world calls this memory *Random Access Memory (RAM).*

Windows NT/2000 also uses paging space to boost the amount of memory on a workstation. *Paging space* is a file that the computer uses to store and retrieve memory information. The combination of RAM and paging space is called *virtual memory.* DB2 takes advantage of virtual memory.

I/O stands for Input/Output, and is used to refer to the interaction of applications or devices with your computer's drives. A certain amount of overhead is associated with I/O. For example, if you have stored a customer's file in a filing cabinet, I/O occurs when you need to look up something on your customer and retrieve the file from the cabinet to find the information. Information first went into the cabinet for storage and later went out again. If you knew all the information about the customer in your head, you would not have to go to the filing cabinet to find out the details. That is memory access.

The amount of memory you require to run a DB2 server depends on the number of DB2 clients that you're planning to concurrently connect to the

DB2 server. We recommend that you have at least 32MB of RAM if you're planning to support five DB2 clients at the same time. For each group of five or more DB2 clients that connect to the DB2 server at the same time, add another 4MB of RAM. So, if 25 DB2 clients are going to connect to your DB2 server at the same time, you need at least 48MB of RAM. Also, if you're planning to use the DB2 management tools to manage your DB2 environment, you should add another 32MB of RAM.

To check the amount of RAM on a Windows NT/2000 workstation, right-click the My Computer icon and choose Properties from the pop-up menu. The System Properties dialog box appears, as shown in Figure 4-3 (the General tab should be the default, but if it isn't, simply click the tab to select it).

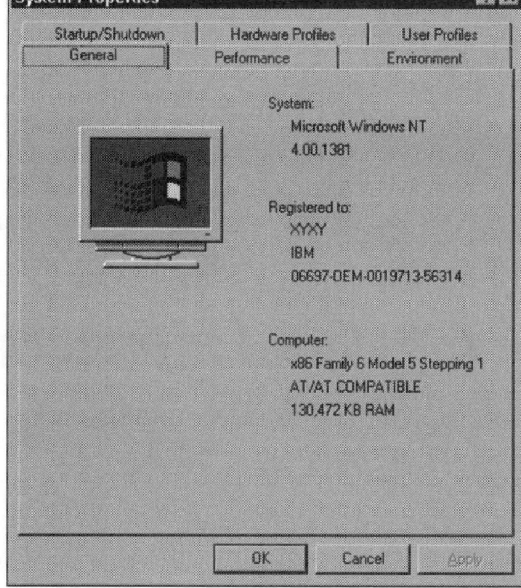

Figure 4-3: The System Properties window shows how much RAM is on your machine.

In Figure 4-3, you can see that we have a very passable 128MB (well, it's 130 actually, shown in kilobytes, but 128 is what you pay for) of RAM on our computer. Unlike the space requirement, however, if you don't have enough memory, the DB2 server still installs correctly. You may even be able to use it, although eventually you are likely to get some sort of "Out of memory" error and need more virtual memory for your machine.

The amount of memory that you need is only a suggestion that doesn't take into account other programs that may be running on your computer. Computers typically come with much more memory than the minimum requirement for DB2. The more programs you need to run on your machine simultaneously, the more RAM you should have.

Operating system

To install a DB2 server by using the CD in the back of the book, you need at least Microsoft Windows NT Version 4.0 with Service Pack 3 (SP3) or later. You can also install a DB2 server on a computer that's running Microsoft Windows 2000. If you want to install your DB2 server on a workstation that is running Windows 2000, you need to apply a FixPack to your installation of DB2. A FixPack is a pack of files that fix a problem after the release of a product. The FixPack you need is called FixPack 2. Of course, we recommend that you also ensure that you copy of DB2 is at the latest FixPack level (these things fix all kinds of problems). You can download FixPacks and get information on how to install them at the following URL:

```
http://www-4.ibm.com/cgi-bin/db2www/data/db2/udb/winos2unix/
        support/index.d2w/report
```

To see which Service Pack is installed on your NT computer (you don't need a service pack for Windows 2000), check out the blue window that you see when Windows boots up. If you have SP3 or higher, you're fine. Otherwise, you need to upgrade (see Microsoft's Windows Web site at `www.microsoft.com/ntserver/default.asp` for details about upgrading your service pack).

Communication software (or protocols)

The computer on which you install a DB2 server should be on a network and have a functional communication protocol running. DB2 supports the following protocols: TCP/IP, NetBIOS/NetBEUI, IPX/SPX, Named Pipes, and APPC (we suggest TCP/IP, which is pretty much universal). The term *protocol* is just fancy computer talk for a language that computers use to talk to each other. If one computer only speaks TCP/IP and another computer only speaks APPC, the two computers cannot talk to each other. To find out whether you have a supported protocol, ask your main computer guru (one hint: about 95 percent of the computers today run TCP/IP).

So that you don't have any problems with the examples in this book, make sure that your computers (the ones for the DB2 server and the DB2 client) can talk to each other by using TCP/IP.

You can quickly check whether you're on a network and using TCP/IP by entering the `hostname` command at the command prompt. This returns the name of your computer, which is usually the same as your computer name (we know this can been confusing, but the computer name is part of Windows and not always the same). Enter the `hostname` command at the command prompt on the computer where you are going to install the DB2 client (which we show you how to do in Chapter 5). Then on the computer where you intend to install the DB2 server, enter the `ping <hostname>`

command (again, at the command prompt), where *<hostname>* is the name that was returned when you entered the `hostname` command on the intended DB2 client machine.

Figure 4-4 shows the successful results of pinging a computer on a network.

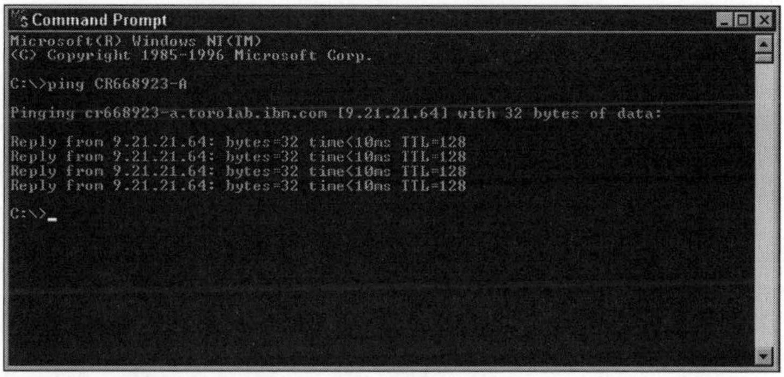

```
Command Prompt
Microsoft(R) Windows NT(TM)
(C) Copyright 1985-1996 Microsoft Corp.

C:\>ping CR668923-A

Pinging cr668923-a.torolab.ibm.com [9.21.21.64] with 32 bytes of data:

Reply from 9.21.21.64: bytes=32 time<10ms TTL=128
Reply from 9.21.21.64: bytes=32 time<10ms TTL=128
Reply from 9.21.21.64: bytes=32 time<10ms TTL=128
Reply from 9.21.21.64: bytes=32 time<10ms TTL=128

C:\>_
```

Figure 4-4: The CR668923-A machine responding to a ping command.

User account

You need a user account to perform the installation. A *user account* is the Windows term for the combination of a username and password, which you most likely use every day when you get to work and log on to your computer.

The user account that you use to install a DB2 server must

- Belong to the *Administrators* group
- Not exceed eight characters in length
- Have the following advanced user rights:
  - Act as part of the operating system
  - Increase quotas
  - Create a token object
  - Replace a process level token

You may need to talk to someone in charge to get the system rights and permissions or to create a new user account. Usually, Administrator authority isn't given out to just anyone, so you may have to pull some teeth at work to get it.

If you want more information on Windows NT/2000 users and groups, refer to the Windows NT/2000 online Help or *Windows NT 4 For Dummies,* 2nd Edition or *Windows 2000 Professional For Dummies,* both by Andy Rathbone and Sharon Crawford (IDG Books Worldwide, Inc.).

Installing a DB2 Server

You're ready to install the DB2 server on your computer, which you can do by using the DB2 CD-ROM at the back of this book. This CD-ROM offers a version of DB2 Workgroup Edition that expires (stops working) after 60 days unless you buy it.

When you install a DB2 server on Windows NT/2000, you have to choose the type of installation that you want to perform. You can select from the following three types of installations:

- **Typical:** The fastest way to get a complete DB2 product installed. All the typical components and settings are installed on your computer, and the setup program takes care of most of the decisions that usually need a guy with four-inch glasses and a pocket protector. Unless you're an expert or need a Compact installation, always install a DB2 server by using a Typical installation.
- **Custom:** Allows you to select specific components and details of a DB2 server installation, giving you complete control over which components get installed on your workstation and which don't. Usually, experienced people with DB2 use this installation method because they know that they will never use a specific option and don't want to hog up hard drive space with these options, or perhaps they need a component that is not part of a Typical installation
- **Compact:** This option is for those people that just don't have the space on their workstation for a DB2 installation and just want to get the bare essentials. This option won't install the DB2 documentation or graphical tools, including but not limited to the Control Center, the Command Center, First Steps, or the Client Configuration Assistant. If you are in a position where you can only install a Compact version of DB2, then you may consider buying a bigger hard drive!

If you choose the Compact install of DB2, you won't be able to follow most of instructions in this book.

Going the easy route with the Typical installation

The Typical installation is probably the way to go unless you have some reason to go with a Custom installation. To quickly install a DB2 server, follow these steps:

1. **Log on to your computer with a user account that meets the requirements for performing a DB2 installation.**

   For information on user accounts, see the "User account" section earlier in this chapter.

2. **Insert the CD-ROM that comes with this book into the CD-ROM drive.**

   The auto-run feature automatically starts the setup program. The setup program determines your computer's system language and launches the setup program for that language.

   If the setup program fails to start, you can manually start it from the command prompt by switching to the CD-ROM drive and entering the `setup` command.

   When the setup program starts, the Welcome dialog box appears, as shown in Figure 4-5.

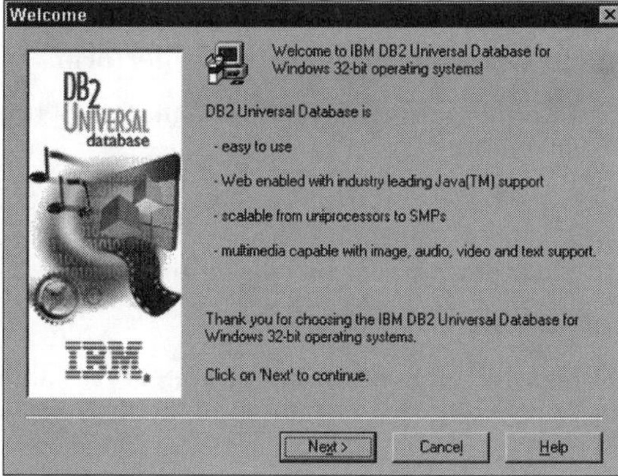

Figure 4-5: The Welcome window — gives you a warm, fuzzy feeling, doesn't it?

3. **Click Next.**

   The Select Products dialog box appears, as shown in Figure 4-6.

4. **Select the DB2 product that you want to install.**

   To highlight a product and read its description, click the product name instead of the check box. If you do so, a check mark does not appear beside the product name.

   Note: To install a DB2 server, click only the DB2 Workgroup Edition check box and be sure that no other check boxes are selected in this dialog box.

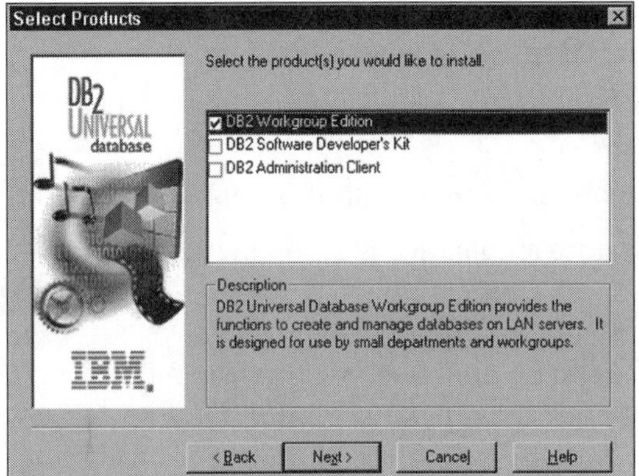

Figure 4-6: Selecting the products you want to install.

5. **Click Next.**

   The Select Installation Type dialog box appears, as shown in Figure 4-7.

6. **Select the type of installation that you want to perform.**

   Beside each installation type is a rough approximation of the hard drive space required to install the product.

   In these steps, we assume that you choose the Typical installation. If you choose Custom or Compact, the rest of these instructions will differ (We briefly discuss the Custom installation later in this chapter).

7. **Click the Typical button.**

   The Choose Destination Location dialog box appears, as shown in Figure 4-8. Note that the Space Required estimated in the figure is for a FAT file system, not an NTFS file system, where the requirements are different.

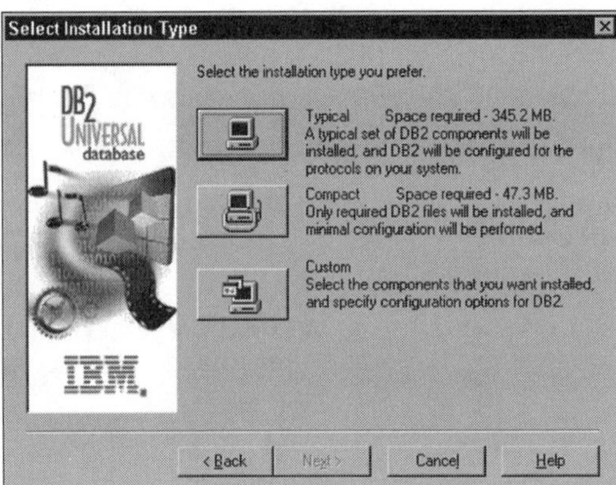

Figure 4-7: Selecting your installation type.

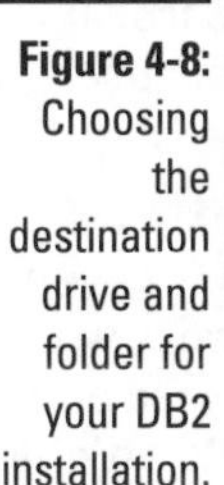

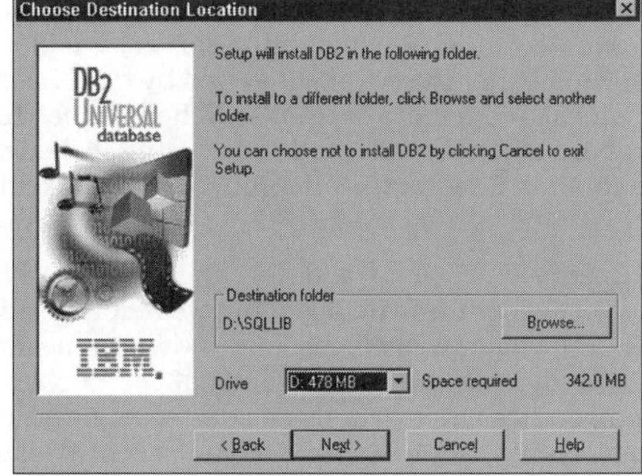

Figure 4-8: Choosing the destination drive and folder for your DB2 installation.

8. **Select the location where you want to install your DB2 server and click Next.**

   You can click the Browse button to select a target drive and directory. Clicking the Drive drop-down list box shows the space available on each of the drives on your system. You can compare this to the Space Required field to ensure that you have enough drive space to install the DB2 server. The information here may help you select a more suitable directory in the Destination Folder box above.

9. **Click Next.**

   The Enter Username and Password for the Administration Server dialog box appears, as shown in Figure 4-9.

   You need to select a username and a password that DB2 uses to log on to the system so that it can start the DAS as a service. That's techie talk, and at this point you don't really need to know anything more than you need a user account for the DAS.

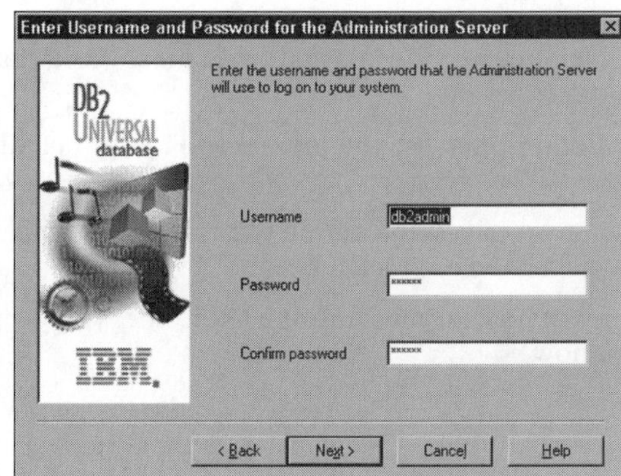

Figure 4-9: The Enter Username and Password for the Administration Server window.

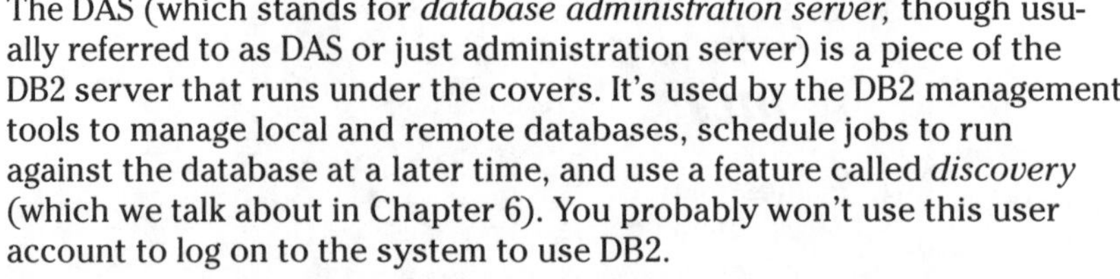

The DAS (which stands for *database administration server,* though usually referred to as DAS or just administration server) is a piece of the DB2 server that runs under the covers. It's used by the DB2 management tools to manage local and remote databases, schedule jobs to run against the database at a later time, and use a feature called *discovery* (which we talk about in Chapter 6). You probably won't use this user account to log on to the system to use DB2.

The default username is `db2admin` and the default password is `db2admin`. You can accept these defaults, but we recommend that you don't. We cannot tell you how many machines we've come across where we used the default `db2admin` username and `db2admin` password and logged on to somebody else's machine. Of course, we never did anything wrong to these machines, but they had a definite security exposure by using those defaults. Get it? If you don't change the password from `db2admin`, everyone knows it because it's the default password for every DB2 server installation.

You can also specify a new username and password, and the setup program will create the user account that you specify. The username you specify cannot be more than eight characters long.

You can specify a username that already exists on your system, but if you do, you have to specify the correct password. Also, the existing username that you specify must have the same rights and privileges as the user account you're using to install DB2. See the "User account" section earlier in this chapter for more information.

10. **Click Next.**

    The Start Copying Files dialog box appears.

11. **Scroll through the Current Settings box to see all the installation options and components that will be installed on your machine.**

    If you're not satisfied, you can click Back to return to the previous installation window and make any changes to your selections.

12. **Click Next.**

    Wait a couple of minutes for the installation to finish (a status bar shows you how much time remains).

13. **When the installation finishes, you must restart your machine before you can use your DB2 server.**

    The setup program gives you the option to restart your machine when the installation is finished or at a later time.

    If you choose to restart your machine at a later time, you cannot use your DB2 server now.

Getting complicated with the Custom installation

For the most part, a Typical installation should be all you need to know about DB2 server installations. Whenever we install DB2, we use a Typical installation because it's easier. But for all you geeks who have to try everything, you can use a Custom installation as well.

A Custom installation allows you to customize the configuration and components that are part of your DB2 server installation. For example, you can choose to install a code page for East-Asian language support, which is not part of a Typical installation. Or, you may not want the setup program to automatically configure all those protocols that are detected on your system, which we discuss in the "Communication software (or protocols)" section earlier in this chapter. You can even use a Custom installation to strip protocols that you don't need.

The process for a Custom installation is the same as for a Typical installation, except that you're presented with more installation options and more decisions. The Custom install would take up an entire chapter if we went through all of the components that you can choose from. Instead, we've included some information to show you how the Select Components window works.

Selecting individual components

If you were to click the Custom button, instead of the Typical button, after the Select Installation Type window (refer to Figure 4-7) opens, the Select Components window would open, as shown in Figure 4-10.

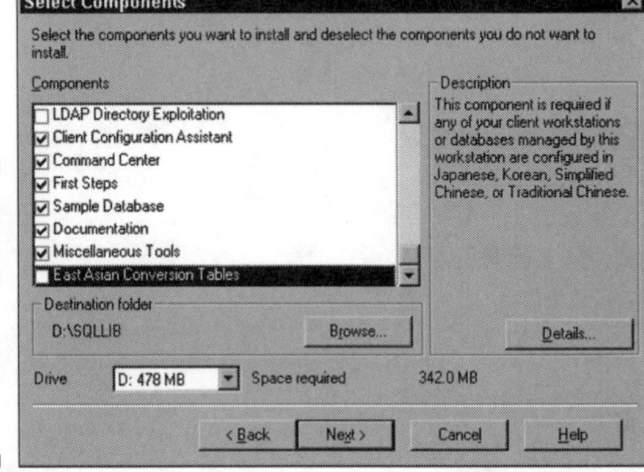

Figure 4-10: Selecting the components you want in a Custom installation.

In this dialog box, you select or deselect DB2 components for installation. For more information about a component, highlight the component and then check out its details in the Description box on the right.

For example, say that you want to perform a Custom installation because the top geek at your company tells you that they're buying a major Japanese software manufacturer and wants you to install code-page support for Japanese.

Code pages are used by DB2 so, for example, people who use DB2 in Japanese can work with people who use DB2 in English. At the beginner level, you don't need to know anything more about code pages than that. Any DB2 installation automatically sets the correct code page for the language that your computer is configured to use.

Notice in Figure 4-10 that the East Asian Conversion Tables check box is not selected as the others are. This is because East Asian conversion tables are not part of a Typical DB2 installation, at least not in the copy you get in North America. To select this component, click in the check box.

When you want to highlight a component, don't click the check box; click the component's name instead. Clicking in the actual check box either selects the component or deselects it, depending on whether the check box has already been checked.

If you only wanted the conversion tables for Japanese, you could select just this one by clicking the Details button.

When you click the Details buttons, the Select Subcomponents dialog box appears listing all the subcomponents that make up a component, as shown in Figure 4-11. Many components have subcomponents that you can include or exclude from an installation. If a component has a subcomponent, the Details button becomes active when you highlight the component; otherwise, the Details button remains grayed out and inactive.

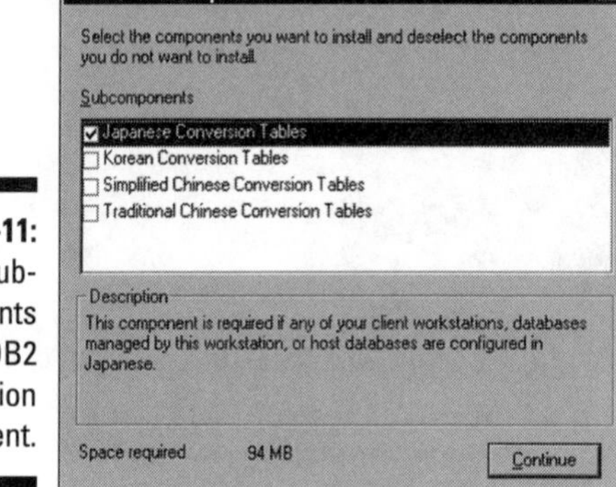

Figure 4-11: Select subcomponents of a DB2 installation component.

For this example, you need to deselect all the check boxes, except for the Japanese Conversion Tables check box, that you want to install.

After you select all the subcomponents for a component, click Continue. You can then move on to other components and repeat the whole sordid process. See why people choose the Typical install? When you have a big enough hard drive, it's worth the few megabytes of hard drive space to not have to haggle with all of these components!

When you finish selecting the components for your installation and specifying the correct target drive and directory, click Next to configure your protocols.

Configuring your protocols

After you finish selecting the components you want, the Configure DB2 Services dialog box appears, as shown in Figure 4-12. This is where you tell the setup program which protocols you want to configure for your DB2 server and set the startup of any instances (which we discuss briefly in Chapter 2 and more thoroughly in Chapter 7).

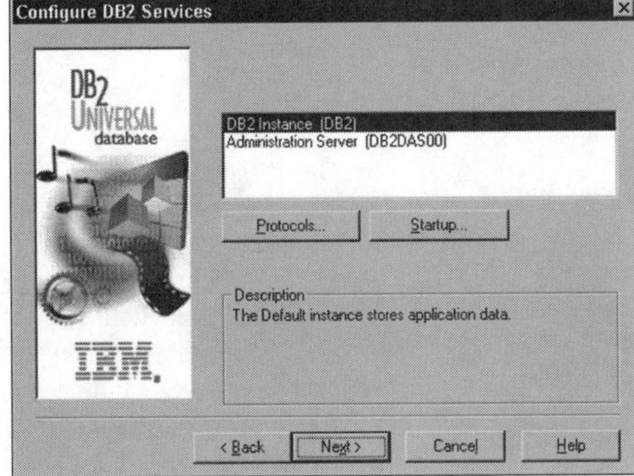

Figure 4-12: Configuring protocols for your DB2 server installation.

The setup program automatically detects and configures all the protocols that are working on your system. This is the best way to install your DB2 server. Our advice: Just click Next at this point because all the default settings are fine. But for you diehards, we show you in the nearby sidebar how to manually select what protocols to configure during a DB2 server installation.

The rest of the installation is the same as a Typical installation (refer to "Installing a DB2 Server" earlier in this chapter and pick up with Step 7) .

Stripping down protocol support

In the Configure DB2 Services dialog box (shown in Figure 4-12), you can set up protocol support for any instances that the DB2 installation program will create. You can have two entries: one for the default DB2 Instance and the other for the administration server's instance (we discuss instances in Chapter 7). The setup program creates one for you and calls it *DB2*. Creative, eh? The administration server (remember that thing we call the DAS?) also has an instance; it's called DB2DAS00. Don't worry too much about it, but if you want only TCP/IP support, you have to follow the same steps for the DB2DAS00 instance as you do for the DB2 instance. Usually, you just let the DB2 installation program detect and configure any protocols on your system for you (this is what a Typical installation does).

To manually select which protocols you want the setup program to configure for your DB2 server, follow these steps:

1. **Select the instance that you want to configure.**
2. **Click the Protocols button.**

   The Customize the DB2 Instance dialog box appears, as shown in the following figure.

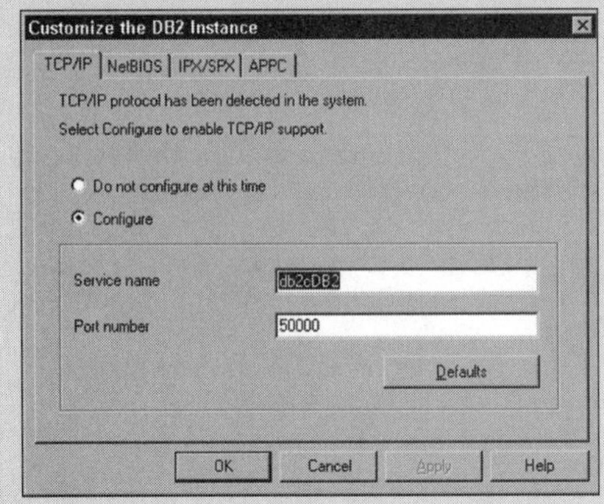

Each protocol has a separate tab, as you can see in the preceding figure. If the setup program detects that a protocol exists on your system, the program generates default values for the protocol and automatically selects the Configure option for each detected protocol.

In the accompanying figure, you can see that the setup program detected TCP/IP on the computer and came up with some default values for it. The values that the setup program provides are fine. We don't talk about these default values because that's beyond the scope of this book. If you want to know more about these settings, check out *Networking For Dummies* by Doug Lowe (IDG Books Worldwide).

If the setup program doesn't detect TCP/IP on the computer, the Do Not Configure at This Time option is automatically selected.

If TCP/IP isn't detected on your system, check the other tabs to see if any other protocols have been detected. Found one? Okay, continue on, but you may not be able to follow the instructions in Chapter 6 word for word because we assume that TCP/IP is running on your workstation. If no protocols are detected, you can still continue, just skip past Chapters 5 and 6 because your DB2 clients won't be able to talk to your DB2 server.

3. **Click the tab for a protocol that you do not want to configure for DB2.**
4. **Select the Do Not Configure at This Time option and then click OK.**

   You're returned to the Configure DB2 Services dialog box (refer to Figure 4-12).

Rebooting your computer

Make sure that you reboot when the setup program asks you to (after the installation is finished, that is). The drama picks up in the next section, where you *finally* get to start using DB2!

Taking Your First Steps with DB2

So you finish installing your DB2 server and reboot. Ten minutes later (ah, the beauty of Windows) your operating system starts up.

Log on to your system after the reboot with the same user account that you used to perform the installation. After you log on, the DB2 First Steps dialog box appears, as shown in Figure 4-13. First Steps is a tool designed to help get you going on DB2. It allows you to create a sample database, start the Command Center (a tool used for inputting DB2 commands and SQL statements) with a predefined script to query the sample database that you created, work with the sample database by starting the Control Center, and view DB2's documentation library.

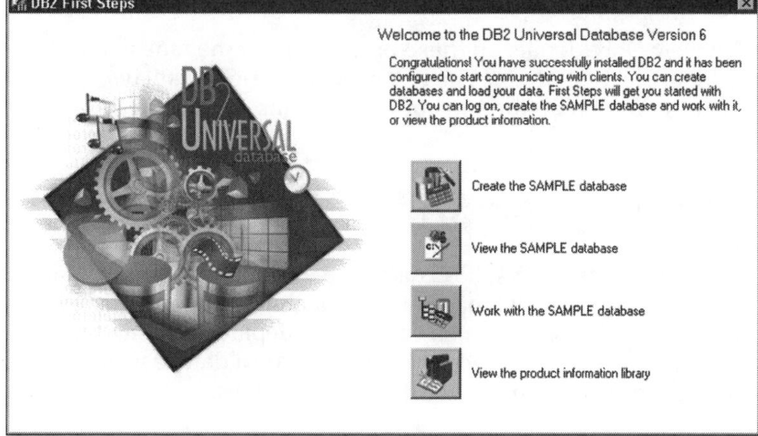

Figure 4-13: First Steps is a tool designed to get you going on DB2.

If First Steps doesn't start or you got scared when the dialog box appeared after you rebooted and shut it down, you can restart it by clicking the Start button and choosing DB2 for Windows NT⇨First Steps. First Steps won't open if you performed a Compact installation or a Custom installation and deselected it, because it won't be there!

First Steps gives you four options, which we describe in detail in the following sections. These four options are

- **Create the SAMPLE database:** Creates a sample database called SAMPLE (aren't you swooning with the sheer creativity?) in the default DB2 instance. (We discuss instances in detail in Chapter 7.) You can use the SAMPLE database to use the other features in First Steps or to experiment without risking important data.
- **View the SAMPLE database:** Launches the Command Center, which is used to enter DB2 commands and SQL statements. When the Command Center starts, a script is preloaded that you can run to retrieve contents from the sample database that you created using the Create the SAMPLE database button.
- **Work with the SAMPLE database:** Launches the Control Center, which is the DB2 graphical management tool. You use the Control Center throughout this book to perform all sorts of management tasks on your DB2 server.
- **View the product information library:** Launches the Information Center, which contains tips, tricks, Web links, samples, and links to the DB2 documentation, including a task-level help feature.

You can also invoke these options outside First Steps as well (except for the creating the SAMPLE database bit), by selecting the appropriate option from the DB2 for Windows option in the Start menu.

To view more details on these options, place the mouse pointer over a button and just let it sit there. The button's hover Help displays, giving you more details on what action the button performs.

Creating the SAMPLE database

You can create the SAMPLE database to get a feel for how databases work in DB2. The SAMPLE database has fictional data about a company, with tables that contain information on sales, staff, departments, and products. In the rest of the book, you find out how to create a database yourself, but for now, we use the sample database that DB2 provides.

To create the SAMPLE database, follow these steps:

1. **In the DB2 First Steps dialog box, click the Create the SAMPLE Database button.**

   Creating the SAMPLE database can take some time, so be patient. In fact, DB2 even warns you of this with a pop-up window.

2. **To confirm that you want to create the SAMPLE database, click Yes in the pop-up window.**

   DB2 creates the SAMPLE database. A not-particularly useful progress dialog box appears, confirming that DB2 is indeed creating this database. Perhaps this is just to give you something to watch while the SAMPLE database is being created.

   If you didn't install First Steps, you can still create the SAMPLE database by entering the db2sampl command at a command prompt.

   A pop-up dialog box eventually appears, informing you that the SAMPLE database has been created successfully.

There you go! You now have a database. Creating a database with real data isn't nearly that easy. First Steps actually calls a script file that creates the database and imports data into it. Later chapters in this book show you how to do this; in the meantime, you can take advantage of the SAMPLE database so that you can work with the rest of this book and not risk damaging your own data.

Viewing the contents of the SAMPLE database

You now have a database and can take a look to see what's inside it. Before you can get data into a database, the instance in which the database resides needs to be started and you must connect to the database. Don't worry about starting the instance because the DB2 installation program sets the default instance to start automatically. (We show you how to start an instance in Chapter 7). If you can connect to your database and get data from it, you know it must be working.

To view your SAMPLE database, follow these steps:

1. **In the DB2 First Steps dialog box, click the View the SAMPLE Database button.**

   DB2 starts the Command Center, which is one of the DB2 tools.

   You can also start the Command Center by clicking the Start button and choosing ProgramsÎDB2 for Windows NTÎCommand Center.

   Whenever you start a DB2 management tool, you have to log on to DB2.

   The Control Center Sign On dialog box appears, as shown in Figure 4-14.

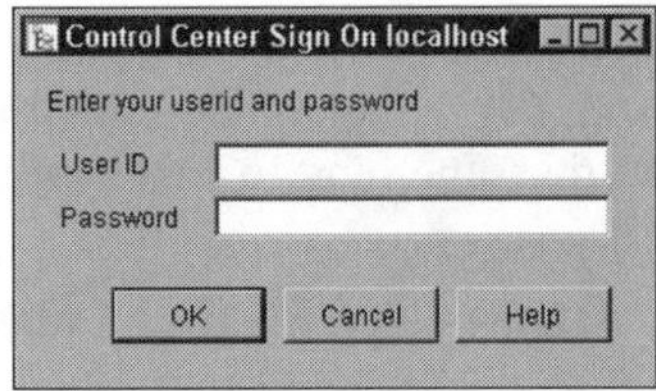

Figure 4-14: The Control Center Sign On dialog box allows you to log on to the Control Center.

2. **Type the user account that you used to install DB2 into the User ID text box.**

   By default, this user account automatically had System Administrative (SYSADM) authority (System Administrative authority is just DB2-speak for a Database Administrator, or DBA). This user account inherits this authority because the account belongs to the Administrators group. You can log on to this tool by using any user account, but then you would have to do deal with authorization issues and other such problems.

   You can also enter the user account that you created when configuring the administration server during your installation.

   As soon as the user account is validated, the Command Center window appears (as shown in Figure 4-15), displaying a default script file with a group of commands that run when you execute them.

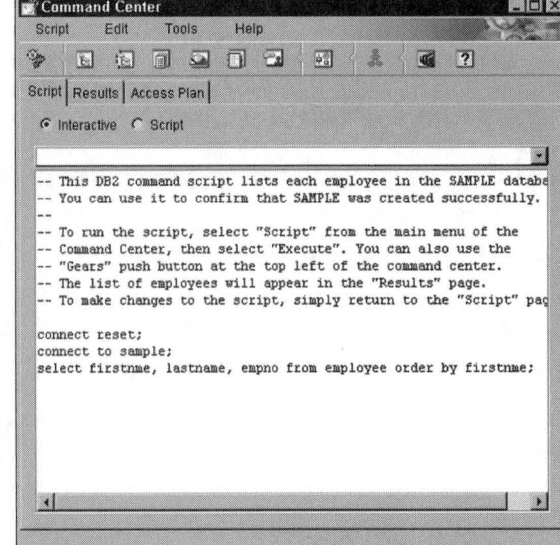

Figure 4-15: The DB2 Command Center with a default script to query the SAMPLE database.

You can see by looking at the DB2 commands that this script file resets any database connections, connects to the SAMPLE database, and then issues a query against the EMPLOYEE table.

The details of these commands aren't important at this point — what is important is that the commands work. If they work, you know that you're running a healthy DB2 server.

You can get detailed information on how to use the Command Center by choosing Help from the menu bar.

3. **Click the gears icon in the top-left corner to run the script.**

   When you place your mouse pointer over this icon, a tool-tip appears and calls this icon Execute.

   You can also start the execution of commands in the Command Center by pressing Ctrl+Enter.

   DB2 first resets the database connection, then connects to the SAMPLE database, and then runs the query. The output looks similar to Figure 4-16, and you have now retrieved data from a database.

```
JASON        GOUNOT       000340
JENNIFER     LUTZ         000220
JOHN         GEYER        000050
JOHN         PARKER       000290
MARIA        PEREZ        000270
MARILYN      SCOUTTEN     000180
MASATOSHI    YOSHIMURA    000170
MAUDE        SETRIGHT     000310
MICHAEL      THOMPSON     000020
PHILIP       SMITH        000300
RAMLAL       MEHTA        000320
SALLY        KWAN         000030
SALVATORE    MARINO       000240
SEAN         O'CONNELL    000120
SYBIL        JOHNSON      000260
THEODORE     SPENSER      000100
VINCENZO     LUCCHESSI    000110
WILLIAM      JONES        000210
WING         LEE          000330

  32 record(s) selected.
```

Figure 4-16: Results of the sample query in the Command Center's Results tab.

Close the Command Center by choosing either Results⇨Close or Script⇨Close (depending on what tab you have selected), or by clicking the X button in the upper-right corner of the window.

Working with the SAMPLE database

First Steps also gives you the option to work with the SAMPLE database by using the Control Center. You can use the Control Center to work with any instance or database, local or remote, as long as it has been catalogued on your system. Following is a brief look at the Control Center. In upcoming chapters, we show you how to use the Control Center to graphically administer your DB2 server and its clients, which is a far easier method than administering your environment by using commands entered in a DB2 command window.

To start the Control Center and work with a database, follow these steps:

1. **In the First Steps dialog box, click the Work with the SAMPLE Database button to start the Control Center.**

   You can also start the Control Center by clicking the Start button and choosing Programs➪DB2 for Windows NT➪Control Center, or entering the `db2cc` command at a Windows command prompt.

   The Control Center is the central management tool for DB2. Throughout this book, you discover all the valuable things that you can do with this tool.

   In the meantime, you can just make sure that it works.

2. **In the Control Center Sign On dialog box that appears (refer to Figure 4-16), log on with the user account that you used to perform the installation.**

   As soon as the user account is validated, the Control Center opens, as shown in Figure 4-17.

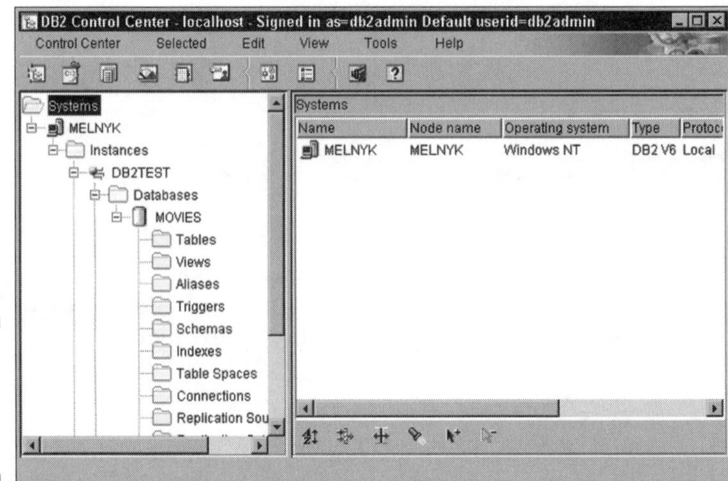

Figure 4-17: The DB2 Control Center.

We don't get into this here, though feel free to explore! We wanted to make sure that it works so that you can perform the rest of the exercises in this book. You find out more about how to use the Control Center in Parts III and IV.

Viewing the DB2 documentation

First Steps also gives you a tour of the DB2 documentation — including books, tasks, notebooks, and so on — via the DB2 Information Center. The Information Center is a central starting point for all the DB2 documentation and is a very useful reference point for discovering more about DB2, performing tasks, and finding more detailed examples of the things you can do with DB2. To start the Information Center, simply click the View the Product Information Library button in the First Steps dialog box.

You can also start the Information Center by clicking the Start button and choosing Programs➪DB2 for WindowsNT➪Information➪Information Center.

Because the Information Center is integrated with the Control Center, you must log on to DB2 again, just as with the Command Center and the Control Center earlier in this chapter.

As soon as the user account is validated, the Information Center appears, as shown in Figure 4-18.

Take some time to experiment and browse through all of the features of the Information Center. Select different tabs and see all the links to valuable DB2 information.

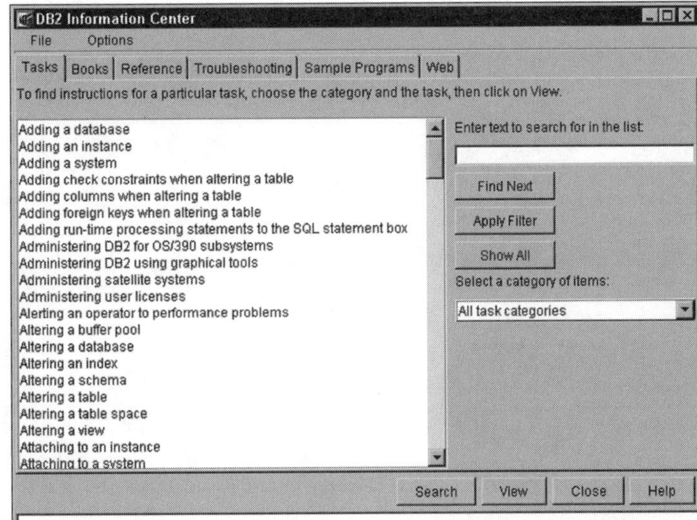

Figure 4-18: The DB2 Information Center.

Chapter 5

Installing a DB2 Client on a Windows NT/2000 Machine

In This Chapter

- Defining a DB2 client
- Understanding run-time clients versus administration clients
- Knowing what you need to install the DB2 client software
- Installing a DB2 client

If you have installed a DB2 server (a process which we discuss in Chapter 4), chances are you need some clients that can work with that server. This chapter introduces you to and shows you how to install a DB2 client — the software used to talk to DB2 servers from remote workstations.

Defining a DB2 Client

A *DB2 client* (not to jump right in or anything) is a piece of DB2 software that runs on a computer other than your DB2 server. The DB2 client software enables your computer to connect to a DB2 server. Many computer geeks call this a *client/server environment* or a *distributed environment.*

Figure 5-1 shows several computers that have DB2 run-time clients installed on them and one computer that has an administration client installed (we discuss these two different types of client later in the chapter). This is so that one administration client operator can manage the DB2 server from their workstation without actually working on the computer where the DB2 server resides. The employees with the run-time clients don't need the administration abilities of the administration client, and so these computers use a stripped-down version of the administration client called a run-time client.

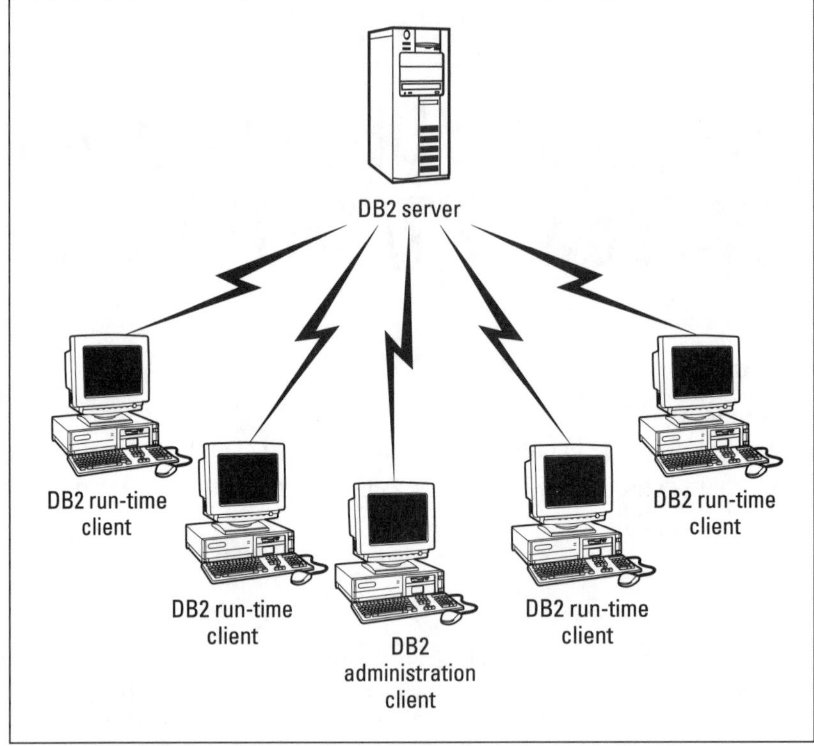

Figure 5-1: An example of several DB2 run-time clients and one DB2 administration client connecting to a DB2 server.

Figure 5-1 shows many computers connected to a remote DB2 server. Each of these computers can access data on the DB2 server because they have a DB2 client installed.

When you install a DB2 server, the installation program always installs a DB2 client behind the scenes. In Chapter 4 we show you how to retrieve information from the SAMPLE database on your DB2 server, which actually involves using a DB2 client.

You can use one DB2 client to access multiple DB2 servers, as shown in Figure 5-2.

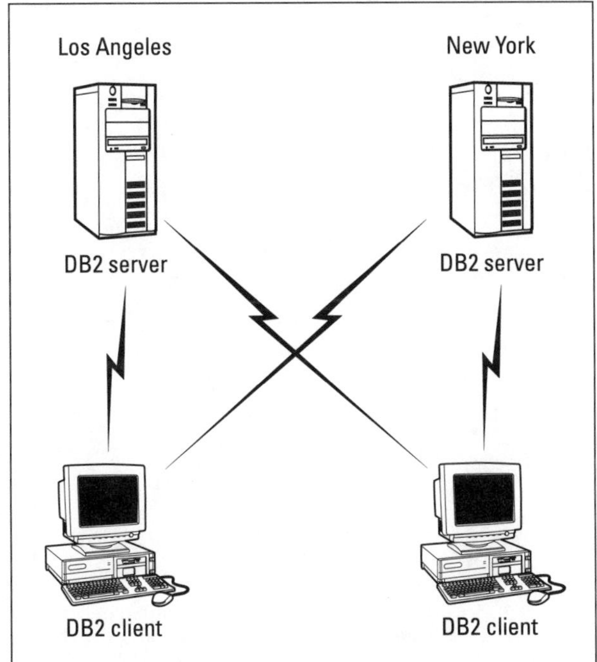

Figure 5-2: Two DB2 clients accessing multiple DB2 servers.

Figure 5-2 represents a typical configuration for a larger company, but it does not use the Internet at all, where the world is moving away from client/server computing to Web-based access.

Figure 5-3 shows an example of a computer that connects to a DB2 server over the Web, and the components that make the connection work. Computer geeks call this a *two-tiered environment.*

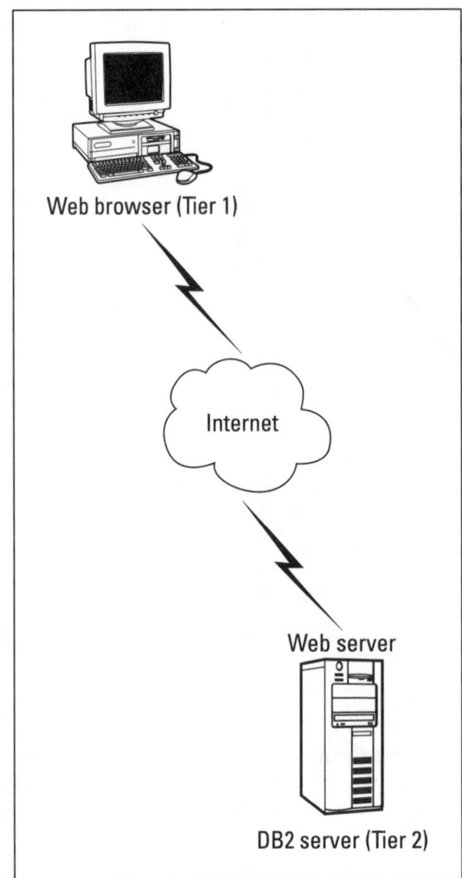

Figure 5-3: Accessing DB2 data over the Web in a two-tiered environment.

Figure 5-4 shows an example of a computer that connects to a DB2 client over the Web, which then connects to a DB2 server. The computer that connects to the DB2 client does not have any DB2 software installed. The connection in handled over the Web. This environment is called a *three-tiered environment.*

You can also use a DB2 client to administer your database or its environment. The type of client you use to administer your database is a special DB2 client called a DB2 administration client (more on that in the next section), with which any computer on your network can access any DB2 server or database and configure it for DB2.

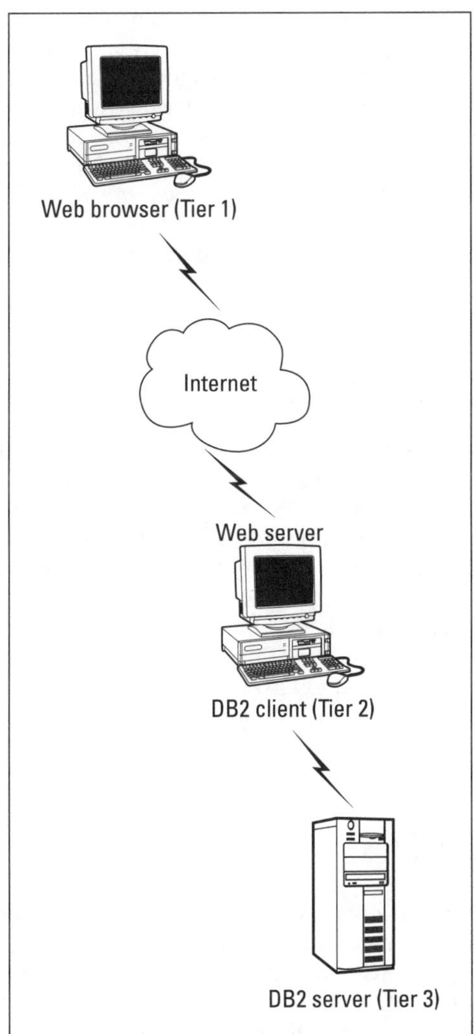

Figure 5-4: Accessing DB2 data over the Web in a three-tiered environment.

Understanding the Different DB2 Clients

At one time, DB2 shipped a single client software package called the DB2 Client Application Enabler (DB2 CAE), which included everything you needed to access or manage a database. But later IBM took a closer look at how clients were being used and realized that in many instances the DB2 CAE was taking up more footprint than necessary. (If you read the word footprint and looked at your feet, see the "Free hard drive space" section later in this chapter.)

As a result, IBM introduced two custom clients: run-time clients and administration clients. While the administration client is roughly equivalent to the old DB2 CAE, the run-time client is stripped down to minimize memory and footprint and maximize performance. This way, administration clients retain the management abilities of the old DB2 CAE only on those machines that need it. It was a good move. DB2 administrators typically install many DB2 run-time clients and only a few DB2 administration clients. The DB2 administration clients are reserved for guys with four-inch thick glasses, or users that need access to the documentation, while the DB2 run-time clients are for the rest of us who couldn't care less.

DB2 administration client

A DB2 administration client contains all the features of a DB2 run-time client, but also includes the DB2 management tools necessary to manage your DB2 environment and some other add-ons when using DB2 in a more complex environment. Because it comes with more tools, a DB2 administration client has a larger footprint than a DB2 run-time client.

For example, a DB2 administration client comes with the Control Center and all of its bundled tools, like the Command Center, the Performance Monitor, and so on. A DB2 administration client also allows you to install such things as documentation, code server support for DB2 thin-clients, and other miscellaneous tools.

DB2 run-time client

When you install a DB2 run-time client, you basically install the code that allows you to run applications that connect to a DB2 server, along with a few other tools. The other tools (the Command Center, the Client Configuration Assistant) allow you to enter DB2 and SQL commands and connect DB2 clients to DB2 servers. These tools are discussed throughout the remaining chapters in this book.

Run-time clients used to be part of what was called a DB2 Client Application Enabler (DB2 CAE). Some people that have used DB2 for years still refer to it as the CAE. This old name is more descriptive of what a DB2 run-time client really is now — it enables client applications. A run-time client is just a stripped-down version of the administration client with only the part that enables client applications to connect to a DB2 server.

Client application is just a stuffy term for program. For example, because your computer is a client and Netscape Navigator is an application running on that client, that makes Navigator a client application.

DB2 run-time clients are usually installed on employee workstations that use DB2, even if the employees don't know it. For example, suppose that a bank uses DB2 to track its customers and their transactions with a program that has a nice graphical user interface (GUI). All the employees have to do is type information into fields, point and click with their mice, and complete transactions. Underneath this GUI is an application that works with a DB2 client to talk to the DB2 server, and the bank employees never once hear the term DB2 or know that their computers interface with it constantly.

DB2 run-time clients don't include any management tools that you can use to administer your DB2 environment. Installing a DB2 run-time client enables you to access data only on remote databases, unless you want to manage DB2 the old fashioned way by using commands.

Knowing What You Need to Install a DB2 Client

To install a DB2 client, you need basically the same things as you do to install a DB2 server (we discuss this process in Chapter 4), but in different proportions or with different characteristics. See Chapter 4 for more information on the general requirements for your basic hardware setup. Table 5-1 lists the different requirements for installing a DB2 client:

Table 5-1: Hardware Requirement for a DB2 Client

Requirement	*Minimum*	*Suggested*	*Optimal*
CPU	Pentium-class CPU	Pentium II or higher	Pentium III or higher
Free Hard Drive Space (for NTFS systems)	11MB	85MB	120MB+
RAM	16MB	32MB	64MB+
Operating System	Windows NT Version 4.0 with Service Pack 3 or higher (or Windows 2000)	—	Windows 2000
Communication Software	TCP/IP, NetBIOS, IPX/SPX, or APPC	TCP/IP	TCP/IP

CPU

The CPU is the heart of your computer, and its speed can make a big difference in how smoothly DB2 runs on your workstation. Make sure that your processor is Intel-compatible (meaning that Intel-compatible processors like AMD's Athlon or Transmeta's Crusoe are okay, too, but that you can't get the DB2 client in the back of this book to run on a RISC processor).

Free hard drive space

As when installing any software on a computer, your amount of available hard drive space is definitely an issue. Those of a geekier bent call the amount of disk space that a program consumes that program's *footprint.* A typical DB2 run-time client installation requires between 11MB and 20MB of available drive space. (See Chapter 4 for instructions to find out whether you have enough free hard drive space available or not.)

Most Windows NT/2000-based computers use the NT File System (NTFS). Some computers may have drives formatted with the File Allocation Table (FAT) file system. If you are using a drive that was formatted as FAT, the footprint requirements may be signficantly (up to three times!) greater than the footprint requirements for an NTFS-formatted drive. The estimates in this chapter are for NTFS-formatted drives.

Because of the DB2 management tools, a DB2 administration client installation is going to have a larger footprint than a run-time client. If you are planning to install a DB2 administration client, make sure that you have about 85MB of available space for a Typical installation. If you perform a Custom or Compact installation, this number can grow to as high as 120MB and be reduced to as little as 11MB.

Memory (RAM)

Your system requires 16MB of memory to run a DB2 run-time client. If you are planning to run a DB2 administration client, you need approximately 32MB of memory. (See Chapter 4 for instructions to find out whether you have enough RAM or not.)

The amount of memory that you need is only a suggestion; it does not take into account other programs that may be running on your computer. Most personal computers today come with more memory than the required minimum (see Table 5-1 earlier in this chapter for the minimum requirements). If you are using your computer at the office, you may even need more memory to install a DB2 client.

Checking out the single-user installation

You can install a DB2 client without the required Administrator authority that you need to install a DB2 server. This is referred to as a single-user installation. Because this book focuses on installing DB2 as an administrator, the single-user installation isn't discussed any further. You can refer to the *DB2 Installation and Configuration Supplement,* one of the DB2 books that is installed with the documentation in a Typical DB2 server or DB2 administration client installation.

We don't recommend that you use a single-user installation unless you really know what you are doing. If you define and install your DB2 client with the same user account that you used to install the DB2 server, you do not have to worry about authentication problems when connecting to the remote DB2 server. If you need access to the DB2 install documentation before installing DB2, you can view it from the CD-ROM.

The single-user installation enables any users of the system (except ones that belong to the Guest group) to install a DB2 client. This ability was added to DB2 because customers often complained that employees without administrator authority on the operating system could not install a DB2 client. After all, many employees may need to access your company's database. Given that database security is usually controlled at the server, where's the harm in allowing nonadministrators to install a DB2 Client?

A single-user installation is for one user only. This means that other users of your system can't use the DB2 client. However, another user can install a DB2 client for their profile, so you may have three users on one machine installing a DB2 client as a single-user. But if an administrator chose to perform an installation, it overrides and wipes out the other single-user installations and creates a global installation of the DB2 client.

Operating system and communication software (or protocols)

The operating system and communication software requirements that exist for a DB2 server and a DB2 client are the same. Chances are, you don't have to worry about this. For more information on how to determine if you have the correct operating system and communication software, see Chapter 4.

User account

You need a user account (and valid password) to perform a DB2 client installation, just as you do when you install a DB2 server.

Installing a DB2 Client

If you're reading this section, our bet is that you are now ready to install the DB2 client on your computer. A DB2 administration client is provided on the *DB2 For Windows For Dummies* CD-ROM. Any DB2 server always comes with a DB2 administration client that you can install. If you want to install a DB2 run-time client, you need to use the DB2 Run-Time Client CD Pack that comes with a licensed copy of DB2, or download one from the Web at the following URL:

```
http://www-4.ibm.com/software/data/db2/db2tech/clientpak.html
```

When you install any DB2 client on a Windows NT/2000 machine, you have to choose the type of installation that you want to perform. The installation options are the same for a DB2 client as they are for a DB2 server. You can select from the following installation types:

- **Typical:** The fastest way to get a complete DB2 client installed. All the typical components and settings are installed on your computer, and the setup program takes care of most of the decisions. Unless you're an expert or need a Compact installation, always install a DB2 client using a Typical installation.
- **Custom:** Allows you to select specific components and details of a DB2 client installation, giving you complete control over what gets installed on your workstation and what doesn't. Usually, experienced people with DB2 use this installation method because they know that they will never use a specific component or need one that is not part of a Typical installation. For helpful information on how to deal with the Custom installation, see Chapter 4.
- **Compact:** This option is for those people that just don't have the space on their workstation for a DB2 client installation and just want to get the bare essentials. This option won't install the DB2 documentation or graphical tools in a DB2 client. If you are in a position where you can only install a Compact version of DB2, then you may consider buying a bigger hard drive!

Saving some hassle with the Typical installation

This section shows you how to install a DB2 client using a Typical installation, which is arguably the fastest, most convenient, and most fool-proof method for a getting a DB2 client on your workstation.

To quickly install a DB2 client, follow these steps:

1. **Log on to your computer with a user account that meets all of the requirements necessary to perform a DB2 installation.**

   If you need a reminder of the details of this user account, see the "Checking out the single-user installation" sidebar earlier in this chapter.

2. **Insert the CD-ROM that comes with this book into the CD-ROM drive. The auto-run feature automatically starts the setup program.**

   If the setup program fails to start, you can manually start it by switching to the CD-ROM drive and entering the `setup` command at a command prompt.

   After the setup program starts, the Welcome window appears, as shown in Figure 5-5.

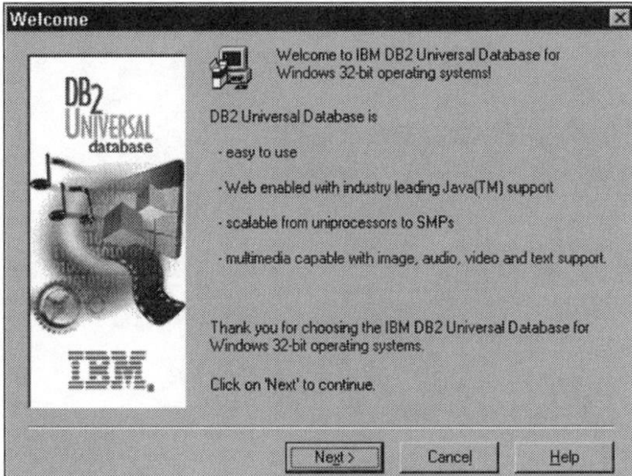

Figure 5-5: The Welcome window for a DB2 client installation.

3. **Click Next.**

   The Select Products window opens, as shown in Figure 5-6.

4. **Ensure that only the DB2 Administration Client check box is selected.**

   Click the check box beside the product that you want to select (so that you see a check mark in the check box) and do the same to deselect a product (so that there's no check mark in the check box). Click the product's name to read a description of that product.

   If you're installing a DB2 client from the CD-ROM in the back of your book, you only have the option to install a DB2 administration client. (There's a URL earlier in this chapter where you can download a run-time client, though.)

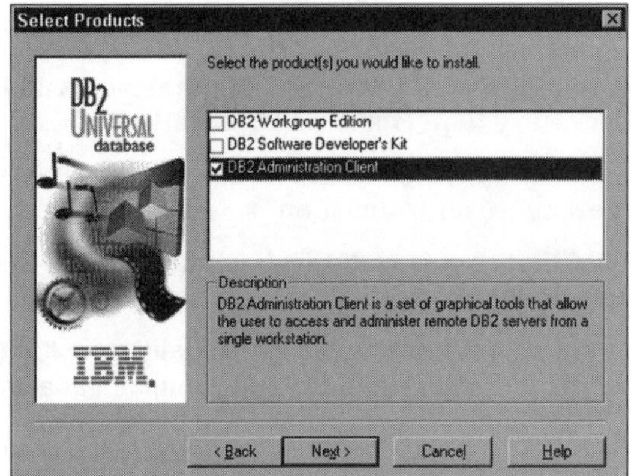

Figure 5-6: The DB2 Select Products window.

5. **Click Next.**

   The Select Installation Type window appears, as shown in Figure 5-7.

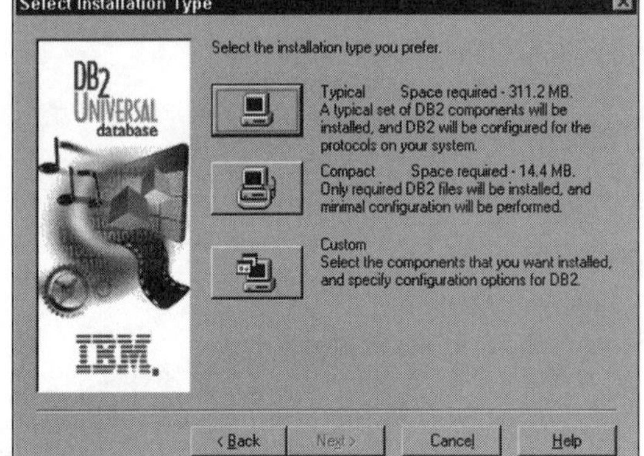

Figure 5-7: The Select Installation Type window.

6. **Click the Typical button.**

   The Choose Destination Location window appears, as shown in Figure 5-8. Note that the Space Required estimated in the figure is for a FAT file system, not an NTFS file system, where the requirements are different.

7. **Select the location where you want to install your DB2 client.**

   You can click the Browse button to select a target drive and directory. Clicking the Drive drop-down list box shows the space available on each of the drives on your system. You can compare this to the Space Required field to ensure that you have enough drive space to install the DB2 client. The information here may help you select a more suitable directory in the Destination Folder box above.

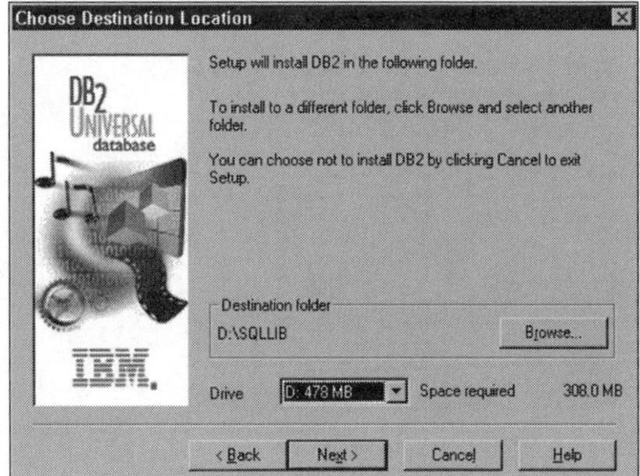

Figure 5-8: The Choose Destination Location window in a DB2 client installation.

8. **Click Next.**

   If you are using the NetBIOS (often referred to as NetBEUI in the wonderful world of Windows) protocol on your network, the Configure NetBIOS window opens, as shown in Figure 5-9. You're not likely to ever need to touch this window, and if you do need to, you know who you are.

   If you are not using NetBIOS, this window does not appear.

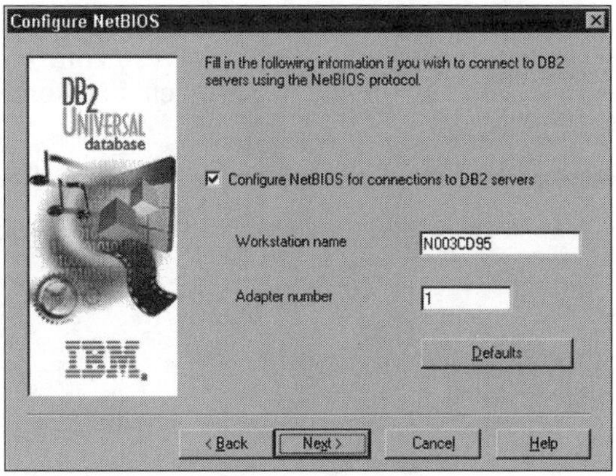

Figure 5-9: The Configure NetBIOS window in a DB2 client installation.

9. **If the Configure NetBIOS window opens, click Next (unless you have a compelling reason to configure NetBIOS).**

   The Start Copying Files window appears, as shown in Figure 5-10.

Figure 5-10: The Start Copying Files window.

10. **Scroll down through the Current Settings box to see all the installation options and components that will be part of the installation.**

    If you're not satisfied, you can click the Back button to return to a previous window and make a change to your selections.

11. **Click Next.**

    Your DB2 client begins installing. Wait a few minutes for the installation to complete; a status bar shows you how much time is left.

    The Setup Complete window appears when the installation finishes. The Setup Complete window gives you the option of restarting your machine now or at a later time. You must restart your machine before you can use your DB2 client.

12. **Choose whether to restart your machine now and then click Finish.**

    If you choose to restart your machine later, you cannot use your DB2 client now.

Chapter 6

Introducing a DB2 Client to a DB2 Server with the CCA

In This Chapter

- Getting a DB2 client to talk to a DB2 server
- Finding a server with discovery
- Testing a connection from a DB2 client to a DB2 server
- Mucking about with DB2 profiles
- Checking out other CCA functions

After installing a DB2 server on one machine and a DB2 client on another machine (or machines, more likely), you must configure your DB2 client (or clients) to talk to the DB2 server by using a supported protocol such as TCP/IP. The Client Configuration Assistant, or the CCA in DB2-speak, is the tool of all tools to help you do this. The CCA automates the discovery and cataloging of remote databases on your network — in other words, enabling you to make a connection from a DB2 client to a DB2 server.

In this chapter, we introduce you to the Client Configuration Assistant (CCA) — which works only on Windows and OS/2 machines — and show you how to use it to connect your DB2 client to a DB2 server.

We also show you how to use the CCA to configure a DB2 client to connect to a DB2 server in two of the three possible ways: discovery and access profiles. The third method, using DB2 catalog commands (which you can do with the CCA as well as a DB2 command prompt), is necessary if you are using a Unix-based operating system (including Linux), although you can also use them with Windows-based workstations. But these catalog commands are very time-consuming and require work to be done on the DB2 server and the DB2 client. Because we are not committed nerds (we just make people think we are), and because this book concentrates on the Windows version of DB2, we don't discuss the DB2 catalog commands here.

Making a Discovery with the Client Configuration Assistant (CCA)

DB2 provides a process called *discovery* that discovers DB2 servers and their databases on a network. When you connect a DB2 client to a DB2 server by using the DB2 catalog commands, you have to know the location and the name of the remote database. With discovery, which DB2 uses under the covers, you don't have to know the location or the name of the remote database to which you are trying to connect — DB2 can find it for you!

There are two types of discovery: known and search. To help visualize the difference between known discovery and search discovery, assume that you want to rent a movie. You have been going to your local video store for years and have the number written beside the phone. To check on a movie's availability, you call the store because you know the number. This is equivalent to known discovery, because you knew where to call. In contrast, if you wanted to call a video store that you were not so familiar with, you would have to look up video stores in the yellow pages and go through each of them asking whether they had the movie that you were looking for — this is much like search discovery. We discuss both types of discovery in the following two sections.

The administration server (DAS) must be running in order for you to use discovery. The DAS responds to discovery when it goes out on the network and searches for remote databases. When you install a DB2 server, the DAS is configured to automatically start each time the machine is booted (unless you specify otherwise in a Custom installation, in which case you must start it by using the `db2admin start` command).

The following two sections show you how to use the CCA to use discovery to make a database connection by using known discovery and search discovery.

Connecting to a remote database using known discovery

Known discovery asks you for information about a remote DB2 server, takes the information that you provide, and goes out on the network to try and find it. This type of discovery is referred to as known discovery because your computer already knows the location of the DB2 server whose databases you are looking for.

Only use known discovery to add a database to your system if you are comfortable with protocols. Otherwise, use search discovery. For information on search discovery, see the next section.

To connect a DB2 client to a DB2 server using known discovery, follow these steps:

1. **Open the CCA by clicking the Start button and choosing Programs⇨DB2 for Windows NT⇨Client Configuration Assistant.**

   You can also start the CCA by entering the `db2cca` command in a command prompt.

   The CCA Welcome window, shown in Figure 6-1, appears if you have not cataloged any databases on your DB2 client, or when you start it for the first time.

   If you already have a database cataloged on your DB2 client, the Welcome window doesn't open. Instead, you see the Client Configuration Assistant's main window, as shown in Figure 6-2. If the Welcome window opens, click the Add Database button.

Figure 6-1: The CCA Welcome window.

2. **Click the Add button to add a database connection to your DB2 client.**

   The Add Database SmartGuide window appears, as shown in Figure 6-3.

3. **Select the Search the Network option and then click Next.**

   The Target Database tab appears, as shown in Figure 6-4. You can invoke known or search discovery by clicking the appropriate plus [+] sign.

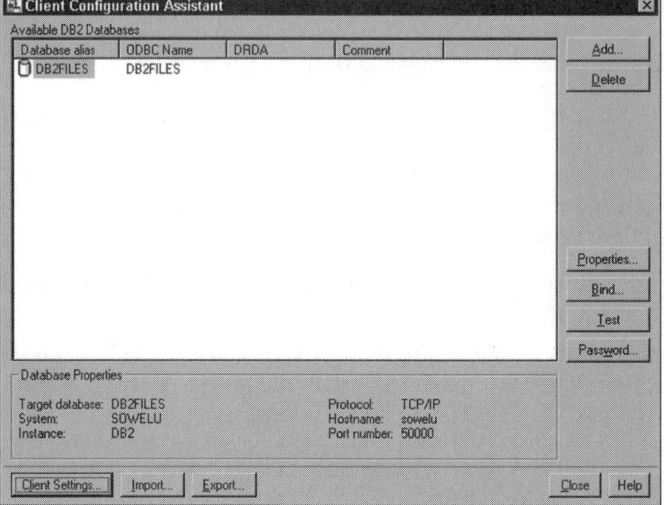

Figure 6-2: The Client Configuration Assistant (CCA) main window.

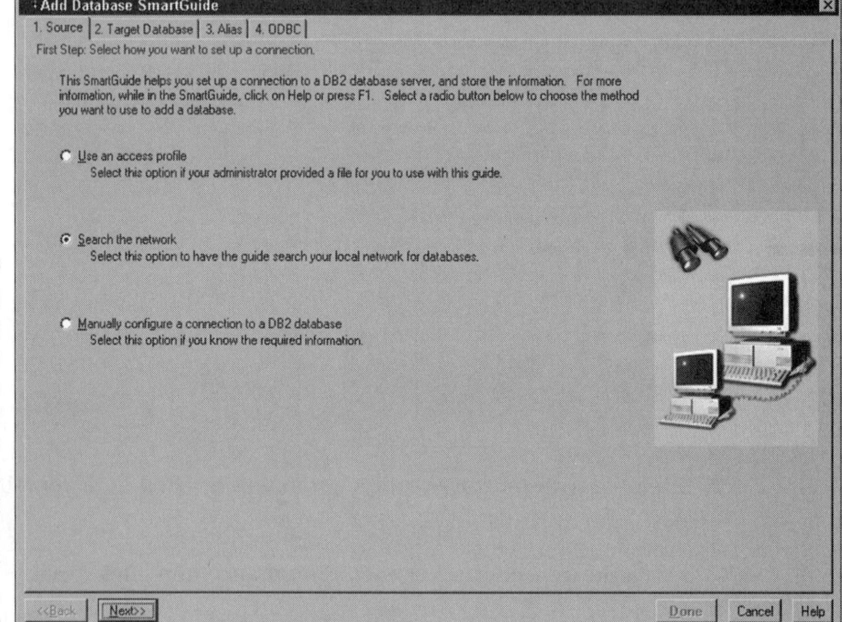

Figure 6-3: Selecting the way you want to catalog the remote database Source tab in the Add Database SmartGuide.

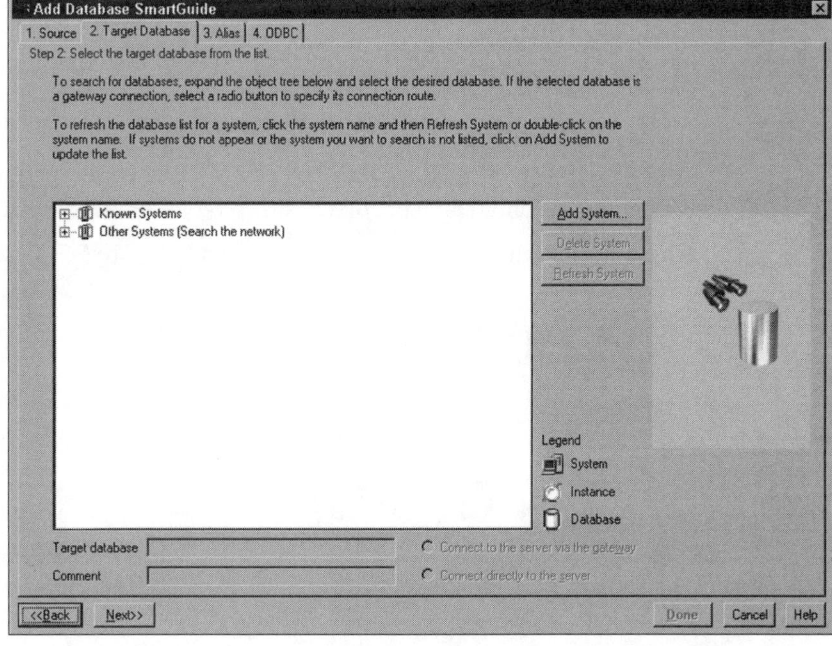

Figure 6-4: Select the target database that you want to catalog on your system in the Target Database tab of the Add Database SmartGuide.

4. **Click the plus sign [+] beside Known Systems.**

   A list of all systems that are known to your DB2 client appears. If this is your first time using the CCA, only your DB2 client machine is shown in the Known Systems list (it's smart enough to know itself). If other databases are cataloged on your DB2 client, the DB2 servers on which they exist appear in this list.

   You can click the plus sign [+] beside a known system to expand or collapse a list of the instances on the known system and the databases within them. The list includes the known DB2 servers' instances, and the databases within them. You can select a database that you want to add from this list.

5. **Click the Add System button if the database that you want to add is not listed in the Known Systems list, and you are familiar with the techie details of the protocol that you are using to try and connect to the DB2 server.**

   If a system does not appear in the Known Systems list, but you know the protocol settings for the remote DB2 server that you are trying to connect to, you can make the system known to your DB2 client by entering that information here. Otherwise, you have to search the network by using search discovery (which is described in the next section).

For example, suppose that the EMPLOYEES database resides on the computer PAULZ, which has an IP address of 9.21.27.122. You can directly enter the hostname or the IP address of the computer PAULZ here to make PAULZ known to the DB2 client without searching the network. You can get to the database that you want quickly because you don't have to search the network, but it requires techie knowledge. When you catalog a remote DB2 server, even by using search discovery, the server automatically becomes known to your DB2 client.

The Add System window appears, as shown in Figure 6-5.

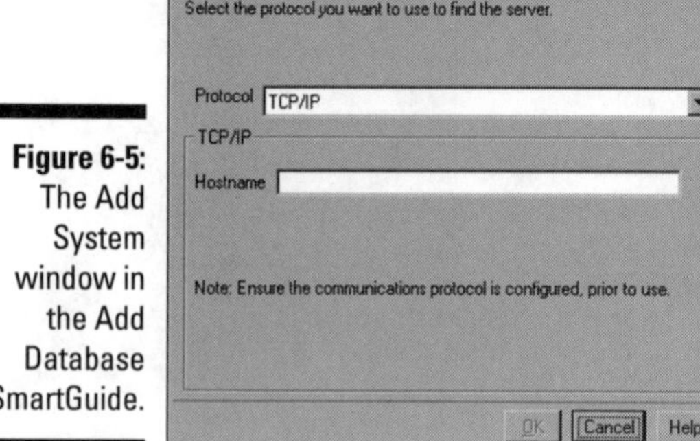

Figure 6-5: The Add System window in the Add Database SmartGuide.

6. **In the Protocol drop-down list box, select the protocol you want to use to find the server.**

   The default protocol for Windows is TCP/IP. Unless you specifically selected to strip TCP/IP during installation, you should have DB2's TCP/IP support installed.

7. **Assuming that you are using TCP/IP, type the hostname or IP address of the remote DB2 server in the Hostname text box.**

   If you selected to use a different protocol to make this connection, you will have to specify different protocol-specific parameters.

   See Chapter 4 for more information on finding the hostname or IP address of a computer.

8. **Click OK.**

   The CCA goes out on the network, finds the DB2 server that you are looking for, and lists the instances and databases that exist on that DB2 server.

9. **Click the plus sign [+] to expand the list of information that is returned, select the database that you want to connect to, and then click Next.**

10. **The Alias tab appears, as shown in Figure 6-6.**

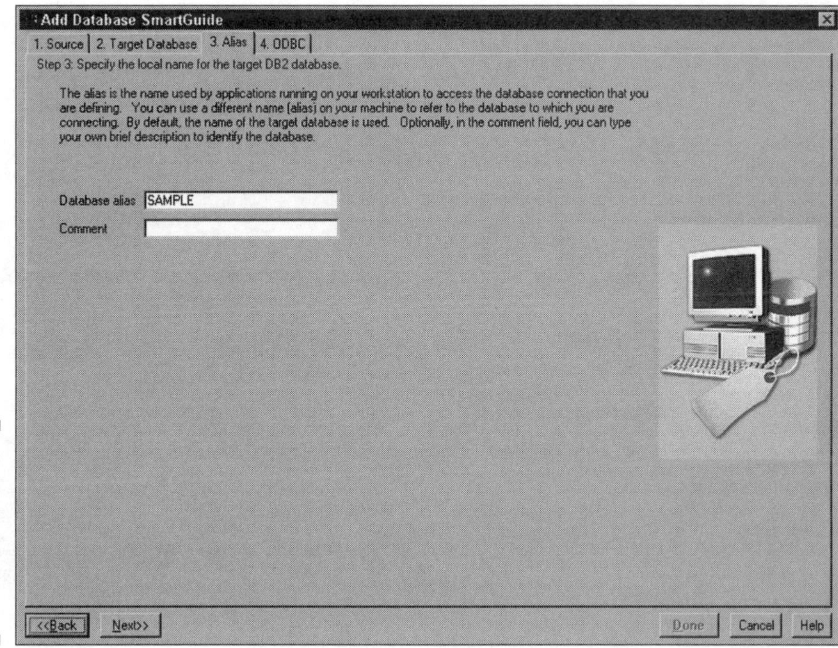

Figure 6-6: The Alias table in the Add Database SmartGuide.

You must define an alias name for the database with which you are trying to connect. By default, the CCA enters the database alias name as the database name in the Database Alias text box.

11. **(Optional) In the Comment text box, enter a few words that describe the database.**

12. **Click Next.**

    The ODBC (Open Database Connectivity) tab appears, as shown in Figure 6-7.

    With this window you can set up connections to a remote database for ODBC applications. You can use ODBC to access a database that resides in a Lotus Approach or Microsoft Access database, or any ODBC-compliant database. ODBC access to remote data sources is outside of the scope of this book.

After you specify a database alias, the Done button becomes enabled. You do not have to specify ODBC-related parameters if you are not planning to use an ODBC application.

13. **Click Done.**

    The CCA catalogs the remote DB2 server and the selected database. A confirmation window opens for the database that you just added to your system, as shown in Figure 6-8.

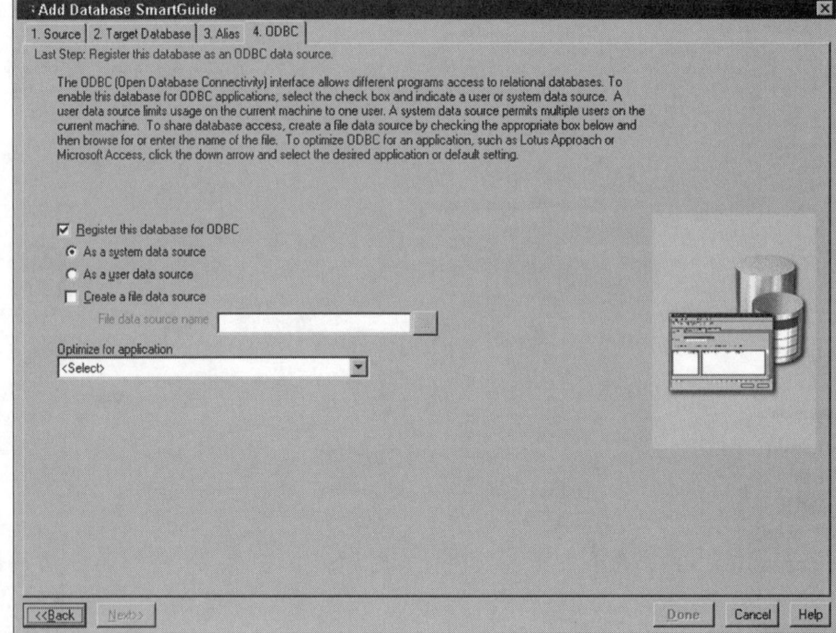

Figure 6-7: The ODBC tab in the Add Database SmartGuide.

Figure 6-8: A Confirmation window appears after you add a remote DB2 database to your system.

Confirmation - MOVIES

The connection configuration for 'MOVIES' was added successfully.

You may now test the connection by selecting Test Connection. Test Connection

Select Change to return to the SmartGuide, or Close to exit the SmartGuide. Change

Add... Close

You can add another database by clicking Add, or change any of the settings that you specified by clicking Change. You may want to change some settings if the add database command failed.

14. **To test the connection to the remote database, click Test Connection.**

    The Connect to DB2 Database window appears, as shown in Figure 6-9.

Figure 6-9: The Connect to DB2 Database window is used to test a connection to an added database.

15. **Enter the user account that you used to install the DB2 server and type the username and password in the User ID and Password text boxes.**

    If in doubt, enter any user account that belongs to the Administrators group on the DB2 server.

    You really need to enter a user account that has access to the database on the remote DB2 server that you are trying to connect to. To make things easier, enter the user account that you used to install DB2; this is because this user account belongs to the SYSADM group (by default) and will definitely be able to access the database.

16. **Click OK.**

    A message returns confirming that you have connected to the remote database.

Connecting to a DB2 database using search discovery

Search discovery goes out on the network and finds any DB2 servers, instances, and databases that are configured for discovery. (You can actually configure a DB2 server, instance, or database so that it isn't discovered). Search discovery basically asks the network "Who's out there with an instance or database that you would like me tell others about?" If the answer is "I am", which is the default for all DB2 servers, discovery returns information to the CCA about the discovered DB2 server and database. If there is no answer, discovery skips the remote DB2 server and goes on to the next one on the network.

To connect a DB2 client to a DB2 server by using search discovery, follow these steps:

1. **Open the CCA by clicking the Start button and choosing Programs⇨DB2 for Windows NT⇨Client Configuration Assistant.**

   You can also start the CCA by typing the `db2cca` command at a command prompt.

2. **Click the Add Database (or Add) button.**

   The Add Database SmartGuide appears.

3. **Select the Search the Network radio button and then click Next.**

4. **Click the plus sign [+] beside the Other Systems (Search the Network) icon.**

   The CCA uses discovery to go out on the network and look for all the DB2 servers. A list that looks something like Figure 6-10 is returned.

   You can click the plus sign [+] beside a system to expand or collapse a list of the instances and the databases within them. The list includes the instances and databases on the discovered DB2 sever.

   From here, start with Step 5 in the numbered list in the previous section. The rest of the instructions there are identical for search discovery.

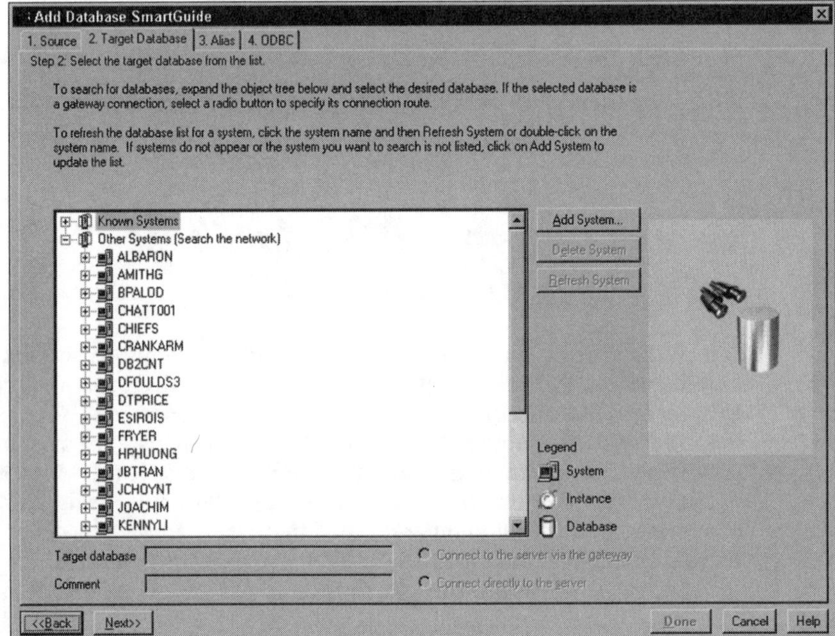

Figure 6-10: The Target Database tab of the Add Database SmartGuide.

Database alias cloak and dagger

If you have ever had a nickname, you are well on your way to understanding database aliases. *Database aliases* are simply nicknames for your database; that is, local synonyms given to local or remote databases. Aliases must be unique to the System Database Directory on your machine. The System Database Directory is where all of the aliases are stored for the databases that are cataloged on your DB2 client. You cannot create a database on a DB2 server that has the same database name as one that already exists. You can, however, have connections on a DB2 client to two different databases that have the same name and reside on different servers, but each would have to have its own database alias name on the DB2 client.

To help you understand this concept, say you know two people named Scott Reid. One Scott Reid is the fellow that works at the bank and the other is your best friend. The one that works at the bank you just refer to as Scott Reid. But you call your friend Scott Reid, "Reido". In this case, Reido would be your friend's alias name. If you ever talk about your friend Scott Reid, you may say something like, "Hey, you won't believe the putt that Reido sank on the eighth hole yesterday!" Your brain (or DB2) houses a list of all the people you know (Database directories in DB2) so that it can convert Reido to Scott Reid who's your friend, not the banker.

Now imagine all the confusion that having two friends with the alias Reido would cause and you can see why no two databases can have the same database alias name with DB2. DB2 can't control the number of databases out there with the same name because different DB2 servers could have databases with the same name. DB2, therefore, uses aliases. If you meet another friend by the name of Scott Reid, and he wants you to call him Reido, you'll have to say no because that name is already taken, and DB2 enforces this as well.

Working with Access Profiles

DB2 access profiles come in two flavors: server profiles and client profiles. You can use a profile to set up database connections between DB2 clients and DB2 servers. Using the CCA, you either know the path to the DB2 server (known discovery) or you stumble your way around the network (search discovery) looking for each DB2 server and the database that you're interested in. A DB2 profile is a map to databases that are either on a DB2 server or have been cataloged on a DB2 client. Administrators use profiles all the time to quickly set up database access between machines.

For example, you can create a server profile for your remote DB2 server and then import it to your DB2 client. Your DB2 client then automatically receives the database connection information for all the databases on the DB2 server. Or, after you set up a DB2 client — provided you want other DB2 clients to have the same access to the remote databases (which is usually the case) — you can create a client profile and import it to other DB2 clients.

Creating a profile

This section shows you how to create a server or client profile. A *server profile* contains information about instances on a server system, and the databases within each instance. The information about each instance includes the protocol information required to set up connections to databases in that instance. A *client profile* contains information such as a client's configuration parameters and database connection information.

The difference between a client profile and a server profile is that the client profile contains client configuration information, as well as database connection information on the client. The server profile only contains server database information. The following two sections show you how to create both types of profiles.

Creating a server profile

You can use the Control Center to create a profile of a DB2 server and use this profile to set up connections to databases on the server where the profile was created.

To create a server profile, follow these steps on your DB2 server:

1. **Open the Control Center by clicking the Start button and choosing Programs⇨DB2 for Windows NT⇨Control Center.**

   You have to log on to the Control Center with a user account that has the correct authorities. For now, log on with the same user account that you used to install your DB2 server. If you need more information, see Chapter 4.

2. **Right-click a DB2 server in the left pane of the Control Center and select Export Server Profile from the pop-up menu.**

   The Export Server Profile dialog box appears.

3. **Choose a filename and location for the profile from the Export Server Profile dialog box and click OK.**

   DB2 server profiles don't use a specific file extension. Many people use the .prf extension, but other programs use this extension for profiles and it may lead to confusion. Choose something obscure, like your initials — unless your name is something like Ernest Xavier Edwards (EXE). There has been talk about creating the .spf extension for DB2 server profiles in future editions of DB2.

   Save this profile to a disk or a shared directory because you are going to need to access it when you import the profile on the DB2 client. You can save the profile to a floppy disk and use that on the DB2 client. You may want to e-mail the file to a user that has access to the DB2 client. You can also FTP the file to the DB2 client workstation if you are familiar with file transfer protocol (FTP).

The Control Center creates a server profile and place it in the directory that you specified.

Creating a client profile

You can use the CCA to create a profile of a DB2 client workstation and then use this profile to set up identical DB2 clients in your network by importing it into other DB2 clients, see the next section for more information.

To create a client profile, follow these steps:

1. **Start the CCA by clicking the Start button and choosing Programs⇨DB2 for Windows NT⇨Client Configuration Assistant.**

   TIP

   You can also start the CCA by entering the `db2cca` command at a command prompt.

2. **In the CCA window, click Export.**

   The Select Export Option window appears, as shown in Figure 6-11.

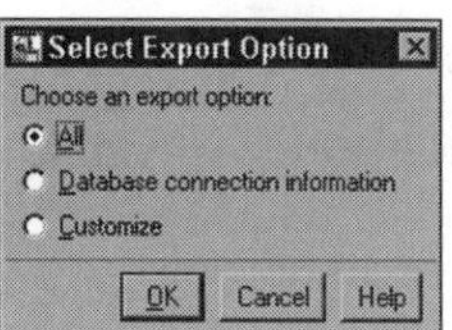

Figure 6-11: The Select Export Option window.

3. **Select the All option and click OK.**

   The Export Client Profile dialog box opens.

   You can customize what is exported in the profile; for example if you just wanted to make a database connection, you could select the Database connection information option. We suggest you just select All to make life easy. If you want to learn more about profile customization, click Help.

4. **Choose a file name and location for the profile from the Export Client Profile dialog box and click OK.**

DB2 client profiles don't use a specific file extension. Many people use the .prf extension, but other programs use this extension for profiles and it may lead to confusion. Choose something obscure, like your initials — unless your initials are EXE or DOC. There has been talk about creating the .cpf extension for DB2 server profiles in future editions of DB2.

Save this profile to a disk or a shared directory because you are going to need to access it when you import the profile on the DB2 client. You can save the profile to a floppy disk and use that on the DB2 client. You may want to e-mail the file to a user that has access to the DB2 client. You can also FTP the file to the DB2 client workstation if you are familiar with file transfer protocol (FTP).

The CCA creates a client profile and place it in the directory that you specified.

Importing a profile

Importing profiles is a great way to add databases to multiple DB2 clients without having to go to each client and search the network for the database that you want to add. Using a profile, you can gather connection information for all the databases that you want your users to connect to, send your users the profile, and give them the instructions to add it to their system. Your users don't have to know anything about DB2, discovery, or any other technical details. Importing a server or client profile on a workstation updates its local configuration and/or catalog directories with the information in the profile.

To import a server or client profile, follow these steps:

1. **Start the CCA by clicking the Start button and choosing Programs⇨DB2 for Windows NT⇨Client Configuration Assistant.**

   You can also start the CCA by typing the `db2cca` command at a command prompt.

2. **Click Import.**

   The Select Profile dialog box appears.

3. **Select the server or client profile that you created from wherever you stored it on this machine (shared directory, disk, and so on) and then click OK.**

   The Import Profile window appears, as shown in Figure 6-12.

   You can either import all of the information in a DB2 profile or you can customize it so that only a subset of the information contained in the profile is imported to your DB2 client. For now, we suggest you select the All option. Click Help if you want to learn more about customizing which info is imported.

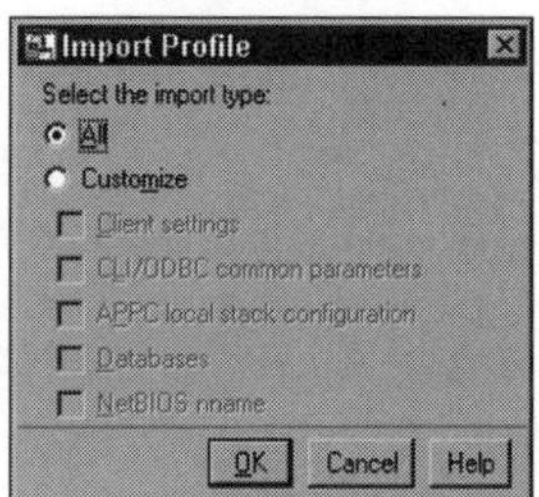

Figure 6-12: The Import Profile window enables you to specify attributes to import a DB2 profile.

4. **Select the All option and click OK.**

   The remote database is cataloged on your DB2 client. If the profile contained configuration information, then the DB2 client is updated with this information as well. For more information on customizing profiles, click the Help button.

Utilizing Other CCA Functions

We could use half this book to describe the CCA's other features. The following is a brief rundown of some other CCA functions. The CCA can:

- Configure database connections that applications on your workstation can use.
- Update or delete existing configured database connections
- Display the information for existing configured connections
- Test a connection to a database
- Enable or disable databases to be configured as Call Level Interface or ODBC data sources
- Update client configuration settings
- Bind user applications and utilities to a database
- Change your server password

If you take on the role of the administrator, you should get to know all the features of this useful tool. To learn more about the other functions that the CCA can do, refer to the CCA's online help.

Part III
Working with DB2

"WELL, SHOOT! THIS EGGPLANT CHART IS JUST AS CONFUSING AS THE BUTTERNUT SQUASH CHART AND THE GOURD CHART. CAN'T YOU JUST MAKE A PIE CHART LIKE EVERYONE ELSE?"

In this part . . .

In this part we take you on an in-depth journey through DB2 and the things that make it work. The stuff in this part is a detailed extension of what we covered in Part I, but this time it isn't all theory. Here we actually tell you how to create database objects instead of just telling you what they are.

This part will make you actually believe that a table isn't just something in your kitchen, and a table space isn't the amount of space your bills hog up on that kitchen table. We also show you how to create and use instances, databases, and all the other stuff that lives in DB2.

Chapter 7

Getting Cozy with Instances

In This Chapter

- Figuring out what an instance is
- Creating an instance
- Listing instances
- Using multiple instances
- Starting and stopping an instance
- Deleting instances
- Instance configuration files
- The administration instance (DAS)

If you've followed the book chapter by chapter until now (and you don't have to), you have likely installed a DB2 server, created a sample database, installed a DB2 client, and configured a connection between the client and the server. Or maybe you just came to this chapter because you're dying to know what an instance is. Either, way, you now stand rank and file with the nerdiest people you know. Be proud! Now you're ready to venture into the heart of DB2 — the instance.

Comprehending Instances

The DB2 documentation defines an instance as a logical database manager environment where you catalog databases and set configuration parameters. That definition doesn't sound too logical to most of us, but it's a very important object that you must understand. Every piece of a database must exist within a DB2 instance. In fact, without an instance, you cannot even have a database.

The best way to describe an instance is to think back to a common experiment you may have conducted in grade school involving a plant, some soil, a seed, some water, and variables. Come on . . . think hard . . . you'll remember it. Here's how it went if you can't remember that far back:

1. Find two pots that are exactly the same size.
2. In each pot, place the same amount of soil.
3. Plant the same type of bean in each pot, making sure they're of equal size.
4. Watch them grow!
5. Experiment with their growth rate by adjusting the amount of sunlight or water (these are the variables).
6. Watch them grow again and note which changed variables increase the growth rate (performance) of your growing plants.

There you have a couple of instances! Each pot is a different environment and can be referred to as an instance. What you do to the plant in one pot doesn't happen to the plant in the other pot, unless you choose to do it there as well. (I bet you didn't know you were such a computer whiz back in grade school, did you?) All of the configuration parameters of the bean plant start the same: the size of the pot, the amount of soil, and the size of the bean. In the bean experiment, maybe you took one instance of the plant and put it in the dark and then took another instance and exposed it to sunlight. Or you may have subjected your plants to other configuration variables, like water, and monitored the effect in conjunction with the sunlight.

As the days passed you monitored the performance of each instance, eventually discovering what changes worked best for the instance. Think of each of those potted plants as instances, and each of the things that you did to the plant as configuration parameters (sort of like the variables in the experiment). You can set and monitor what effects a change to an instance's configuration (water and sunlight) has on performance (plant growth) and other factors. Consider the growing plant as the equivalent to your database; depending on how you tune your instance, your plant grows quickly or slowly. If you accidentally poured acid in one pot (or instance), you would only kill one plant (or database) and the other would be fine because you didn't pour acid into the second pot. Needless to say, with instances, administrators sometimes maintain backup pots!

If you want, you can plant two bean plants (databases) in the same pot (instance). This means that an instance can contain more than one database. Because you can't plant a pot in a plant, a database cannot contain an instance; it can only belong to one. A database can only belong to one instance, because it can only grow from one pot.

Each instance has its own configuration file, called the *database manager configuration* (`dbm cfg`) file. This file contains parameters that are used to control the instance. For example, you can tune an instance for performance or configure it for communications.

The settings for an instance are for that instance only and affect all of the databases within the instance. A *one-to-one* relationship exists between an instance and the `dbm cfg` file, (We discuss these relationships back in Chapter 2), meaning that:

- An instance can only have one configuration file.
- A configuration file can belong to only one instance.

Whenever you create an instance, a new configuration file is generated with the default settings. An instance can have many databases, but a database can only belong to one instance.

If you want to really impress a database geek, say "There is a *one-to-many* relationship between instances and databases." Figure 7-1 illustrates the relationship between instances and databases.

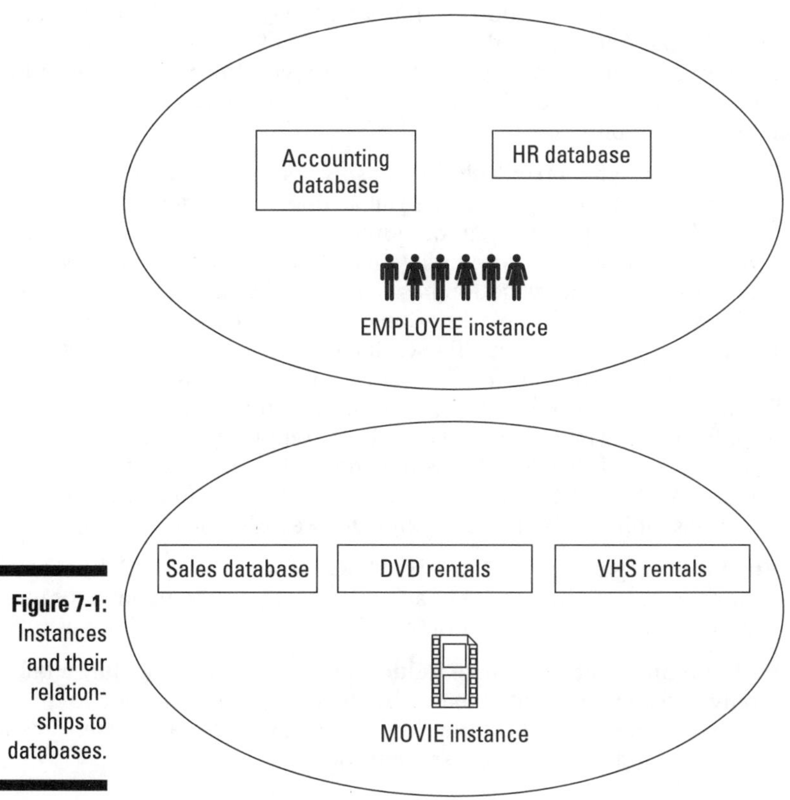

Figure 7-1: Instances and their relationships to databases.

Following are some of the many reasons that a database administrator would want to have more than one instance:

- **Separate departmental data.** For example, you may want your Human Resources department's data to be completely separate from the Accounting department's data. Now, of course you could separate the data by using two databases, but they would not be completely separate because they share the same instance.
- **Separate a production environment from a test environment.** With many large organizations, it would not be uncommon for the Human Resources department to have the exact same databases and data that are in their main instance also in a test instance. This way, the database administrators could set trial performance parameters and monitor their effects before applying the changes to the database that is used in critical day-to-day operations.
- **Tune and optimize an instance for a particular environment.** For example, your Human Resources computers may be in an SMP environment while the Accounting department's computers are just plain uniprocessor computers. You may want to exploit the SMP configuration for the Human Resources department, but it is not available for the Accounting computers.

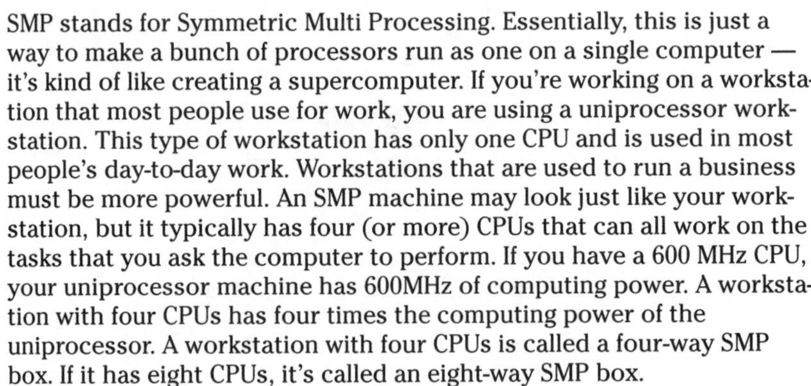

SMP stands for Symmetric Multi Processing. Essentially, this is just a way to make a bunch of processors run as one on a single computer — it's kind of like creating a supercomputer. If you're working on a workstation that most people use for work, you are using a uniprocessor workstation. This type of workstation has only one CPU and is used in most people's day-to-day work. Workstations that are used to run a business must be more powerful. An SMP machine may look just like your workstation, but it typically has four (or more) CPUs that can all work on the tasks that you ask the computer to perform. If you have a 600 MHz CPU, your uniprocessor machine has 600MHz of computing power. A workstation with four CPUs has four times the computing power of the uniprocessor. A workstation with four CPUs is called a four-way SMP box. If it has eight CPUs, it's called an eight-way SMP box.

- **Control the assignment of SYSADM, SYSCTRL, and SYSMAINT authority**. For example, a different set of administrators can be defined for each department. For more information on DB2 authorities, see Chapter 2.
- **Limit the impact of an instance failure.** In the event of an instance failure, only one instance is affected. Other instances can continue to function normally. For example, if the Human Resources instance goes down, the Accounting people can access their own data.

Using multiple instances carries some disadvantages as well. For example, additional system resources, such as virtual memory (RAM) and disk space, are required for each instance, and additional instances require more administration to manage.

Working With Instances

Databases are dependent on instances, and this section shows you how to create, drop, list, start, stop, and work with instances.

Creating an instance

To create an instance, you must log on to the system with a user account that belongs to the local Administrators group, as defined by the Windows User Manager. You use the db2icrt command as follows:

You can only create an instance by using the db2icrt command. You cannot create an instance by using the Control Center.

You create an instance called DB2 when you install DB2 Universal Database.

1. **Log on to your system with a user account that belongs to the local Administrators group.**
2. **At a Windows command prompt, type** db2icrt *<instance name>* **and press Enter.**

   where *<instance name>* is the name of the instance you want to create.

Dropping an instance

You can only drop an instance by using the db2idrop command. You cannot drop an instance by using the Control Center. When you drop an instance, you must specify the name of the instance to be dropped, so it doesn't matter what DB2 thinks is the current instance (more on that in a bit). An instance must be stopped before it is dropped (we describe how to stop an instance in the "Stopping an instance" section later in this chapter).

To drop an instance, you must log on to the system with a user account that belongs to the local Administrators group, as defined by the Windows User Manager.

To drop an instance, follow these steps:

1. **Log on to your system with a user account that belongs to the local Administrators group.**
2. **At a Windows command prompt, type** db2idrop *<instance name>* **and press Enter.**

   where *<instance name>* is the name of the instance you want to drop.

Starting an instance

To access a database that resides in an instance, make sure that the instance is running. You can start an instance by using the Control Center. You can also start an instance by entering the `db2start` command at a command prompt. If you use the Control Center to start an instance, you do not need to worry about what the current instance is.

Of course, I'm assuming here that DB2 is your default instance, as defined by your Typical installation of DB2. If it is not the default instance, see the "Working with Multiple Instances" section later in this chapter.

The Control Center can also be used to start or stop an instance. If an instance that you created does not appear in the Control Center, read the "Figuring out what to do if your instance isn't showing in the Control Center" section later in this chapter.

To start an instance, follow these steps:

1. **Open the Control Center by clicking the Start button and choosing Programs⇨DB2 for Windows NT⇨Control Center.**
2. **Click the plus sign [+] beside the name of the system you're working with.**

   The name of your system is usually the same as your computer name.
3. **Start an instance by right-clicking the instance that you want to start and selecting the Start option from the pop-up menu.**

   If you try to start an instance that isn't the default instance, notice that you do not have to concern yourself with the active instance. If you were using the DB2 CLP (command line processor) or the DB2 Command window, you would have had to set either the `DB2INSTANCE` environment variable or the `DB2INSTDEF` DB2 registry value. The Control Center takes care of this for you. For more information, see the "Figuring out what to do if your instance isn't showing in the Control Center" section later in this chapter (and say that section name ten times fast!).

   If you try to start an instance that has been set to autostart at log in time (such as the DB2 instance that is created by the installation program that has already been started), you receive a message noting that the instance has already been started. We talk about setting an instance to autostart later in the "Auto-Starting an Instance" section of this chapter.

Stopping an instance

You can stop an instance by using the Control Center. You can also stop an instance by entering the `db2stop` command at a command prompt. If you use the db2stop command, the current instance is stopped. If you use the Control Center to stop an instance, you do not need to worry what the current instance is.

You can stop a DB2 instance the same way you start an instance in the preceding section, only this time, select the Stop option from the pop-up menu. A window opens asking you to confirm the instance you want to stop. If you want to stop the instance select OK. A message appears noting that the instance was successfully stopped.

Listing instances

You can list all of the instances on your workstation by entering the db2ilist command at a command prompt. This command lists any instances on your local system. Of course, the easiest way to see the instances on your workstation is to look at the Control Center's main window; however, sometimes instances that exist don't always show up (if that is the case, see the "Figuring out what to do if your instance isn't showing in the Control Center" section later in this chapter). This is the best way to make sure what instances exist on your system.

When you enter the db2ilist command in a command prompt, DB2 lists all of the names of the instances that exist on your system.

Because an instance called DB2 is created when you install DB2, expect to see this instance (along with any you've created for testing purposes) to be returned when you enter this command. There is one exception however; the administration server's instances is not listed. To list this instance, you would enter the db2admin command at a command prompt.

Instances are always listed from newest to oldest when you run the db2ilist command.

Determining the current instance

When you have more than one instance, you need to know which instance you are working with. The current instance is the instance where all of the commands you enter are run. If you want to work with a certain instance, you need to ensure that DB2 is working with that instance. You can enter the db2 get instance command at a DB2 command prompt to determine the current instance you're working with.

For example, if you enter the db2 get instance command, you should receive the following output:

```
The current database manager instance is: <instance name>
```

where *<instance name>* is the name of the current instance.

Figuring out what to do if your instance isn't showing in the Control Center

Sometimes, the Control Center doesn't realize that you have added an instance to your system and the new instance therefore doesn't appear. This absence is no big deal. To add an instance to the Control Center, follow these steps:

1. **Right-click on the Instances folder in the appropriate System folder where the instance resides and select Add.**

   The Add Instance dialog box appears, as shown in Figure 7-2.

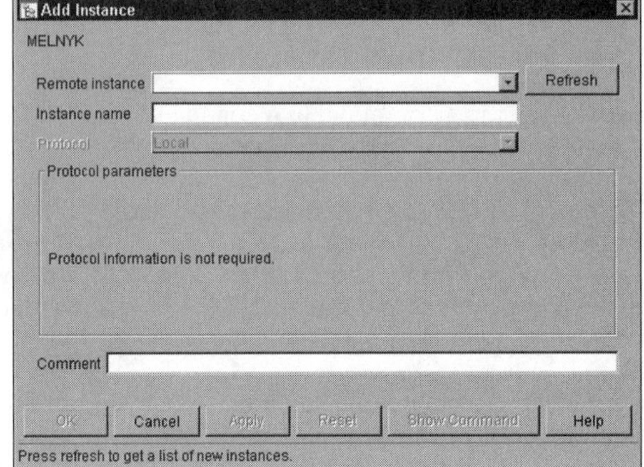

Figure 7-2: The Control Center's Add Instance dialog box.

2. **Click the Refresh button.**

   A list of all instances on your system is returned.

3. **Select the instance that you want to add from the Remote Instance drop-down list.**

   This box's label can be confusing. If you are adding an instance that resides on a remote machine, it makes sense. In this case the instance is a local instance, because the system that we are working with is local (meaning it's ours), but the box still says remote instance, go figure?

4. **(Optional) Enter the same name as the instance name in the Instance Name text box. This name is shown for this instance in the Control Center.**

5. **(Optional) Add a comment describing the instance in the Comment text box.**
6. **Click OK.**

Setting DB2 straight about which instances really are on your system

Sometimes the Control Center can get confused with instances that are on your system. If you dropped an instance, it may still show up in the Control Center. If it does, follow these steps to remove it from the Control Center:

1. **Right-click the instance that you want to remove from the Control Center and select Remove.**

   The window shown in Figure 7-3 opens, and the Control Center asks you to verify that you want to remove the instance.

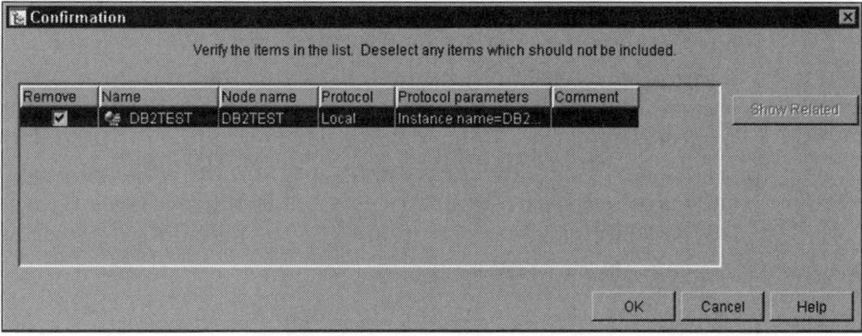

Figure 7-3: The Control Center Confirmation window asks you to verify that you want to remove the selected instance.

2. **Click OK.**

   Removing an instance for the view of the Control Center does not drop the instance; it still exists! If you listed the instances on your system by using the `db2ilist` command, this instance would still show up.

Auto-Starting an Instance

The DB2 setup program sets the default DB2 instance to automatically start (hence the term *auto-start*) each time you log on to the system. Auto-starting eliminates the need to enter the `db2start` command for the instance that you want to start. To configure an instance to auto-start, you must set the service to auto-start at login time.

To set an instance to auto-start each time you log on to the system, follow these steps:

1. **Click the Start button and choose Settings⇨Control Panel.**
2. **Double-click the Services icon.**

   The window shown in Figure 7-4 appears.

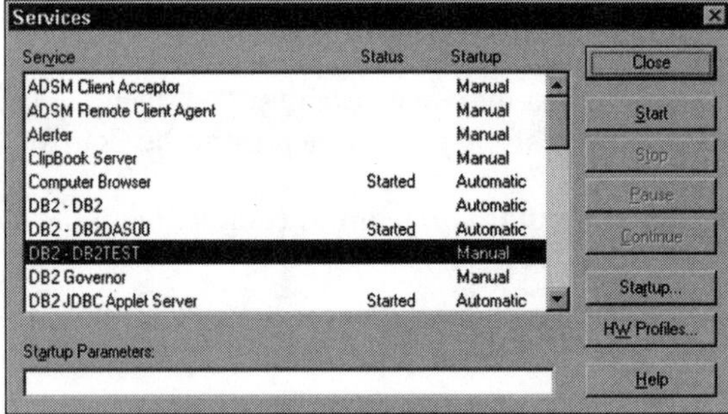

Figure 7-4: The Windows NT/2000 Services dialog box.

All DB2 services (instances) are prefixed with the word DB2; for example, the DB2 instance appears as DB2 – DB2. Note that the DB2 instance's startup option is set to Automatic. If you created another instance by using the `db2icrt` command, it would be set to Manual, which is the default setting for a new instance not created by the installation program. The DB2 installation program set up the DB2 instance to automatically start each time your workstation is started. Because the DB2 — DBTEST instance was not created by the installation program, its Startup column is Manual.

3. **Select the instance you want to auto-start and click Startup.**
4. **In the Startup Type box, select the Automatic option.**
5. **Click OK.**
6. **Click Close.**

From now on, each time you log on to the system, the instance you set up to auto-start automatically starts.

When you drop a DB2 instance, its entry is removed from the Services menu.

Viewing and Modifying Instance Configuration Files

Any parameters (like the sunlight and the water variables that we talk about at the beginning of the chapter) for an instance are set in the instance's database manager configuration file (`dbm cfg`). These settings affect all databases that are created within the instance, although some settings can be overwritten with the database configuration file.

You can view or update the `dbm cfg` file by using the Control Center or the command line processor (CLP). For the rest of the book, most of the examples focus on the GUI tools. We talk a lot about the CLP earlier in this chapter because you cannot create an instance with the Control Center.

To view the database manager configuration file, right-click the instance of the configuration file with which you want to work and then select the Configure option from the pop-up menu. The Configure Instance window opens as shown in Figure 7-5. For the purposes of our example, select the Diagnostic tab.

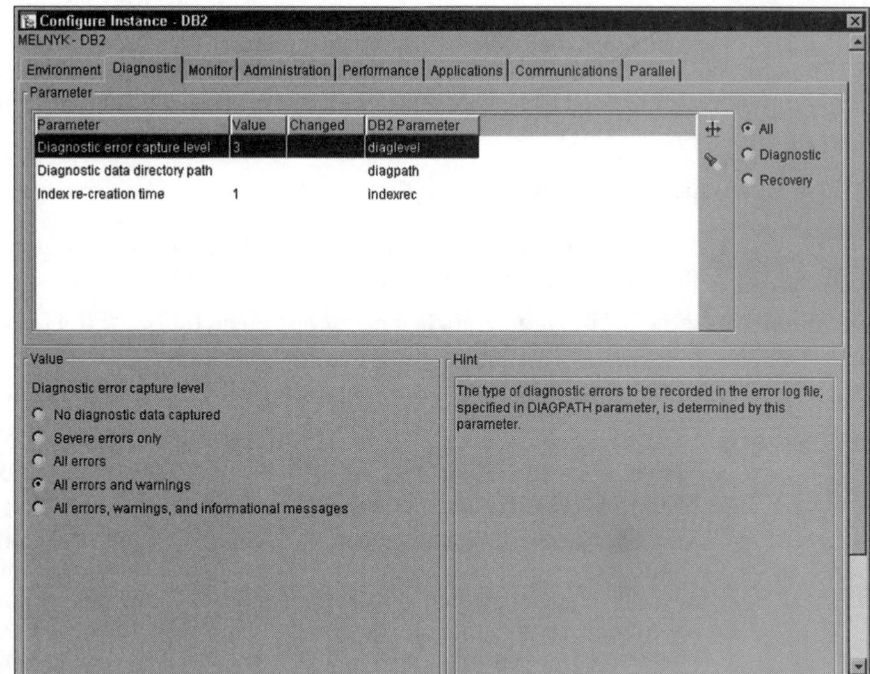

Figure 7-5: The Control Center's Configure Instance notebook.

All of the instance's configuration parameters are logically placed into groups that are denoted by tabs at the top of the window. The advantage to using the Control Center's interface into the `dbm cfg` is the available online help, search facilities, and the hints provided with each parameter.

To view the configuration file for the current instance, type the following command at a DB2 command prompt:

```
db2 get database manager configuration
```

You can use abbreviations in this command. The term *database manager* can be abbreviated as *dbm* and the term *configuration* can be abbreviated as *cfg*. Therefore, entering the `db2 get dbm cfg` command returns the same output. You can use these abbreviations for any DB2 commands that have these terms in them.

Enter the `db2 get dbm cfg | more` command in a DB2 command prompt to make the results of this command break at each full page on your screen. The | symbol is called a pipe in the Windows world. A *pipe* simply tells the computer to move the command, or pipe the command, to the program that follows, which in this case is called `more`. `more` is a Windows program that takes long output and breaks it down into pages, so that you can read it without all the information flying by in one fast shot!

An instance has many configuration parameters. The *DB2 Administration Guide* details them well. In other chapters of this book we discuss the parameters that need to be changed in order to enable a certain function, but for now we just show you how to change them.

To change a parameter, follow these steps:

1. **Select the tab where the parameter that you want to change resides (for example, the Diagnostic tab in Figure 7-5).**

   If the list of parameters is long for any given tab, click the Find icon (the flashlight to the right of the parameter box), and enter the name there.

2. **In the value box, select the option that corresponds to the setting that you want.**

   Depending on the parameter that you want to change, you may not have an option to click; you may have to enter a value, for example.

   An *X* appears in the Changed column after you change the setting for a configuration parameter, indicating that you have asked for this parameter to be changed, which is useful because you can change more than one parameter at a time. If you scroll down the list or decide to change another parameter in another tab, you can quickly identify which parameters you change.

   If you changed a value and you want to set the value back to its setting before you made any changes, select the parameter and click Reset.

Keep in mind that this resets the setting back to the value for the `dbm cfg` when you opened it for editing. If you change a default setting (for example, from 1 to 2) and save the changes, reset sets the value to 2, which was the value of the parameter when you opened `dbm cfg`. (That was a mouthful!)

If you want to restore a parameter value to the default setting for every DB2 instance, select the parameter and click Default.

3. **Click OK.**

   Any time you change a parameter in the `dbm cfg` file, you *must* stop and restart the instance.

4. **Stop the DB2 instance.**

   We show you how to stop an instance in the "Stopping an instance" section earlier in this chapter.

5. **Start the DB2 instance.**

   We show you how to start an instance in the "Starting a DB2 instance" section earlier in this chapter.

   The parameter is now set to whatever setting you selected in Step 2.

Now, some of you more experienced computer geeks want to know the command for this. I can see you now, trying to think of ways to show-off . . . "Look ma, no hands," . . . "Look boss, no interface!" This once, we begrudgingly give you the commands to complete the preceding tasks (enter them in a DB2 command prompt):

```
db2 get dbm cfg
db2 update dbm cfg using diaglevel 4
db2stop
db2start
```

You can verify that this was changed by entering the following commands in a command prompt:

```
db2 get dbm cfg | more
db2 reset dbm cfg
db2stop
db2start
```

The `db2 rest dbm cfg` command resets the `dbm cfg` file to the original settings that are part of a Typical DB2 installation.

Pretty easy to appreciate the Control Center, isn't it? You didn't have to worry about the current instance; you had explanations for each parameter; you could access online help; and you could view the parameter values in a more organized fashion.

Identifying the Default Instance by Using the Command Center and the DB2 CLP

Using the Command Center or the DB2 CLP with different instances can be somewhat confusing. When you start the Command Center or the DB2 CLP, each utility is always started according to the current instance setting, which by default is the `DB2INSTANCE` environment variable that was set during installation.

To start the Command Center to work with an instance other than the default instance, you have to start the Control Center from a different window and then start the Command Center. To do so, follow these steps:

1. **Open a command prompt.**
2. **Set the** `DB2INSTANCE` **environment variable to the instance that you want to be the current instance by entering the following command:**

   ```
   set DB2INSTANCE=<instance name>
   ```

   where *<instance name>* is the name of the instance that you want to be the current instance.
3. **Open the Control Center by clicking the Start button and choosing Programs⇨DB2 for Windows NT⇨Control Center.**

   You have to log on to the Control Center when you start it, use the user account that you used to install your DB2 software.
4. **Click the Command Center icon in the Control Center's toolbar menu.**
5. **Type** get instance **and press Ctrl+Enter.**

   You receive the following output:

   ```
   The current database manager instance is: <instance name>
   ```

   where *<instance name>* is the name of the current instance.

To start the DB2 CLP to work with an instance other than the default instance, follow these steps:

1. **Open a command prompt.**
2. **Type** db2cmd **and press Enter.**

   A DB2 command prompt appears.

3. **Set the** DB2INSTANCE **environment variable to the instance that you want to be the current instance by entering the following command:**

   ```
   set DB2INSTANCE=<instance name>
   ```

   where <*instance name*> is the name of the instance that you want to set as the current instance.

4. **Type** db2 get instance **at the command prompt and press Enter.**

   You receive the following output:

   ```
   The current database manager instance is: <instance name>
   ```

   where <*instance name*> is the name of the current instance. It should now be the instance that you just set as the current instance in Step 2.

Working with Multiple Instances

When you have more than one instance, you need to understand how DB2 decides which instances to work with. When you install DB2, a system environment variable called DB2INSTANCE is created and set to the default instance DB2. To view your system's environment variables, right-click the My Computer icon and select Properties from the pop-up menu. When the System Properties window opens, select the Environment tab as shown in Figure 7-6.

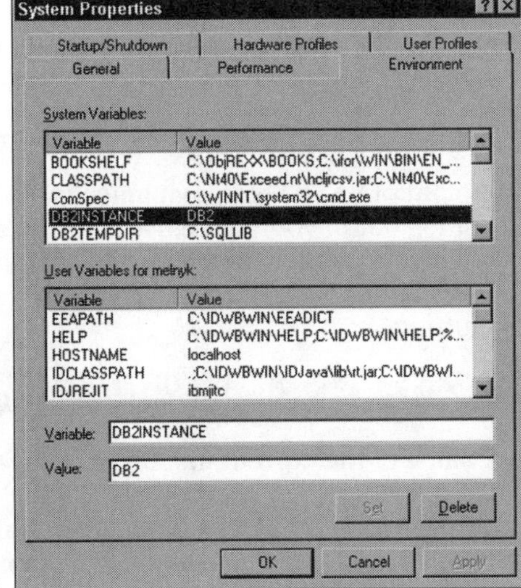

Figure 7-6: The Environment tab in the System Properties box.

The DB2INSTANCE environment variable determines the default instance for your system. Each time you log on to your system, the current instance is set as the default instance. The current instance, by default, is always the DB2 instance. This default setting can be changed permanently or for a particular session, which we describe in the following sections.

Changing the current instance permanently

To change the default setting of the DB2INSTANCE environment variable for all users and sessions, follow these steps:

1. **Log on to your system with a user account that belongs to the local Administrators group.**
2. **Click the Start button and choose Settings➪Control Panel.**

   The Control Panel window appears.
3. **Double-click the System icon.**

   The System Properties window appears.
4. **Select the Environment tab.**
5. **Scroll down the System Variables box and select the** DB2INSTANCE **variable.**
6. **Click the Value field and change it to the name of the instance that you want to become the default instance each time you log on to your workstation.**
7. **Click the Set button and then select OK.**

System environment variables cannot be changed dynamically. For DB2 to read this new setting, you must log out of your system and log on again by using the same user account. When you enter the `db2 get instance` command in a DB2 command window after you log back on to the system, you should receive the following output:

```
The current database manager instance is: <instance name>
```

where *<instance name>* is the name of the current instance.

If you changed the setting for the DB2INSTANCE environment variable, follow the preceding steps and set the DB2INSTANCE environment variable so that the DB2 instance is once again the default.

Set the DB2INSTANCE environment variable to the instance that you want to use most.

Changing the current instance for a session

Changing instances can be quite an inconvenience. If you plan to always work with a particular instance, set the DB2INSTANCE environment variable to this instance as described in the last section. Sometimes, however, you may want to work with an instance for only a brief period of time, or you may even need to start two instances at the same time. With the previous method, how can you start the DB2 instance and another instance at the same time when you have to log out of the system each time you want to work with a different instance? The answer, of course, is changing the current instance for a window.

To be more technical, geeks often refer to the window as a *session.* For example, opening a command prompt and then closing it is a session; you can have many sessions running at the same time. I call a session a window. Just understand this concept in case you find it necessary to showcase your new skills.

You can set an instance for a current window by entering the `set DB2INSTANCE=instance_name` command in a DB2 command window. This command changes the current instance until the window is closed.

Because the DB2INSTANCE environment variable is defined in uppercase letters, you must also use uppercase letters when setting this environment variable.

In the following example we assume that you have two different instances. If you do not have one, create another instance using the `db2icrt` command (see the "Creating an instance" section earlier in this chapter for more info).

For example, to change the current instance for a current session, follow these steps:

1. **Open a command prompt and type the following command :**

   ```
   db2cmd title <window name>
   ```

   where <*window name*> is whatever you want to name the window. For example, to name the window Window A (exciting stuff here!) you enter the following command:

   ```
   db2cmd title Window A
   ```

   This command opens a window called Window A (surprise!)

The title flag used with this command is actually a Windows command option. You can use the title flag to set a name for any command prompt window. We used the title flag with Window A to help show an example. You could just enter the `db2cmd` command without the option if you can keep track of the different sessions.

When you enter the db2cmd command in a command window, it launches a DB2 command window that you use to enter DB2 commands. You can also launch a DB2 command window by clicking the Start button and choosing DB2 for Windows NT⇨Command Window.

2. **At the Window A command prompt, type** db2 get instance **and press Enter.**

   You receive the following output:

   ```
   The current database manager instance is: <instance name>
   ```

DB2 will probably be your current database manager, because the `DB2INSTANCE` environment variable was set to DB2 when DB2 was installed. Any window opened uses the DB2 instance because you set it at the environment variable level, which is read at system logon time.

3. **At the Window A command prompt, type** set DB2INSTANCE= *<instance name>* **and press Enter.**

   where *<instance name>* is the name of another instance that you want to be the default instance for this session.

4. **At the Window A command prompt, type** db2 get instance **and press Enter.**

   This time, you receive the following output:

   ```
   The current database manager instance is: <instance name>
   ```

   where *<instance name>* is the name of the instance you just changed the default instance for this session to.

5. **Start another DB2 command window from the same session where you started the last one (Window A in our example) by entering the following command:**

   ```
   db2cmd title <window name>
   ```

   where *<window name>* is whatever you want to name the second window.

   For example, if you wanted to name your window Window B, you enter the following command:

   ```
   db2cmd title Window B
   ```

   This command opens another DB2 command window called Window B (or whatever you named it).

6. **In Window B, type** db2 get instance **and press Enter.**

   You receive the following output:

   ```
   The current database manager instance is: <instance name>
   ```

   where *<instance name>* is the name of the current instance for Window B.

   Your first window works with one instance, but your second window is working with another instance because you changed the setting for the DB2INSTANCE environment variable for only the first window. All other windows (new or old) always default to the instance specified by the DB2INSTANCE environment variable.

   Now you can work with both instances without having to globally set the DB2INSTANCE environment variable, log out of the system, and then log back in. If you're using the Control Center, you can always work with both instances, as it attaches to each instance for you.

   The changed instance is only set for the duration of the window. After you close Window A.

So many ways to set the current instance: Who's in charge here anyway?

With so many ways so set the current instance, you can easily get confused as to which setting DB2 adheres to and which it ignores. Here is the order in which DB2 determines the current instance:

1. If the DB2INSTANCE environment variable is set for the current session, DB2 adheres to the session's setting and overrides any other settings.
2. If the DB2INSTANCE environment variable is not set for the current session, DB2 uses the setting for the DB2INSTANCE environment variable from the system environment variables that are read at boot time.
3. If the DB2INSTANCE environment variable is not set at all, DB2 uses the DB2INSTDEF DB2 registry variable.

For example, if you set the current session's DB2INSTANCE environment variable to an instance — even if the system's setting for the DB2INSTANCE environment variable was for a different instance — DB2 would interact with the instance that you set the current session's variable to.

This order is why the DB2INSTDEF DB2 registry variable is not recommended for setting the active instance. If the DB2INSTANCE environment variable is defined (which is the default during any DB2 installation), the setting for DB2INSTDEF is never considered.

Telling DB2 the current instance with the Registry

DB2 must always know the current instance. DB2 has its own set of variables, just like the environment variables that Windows has, that are used to set DB2-related parameters. If DB2 cannot find a global or session-level setting for the `DB2INSTANCE` environment variable, it looks in the DB2 registry for the setting of `DB2INSTDEF`. It DB2 cannot find a setting for the default instance, you receive an error. By default the installation program sets the `DB2INSTANCE` environment variable. If for some reason you remove this from your system's settings, you must use the DB2 registry variable `DB2INSTDEF` to let DB2 know what the current instance is.

You can set the `DB2INSTDEF` registry variable globally by typing the following command at a command prompt:

```
db2set DB2INSTDEF=<instance
    name> -g
```

where *<instance name>* is the name of the instance that you want to make current.

Managing DB2 Servers with the Administration Instance

The database administration server (DAS) is a special instance that is used to manage DB2 servers. Each DAS manages its own local instances on a DB2 server. It serves as an administration control point. You never use the DAS directly, you don't create databases in it, and you usually don't have to concern yourself with its configuration and management. A DAS is created for you when you install DB2.

You must have a running DAS to use the Client Configuration Assistant (CCA) or the Control Center. The DAS assists the CCA and the Control Center when working on the following administration tasks:

- Enabling remote administration of DB2 servers.
- Providing a facility for job management, including the ability to schedule the execution of both DB2 and operating system command scripts. These command scripts are user-defined. The Control Center is used to define the schedule of jobs, view the results of completed jobs, and perform other administrative tasks against jobs located either remotely or locally to the DAS.
- Providing a means for discovering information about the configuration of DB2 instances, databases, and other administration servers in conjunction with DB2 discovery. (For more info on discovery, check out Chapter 6.) This information is used by the CCA and the Control Center to simplify and automate the configuration of client connections to DB2 databases.

You can have only one DAS on a machine. The DAS is configured during DB2 installation to start automatically each time you log on to the system. When you administer a DB2 server from a remote workstation, all the commands are sent to the DAS.

The DAS is an instance, but you really don't need to be concerned with it. You can see the name of the DAS by entering the `db2admin` command. Enter this command now. You should receive the following output:

```
DB2DAS00
```

as `DB2DAS00` is the name of the default DAS in Windows NT/2000.

Starting and stopping the Administration Server

You can start and stop the DAS by using the `db2admin start` and `db2admin stop` commands. When you enter these commands, you don't need to be concerned with the current instance; the DAS is a special instance that is not designed for user interaction; except indirectly through DB2.

To stop the DAS, type the `db2admin stop` command. You should receive a message confirming that the DAS was stopped successfully.

If you stop the DAS, you can't remotely administer a DB2 workstation or schedule jobs to run unattended.

Start the DAS so that the Control Center can be used to administer the system. To start the DAS, enter the `db2admin start` command at a command prompt. You should receive a message stating that the Administration Server was started successfully.

Creating the Administration Server

The DB2 setup program creates the DAS for you during installation. If for some reason the DB2 setup program failed to create the DAS during the installation, or the DAS becomes corrupt and you are forced to recreate it, you will need to create a new DAS.

To create a DAS, follow these steps:

1. **Log on to your system with a user account that belongs to the local Administrators group.**
2. **Type** db2admin create **at a command prompt and press Enter.**

   The administration server is created on your machine.

You can optionally associate the DAS with a user account. You may want to do this to limit the users that have access to this service, after all, you don't want anyone stopping this thing when DB2 tools rely on it so heavily. To create the DAS and associate it with a user account, type the `db2admin create` command as follows:

```
db2 admin create /user:<username> /password:<password>
```

After you create the DAS, you can establish or modify its ownership by providing a user account name and user password with the `db2admin setid` command. To associate a username and password with the DAS, the command is:

```
setid db2admin <username> <password>
```

where *<username>* and *<password>* are the username and password that you want to associate with the DAS.

Dropping the Administration Server

If for some reason you need to drop the DAS, follow these steps:

Don't follow these steps until you are really comfortable with your DB2 skills. If you drop the DAS, you will not be able to use some of the DB2 tools and their functions.

1. **Log on to your system with a user account that belongs to the local Administrators group.**
2. **Type** db2admin stop **at a command prompt and press Enter.**

   The DAS stops.
3. **Type** db2admin drop **at a command prompt and press Enter.**

   The DAS is dropped.

Configuring the Administration Server

Like a normal instance, the DAS has its own configuration file called `admin cfg`. To view this file, type **db2 get admin cfg** at a DB2 command prompt. You should receive something similar to the following output:

```
Admin Server Configuration

 Node type = Database Server with local and remote clients

 Database manager configuration release level       = 0x0900

 Diagnostic error capture level              () = 3

 Notify Level                         (NOTIFYLEVEL) = 2
.
.
.
 Discovery mode                         (DISCOVER) = SEARCH
Discovery communications (DISCOVER_COMM) = NETBIOS,TCPIP
```

You can update any of the parameters in this file the same way you update the `dbm cfg` file using a DB2 command prompt. For example, to update the `NOTIFYLEVEL` parameter to 4, type the following commands:

```
db2 update admin cfg using notifylevel 4
db2admin stop
db2admin start
```

To reset all of the settings in the DAS configuration file, type **db2 reset admin cfg** at a DB2 command prompt.

When you really get to know DB2, you may have to set some of the parameters in this file. For example, you may add a protocol to your network and need to make some changes to this configuration file to get the Administration Server to work on the new protocol. The default settings in this file are fine for this book.

You don't need to update the `admin cfg` file for the examples in this book. For more information on this file, refer to the *Administration Guide* in the Information Center. You can access the Information Center by clicking the Start button and choosing Programs➪DB2 for Windows NT➪Information➪Information Center.

Chapter 8

Working with Databases

In This Chapter

- Creating databases
- Dropping databases
- Altering databases
- Adding and removing databases on your system
- Configuring databases

Ah yes, databases. You are presumably reading this chapter because you either want to know more about them, or create one for yourself! Before you read this chapter, you may want to check out Chapters 2 and 3, and get up to speed with the basics of databases, which we discuss in those chapters.

This chapter tells you all you need to know about databases. You will find out how to create them, drop them, alter 'em, add 'em to your system, configure 'em, cook and fry 'em . . . okay, maybe not the last two. But this chapter will show you the things you need to know about databases.

Creating a Database Faster Than Greased Lightning

This section shows you how to create a database using the Create Database SmartGuide, which is the easiest way to create a database, You can also create a database by using the `create database` command. In order to create a database, you must log in to the system as a user with SYSADM or SYSCTRL authority. (If you need a refresher on authorities, refer to Chapter 2.)

We recommend that you log on to your system with the user account that you used to perform the installation. This user by default has SYSADM authority.

During database creation, you can choose to create a simple database that uses many of the default settings, or choose to specify advanced options, such as table spaces and collating sequences.

To create a database, use the Create Database SmartGuide. You can start this SmartGuide in the Control Center by right-clicking the Database folder in the instance where you want the database to reside, and then selecting the Create Database Using SmartGuide option from the pop-up menu.

Figure 8-1 shows the Create Database SmartGuide window.

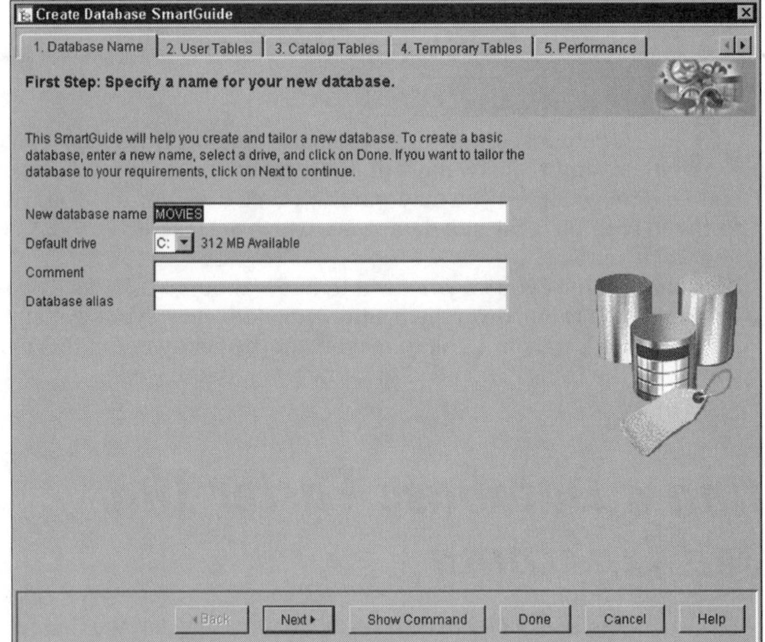

Figure 8-1: The main tab in the Create Database SmartGuide window.

To create a database, follow these steps:

1. **In the New Database Name text box, type a name for the database that you want to create.**
2. **In the Default Drive drop-down list box, select the drive where you want this database to be physically created on your system.**

The SmartGuide shows the amount of free disk space to the right of the drop-down list box for the drive that you specified.

You cannot create a database on a floppy or CD-ROM drive. If you select anything other than a drive, the SmartGuide returns the words `Not Ready` as the amount of free disk space. If you try to create the database on a drive where the SmartGuide notes the available disk space as `Not Ready`, you receive an error noting that the file or directory can't be accessed.

3. **(Optional) In the Comment text box, type a comment describing the database.**
4. **In the Database Alias text box, type an alias name for the database.**

   If you do not specify an alias name for your database, the alias name defaults to the same as the database name. For more on database alias names, check out the sidebar in Chapter 6.
5. **Click Done.**

   The SmartGuide starts to create your database.

All you need to create a simple database is to fill in the Database Name text box. Typing a database name in this text box makes the Done button become available. We recommend, however, that you fill in all the fields listed in the Database Name tab of the Create Database SmartGuide before creating a simple database.

Look at the Control Center's view of the instance where you just created your database. A new database should appear in the Control Center. For example, the MOVIES database is shown as a new database in Figure 8-2.

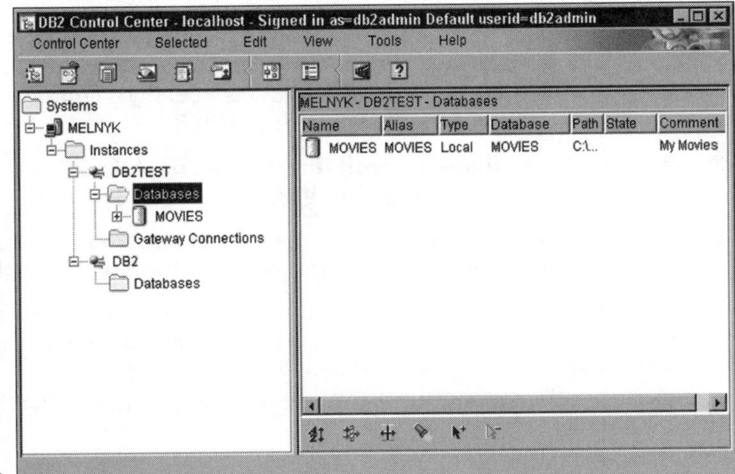

Figure 8-2: A new MOVIES database in the Control Center.

Aspiring to Geekdom: Creating a Database the Advanced Way

As you may have noticed when you created a database the easy way with the Create Database SmartGuide, there were a bunch of tabs that we did not take you through. Well, they aren't there for fun! They are there for people that understand the database creation task. This section briefly looks at these options and shows you how to create a database using these tabs. The Advanced method can save you time when you know what you are doing, because many of these tasks would have to be performed after you created the database.

To create a database by using the Advanced method, you need to have started the Create Database SmartGuide and be on the first tab (the Database Name tab).

You can start this SmartGuide in the Control Center by right-clicking the Database folder in the instance where you want the database to reside, and then selecting the Create Database Using SmartGuide option from the pop-up menu.

Follow these steps to create a database the advanced way:

1. **Enter the required information into the Database Name tab, as described in Steps 1 through 4 of the previous section, and then click Next.**

   The next three tabs, (User Tables, Catalog Tables, Temporary Tables) all give you the option to specify table space characteristics. You should read Chapter 9 before using these panels in the SmartGuide.

   Chapter 9 can help you understand how you can define many of the table space settings during database creation, as opposed to after the database is created. Each individual tab is actually a combination of panels from the Create Table Space SmartGuide.

2. **Click Next three times to scroll through the next three panels (we suggest you change something only if you know you have to.)**

3. **On the Performance tab you can define some regional characteristics for the database that you are creating. including the following.**

   In the Database locale box, you can select the country, territory, and code set for the database that you are creating. The territory and code set are used for string comparisons (default collating sequence) and character conversions. Refer to this SmartGuide's help if you need more information.

Usually the defaults are fine, but you should be aware that once you have created the database, you cannot go back and change these values. You would have to create another database.

To specify the database locale for the database you are creating, click the Country (Language) drop-down box and select the country who's territory and code page you want to use. The default option uses the territory and code page for the country that your operating system is set to.

When you select the country, the Territory and Code Set fields are automatically updated. Some territories give you the option to use different code sets. If your territory has more than one code set, you can click the Code Set drop-down box and select the code set that you want to use.

Finally, you need to define the string comparison technique used for your database. Select an option from the Strong comparison box to specify how characters are sorted, merged, and compared. You should pay some attention to this option as the string comparison method (or collating sequence) cannot be changed once the database is created.

If you select the Local Alphabet (Recommended) option, items are sorted according to the database locale and characters are compared by using the database code set and locale. In DB2-speak, this is called a System Collating Sequence. An example of this sorting sequence is: AaBbCcDd on through Zz.

If you select the Byte for Byte option, items are sorted to their binary representation. In DB2-speak this is called an *identity collating sequence.* An example of this sorting sequence is: ABCDE or zabcde and so on.

4. **Click Done when you're finished.**

   Your database is created.

Dropping a Database

Dropping a database deletes the database from your system. This is different from removing a database from the view of the Control Center, which only hides that database from the Control Center's view (more on that in a bit). To drop a database, follow these steps:

If you drop a database you will lose all of the data that you had in it. Only do this if you really don't want to see your database again!

1. **Right-click the database that you want to drop, and choose the Drop option from the pop-up menu.**

   A Confirmation window appears, similar to that shown in Figure 8-3, asking you to confirm that this is the database you want to drop.

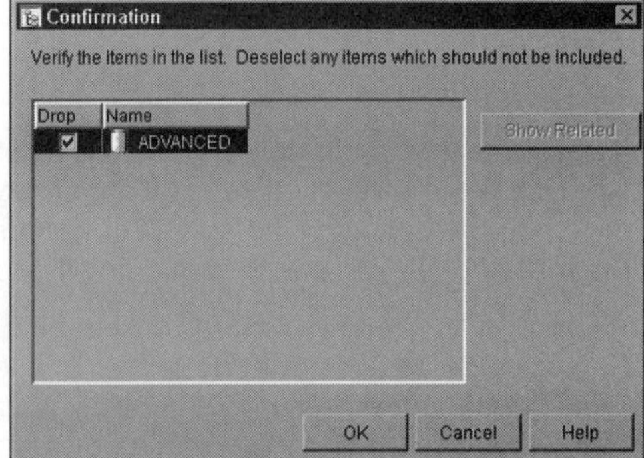

Figure 8-3: The Confirmation window asks if you're sure you want to drop a database.

2. **Click OK.**

   The database is dropped.

Adding a Database to the Control Center

Sometimes databases that you create do not appear in the Control Center for your system. This section shows you how to add a database that exists on your system, but does not show up in the Control Center, to the Control Center's view.

To add a database to your system, follow these steps from the Control Center:

1. **Right-click the Database folder in the instance where the database that you want to add resides, and then choose Add from the pop-up menu.**

   The Add Database window appears, as shown in Figure 8-4.

Figure 8-4: The Add Database window.

2. **Click Refresh.**

   The name of a database appears in the Database Name drop-down list box. If you have more than one database on the system, you can click the drop-down list box and select the database that you want to add. If the database does not appear after you click the Refresh button, type its name in the Database Name field.

3. **Type an alias name for the database in the Alias text box.**

   If you don't remember or aren't sure what a database alias is, see the sidebar in Chapter 6.

4. **(Optional) Type a comment describing this database in the Comment text box.**

5. **Click OK.**

   You're back where you started from, only this time your database is shown in the instance in which you created it.

Removing a Database from the Control Center

Suppose that you don't want to drop a database that you created, but you do want to remove it from the view of the Control Center. To remove a database from the view of the Control Center, follow these steps:

1. **Right-click the database that you want to remove from the Control Center and choose Remove from the pop-up menu.**

   A Confirmation window appears (similar to the window shown in Figure 8-3) asking you to confirm that you want to remove this database from the view of the Control Center.

2. **Click OK.**

   The database is now hidden from the Control Center.

Altering a Database

After creating a database, the comment describing the database is the only part that you can alter. To alter a database, you must log in to the system with the same set of user rights that you use to create a database.

To alter a database, follow these steps:

1. **Right-click the database icon for the database that you want to alter and choose Alter from the pop-up menu.**

   The Alter Database window appears, as shown in Figure 8-5.

Figure 8-5: The Alter Database window.

2. **Change what you need to and click OK.**

You can alter the alias of a database, but you cannot do this by using the `alter` command. Instead, you have to remove the database from the Control Center and then add it again specifying a different alias name. This way the database isn't lost. If you drop the database, the database and all of its contents are lost.

Configuring a Database

It would take a whole book to cover the topic of configuring a database. Trust me, this is not fun work. Because database configuration can be a pretty complex task, DB2 (thankfully) comes with a Configuration Performance SmartGuide that you can use to configure your database. The SmartGuide takes you through a series of tabs and asks you for information describing your database and its environment.

To start the Performance SmartGuide, right-click the database that you want to configure and select the Configure Performance Using SmartGuide option from the pop-up menu.

Database parameters affect the performance and operation of your database the same way database manager parameters affect the performance and operation of your instances. The *DB2 Administration Guide* details each parameter; as well, additional information can be found in the online help available with the Control Center.

Each database has its own set of parameters. When DB2 geeks refer to the parameters for a database, they are referring to the database configuration file (`db cfg`). These same geeks refer to the configuration parameters of an instance as the database manager configuration file (`dbm cfg`). For more information on the configuration parameters of an instance, see Chapter 7.

Any parameters for a database must be set in the database's configuration file. Each database has its own database configuration file, and a database configuration file can be used with only one database. In DB2, this translates as a one-to-one relationship between a database and a database configuration file.

The database configuration settings affect all the objects within the database, but they do not affect other databases. While instance settings affect all databases within the instance, if you want to change a database setting for all your databases, you must change the desired setting in each database's configuration file, as I show you generally how to do in the next section (describing how to change every possible setting would be impossible here).

Checking out the Configure Database Notebook

You can use a notebook to configure your database. If you do not use the notebook, you have to use the command line interface and cope with all sorts of messy syntax. A notebook gives you a graphical interface into the task that you are trying to perform, which in this case is the task of configuring a database.

The Notebook and the SmartGuide mentioned earlier in the chapter are different things. A Notebook gives you a graphical interface into an object, while a SmartGuide is designed to help you complete a task as easily as possible. We don't get into the specifics of the questions that the SmartGuide will ask you. We do show you how to change the configuration of your database with the notebook. The configuration parameters of the SmartGuide are specific, we just show you how to change them and give an example.

To view a database's configuration file, right-click the database that you want to configure and choose Configure from the pop-up menu. The Configure Database Notebook appears, as shown in Figure 8-6.

The database's configuration parameters are logically placed into groups denoted by tabs at the top of the window. The advantage to using the Control Center's interface into the `db cfg` file is the available online help, search facilities, and the hints provided with each parameter.

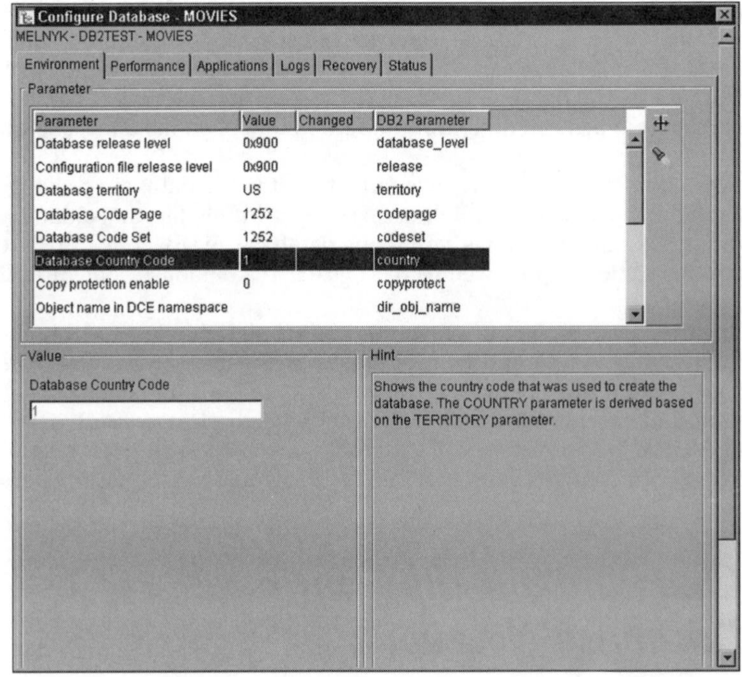

Figure 8-6: The Configure Database notebook.

You can't change some database settings after the database is created. Settings you cannot change have a grayed out value box.

To view the `db cfg` file by using the DB2 command line processor, type the following command in a DB2 command window:

```
db2 get database configuration for <database name>
```

where *<database name>* is the name of the database whose configuration you want to look at.

You can use abbreviations in the get database configuration command. You can abbreviate the term database as `db` and the term configuration as `cfg`. Therefore, entering the `db2 get db cfg for <database_name>` command returns the same output as the `db2 get database configuration for <database_name>` command. You can use these abbreviations for any DB2 commands that contain these terms.

Changing db cfg parameters

Sometimes you need to change `db cfg` parameters, especially later in the book. For now, we just show you how to change them generically. Suppose that you want to change the number of primary log files assigned to a database when it is started. To accomplish this task, open the Configure Database Notebook (follow the instructions in the previous section) and then follow these steps:

1. **Select the tab where the parameter that you want to change resides.**

   If the list of parameters is long for any given tab, click the Find icon (the flashlight to the right of the parameter box) and type the name there.

2. **In the value box, type the new value for the parameter that you want to set.**

   In some cases, a parameter only has a choice of specific settings, In this case, you are presented with a list of options; choose one.

3. **If you changed a value and you want to set the value back to its setting before you made any changes, select the parameter and click Reset.**

   Keep in mind that this resets the setting back to the value for the `db cfg` when you opened it for editing. If you want to restore a parameter value to the default setting for every DB2 database, select the parameter and click Default.

4. **Click OK.**

   You receive a message noting that all applications that are currently connected to the database must disconnect before the changes take effect.

5. **Right-click the database and choose Restart from the pop-up menu.**

   The database restarts.

Chapter 9

Places for Table Spaces

In This Chapter

- Defining a table space
- Containers and extents
- Performance considerations
- Types of table spaces
- Types of data in a table space
- Default table spaces
- Creating a table space

If we told you that a table space is the space where you store your tables, it would probably remind you of a time when you rephrased a term when trying to explain it to your teacher. Your teacher's likely response was a decidedly unimpressed look. The difference is that in this case, rephrasing the term actually works!

In this chapter, you'll find out about table spaces and how they work in DB2. You also see the different types of table spaces that exist in DB2, and when to use them. Finally, you find out about the default table spaces that are created each time you create a database the easy way (check out Chapter 8) and how to create your own table spaces.

Dealing with Table Spaces

A *table space* is the physical mapping between the logical data that is stored in your databases and the physical location of that data on your storage media. A table space tells DB2 where the data and objects in your tables physically reside on your system. In DB2, all tables must be stored in a table space. Aside from just placing the data and objects physically on your system, table spaces play an important role in the layout of your database.

DB2 has a variety of table spaces that you can use to store different types of table data. Many administrators place frequently used tables, or specific data in a table, on table spaces that exist on faster drives, while other less frequently accessed tables may reside on slower drives. To be a database administrator, you need to understand table spaces and how to use them in your database.

DB2 also allows you to back up your database at the table space level. This provides more granularity and control when backing up or restoring data on your system. For example, instead of backing up an entire database, you have the option to just back up a table space and whatever tables reside in it. This can save time when backing up large databases. (Backup issues are covered in Chapter 13.)

A table space consists of containers. Depending on the type of table space that you're using, a container can be a file, directory, or raw device on your system. A table space uses a container to store the data that is assigned to the table space.

A *raw device* is a storage medium on your system. In Windows, a raw device would be a partition. Your drive, if it was formatted on a full partition, could be a raw device. You should be aware, however, that many partitions have two drives on them. Each drive could not be used as a table space container. To see the partitions on your system, click the Start button and choose Administrative Tools (Common)⇨Disk Administrator.

Contemplating containers

A *container* is the place on your system where DB2 physically stores a table's data. A container is made up of extents, which are made up of pages (more on extents and pages in a bit).

DB2 uses the word *container* to describe something that you use in your system everyday. When you install Windows, you decide which drive to place the files. When you save a file, you place it in a directory. When you write a letter to your mother, you save the data in a file. Depending on the type of table space, you can ask DB2 to physically place your data on a raw device, directory, or in a large file.

On Windows, depending on the type of table space, a DB2 container can be a file, directory, or a raw device.

A table space can have many containers, which is what DB2 folks call a *one-to-many relationship* between a table space and containers. But a container can only belong to one table space, which is called a *one-to-one relationship.*

Figure 9-1 illustrates the relationships between table spaces and containers, where table space A uses files, while table spaces B and C use raw devices (or hard drives in the case of the figure).

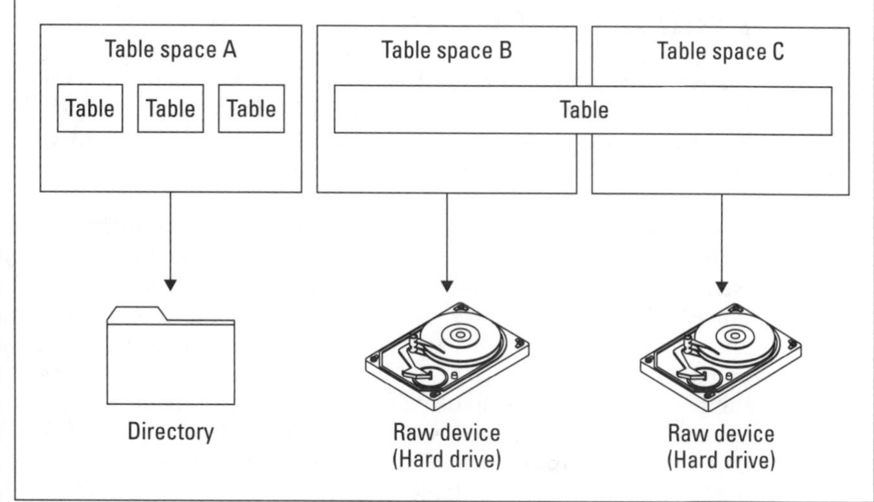

Figure 9-1: The relationship between containers and table spaces.

Depending on the type of table space, you can mix containers for a table space. For example, a table space can have a file container and a raw device. This is not, however, recommended for performance reasons.

The type of container that you can assign to a table space depends on the type of table space that you are using. (We discuss the two types of table spaces in the next section.)

- If you are using an SMS table space, a container can only take the form of a *directory* because this type of table space is managed by the operating system.
- If you are using a DMS table space, a container can be a file or a raw device because this type of table space is managed by DB2.

You decide the size of a container by estimating how much space your data will take up in your tables. This is no easy task. You can find information on how to estimate the size of the tables in your database in the *DB2 Administration Guide* (available from the Information Center).

You can see the size of your raw device in bytes by using the Disk Administrator tool. (To start the Disk Administrator tool, click the Start button and choose Administrator Tools (Common)➪Disk Administrator. To view the size of an SMS container (a directory), enter the `dir` command in a command prompt.

Examining extents

An *extent* is a unit of space within a container that is defined for a table space. DB2 stores data in pages (except for LOBs and LONG VARCHAR data). The extent size is equal to the number of pages that DB2 writes to a container (see the next section for more info on pages).

When you create a table space, you decide how big to make an extent by using the EXTENTSIZE parameter. After you create a table space, you cannot easily alter its extent size. The default extent size for a table space is determined by the DFT_EXTENT_SIZE database configuration parameter. Any table space that you create uses an extent size that is equal to this setting, unless you specify otherwise with an advanced database creation option. To change the default extent size that DB2 assigns to a table space, you need to specify the extent size during table space creation or change the DFT_EXTENT_SIZE database configuration parameter. For more information, refer to the *Administrators Guide* (available through the Information Center). The default extent size for a table space is 32. You can set an extent size between 2 and 256 pages.

Figure 9-2 shows a container, a page, and the default number of extents.

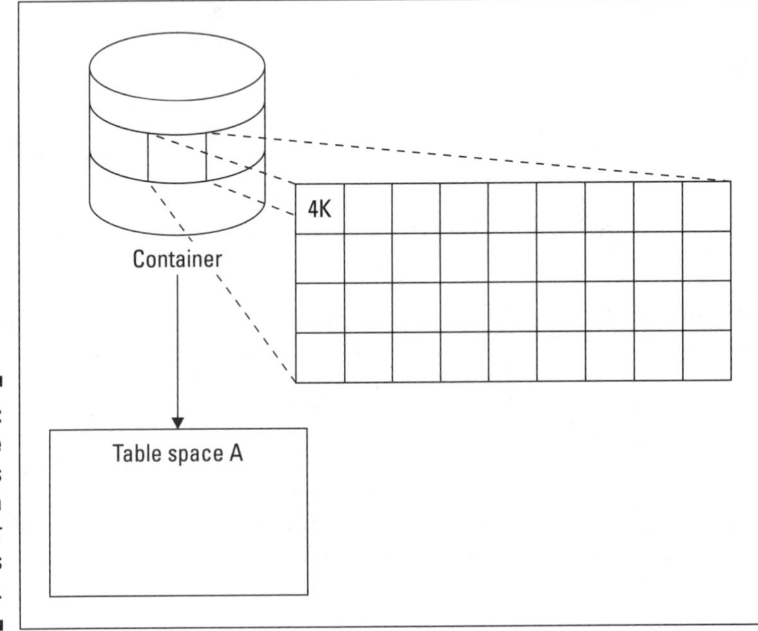

Figure 9-2: The components of a container — extents and pages.

With SMS table spaces, DB2 writes to containers in a round-robin fashion, though the container it writes that data to first does not necessarily have to be the first container defined for the table space. For example, if DB2 starts to write data to container A, it would then write to container B, and then C. After DB2 writes data to all the containers, it starts back at the first container it wrote to, which in this case is A. Note, however, that the first container that DB2 writes to does not have to be A; it can start at B. If it started at B, it would go from B to C to A and then back to B.

DB2 does this so that it can attempt to evenly balance the storage used for each container. Figure 9-3 illustrates how DB2 writes data to a container.

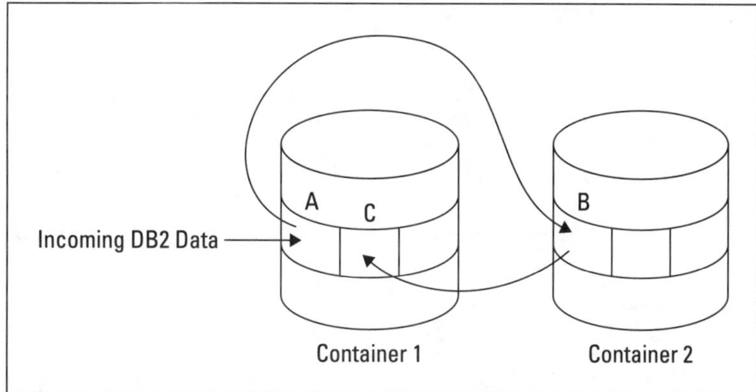

Figure 9-3: The round-robin fashion of writing to a container.

In the preceding figure, you can see that an extent is written to each container before another extent is written back to the first container. This is referred to as *striping* of your data on the containers defined for a table space. When a container defined for a table space becomes full, DB2 doesn't write to any other containers — even if space is available on another container — but instead stops writing data to the container altogether and returns an error to the user.

Pondering pages

A *page* is an allocation of memory that is used to transfer data from physical storage to the database manager's memory. Each container has a defined number of extents and an extent is made up of these pages. The number of pages that make up a container is determined by the extent size (determined by default through the database configuration file or specified when you create the table space.). DB2 supports different page sizes. By default, a page is equal to 4,096 bytes, or 4KB of memory. You would use larger page sizes for workloads that tend to access rows sequentially; for example, in a data warehouse environment. Smaller page sizes would be used for transaction-based databases; the kind that are used to run a business. For example, an airline's flight reservation database would typically use smaller pages.

For the most part, unless you are really looking to indulge yourself in geekdom, don't concern yourself with pages at this time. If you really want to learn more about them, refer to the *DB2 Administration Guide* in the information center.

Deciding Between SMS or DMS

You can have either the operating system or DB2 manage a table space. If the operating system manages the table space, the table space is referred to as a System Managed Space (SMS) table space. If DB2 manages the table space, it is referred to as a Database Managed Space (DMS) table space.

Table 9-1 summarizes the differences between an SMS and DMS table space:

Table 9-1: Comparing SMS and DMS Table Space

Table Space Capabilities	*SMS Table Space*	*DMS Table Space*
Add containers to table space after creation	x*	✓
Store INDEX data in a separate table space	x	✓
Store LONG data in a separate table space	x	✓
One table can span multiple table spaces (for example, indexes in one table, long data in another, and regular data in another)	x	✓
Space is obtained as needed (not preallocated)	✓	x

** You can add a container to an SMS table space during a redirected restore.*

SMS table spaces

Each container in an SMS table space is a directory on your system that will consist of files that are put there by DB2. Never touch them! With an SMS table space, the operating system controls the storage space required for your DB2 data. The storage space is not preallocated, it is obtained as it is needed. As your tables get more and more data, the operating system assigns more and more storage space to the table space.

This storage method is no different than what you are used to with a regular directory. If you have a directory called `c:\temp`, each time you move a file into this directory, the operating system gives the `c:\temp` directory the needed space — of course, space is always limited by the total size of your hard drive. This is how an SMS table space works. The more space that is required by DB2 to store data, the more space that is allocated by the operating system to the container.

You may want to use an SMS table space if:

- You have a limited amount of space on your system and the size of your database is unknown. Because the SMS table space uses storage space only as it needs it, the total available space on your drive can still be available to other applications.
- You do not have the resource or skill to devote to table space administration. SMS table spaces are easier to administer than DMS table spaces.
- Your database does not require optimum performance. Generally, SMS table spaces are not used for online analytical processing (OLAP) databases.
- You are creating a temporary table space.

Database administrators must pay special attention when creating an SMS table space. You must specify the total number of containers for an SMS table space when you create the table space; you cannot add containers to an SMS table space after it is created.

For example, a drive may have 150MB of free space available. If a container that you assign to your SMS table space is a directory on this drive, then you only have 150MB of available space to store your data. If the tables you assign to this table space grow rapidly, you can easily run out of space and you would not be able to add more containers to handle the problem; however, if you had a DMS table space, you could do so (DMS tables spaces are covered in the next section).

One situation where you can add a container to an SMS table space is called a redirected restore. This option is available to you when you restore a table space from a backup. Chapter 13 discusses backing up a database.

When a table is assigned to a particular SMS table space, all the data for that table must reside in the table space. Two types of data are allowed in an SMS table space: regular data and temporary data. *Regular data* consists of tables, indexes, large objects, and so on, that you create in your tables. With SMS table spaces, all data that is not temporary data is considered regular data. *Temporary data* consists of tables and objects that DB2 creates to satisfy requests for data. The tables and objects are temporary and are used internally to process and organize a user's request. Any temporary tables or objects are dropped when the results are returned to the user.

Dropping an SMS table space causes the allocated storage space to be erased and given back to the operating system.

DMS table spaces

Using a DMS table space has three advantages. The biggest advantage is the ability to span data for a single table across multiple table spaces. DMS table spaces allow you to store large objects (LOBS) and indexes separately from the regular data. In an SMS table space, you cannot do this.

A DMS table space can contain temporary data, regular data, long data, and index data. Long data and index data are subsets of regular data and can only be isolated in a DMS table space. You can refer to long data as any large objects, for example: binary large objects (BLOBs), character large objects (CLOBs), or LONG VARCHAR data columns. (For more information on data types, see Chapter 2.)

DMS table spaces are more complex to work with and administer. Until you get comfortable with DB2, to the point where you have ventured into the *DB2 Administration Guide* for really geeky information, it's a good idea to stick with SMS table spaces.

Following is a list of some of the main differences between DMS and SMS table spaces:

- A DMS table space typically performs better than an SMS table space because DB2 does not have to interact with the operating system's file system to locate the data. Each container in a DMS table space is a file or raw device on your system. DB2 must control the data within this type of table space, which is why the table space is considered to be managed by the database. Because DB2 manages the table space, DB2 is more aware of the placement of that data in the operating system.

- Storage for each container is preallocated when the container is created. Unlike the SMS table space, only a set amount of storage space is available. When you create a DMS table space, you specify the size of the containers.
- DB2 doesn't have to compete with other applications for storage space because the storage space is preallocated at table space creation time.
- You can dynamically add more containers to a DMS table space. If you have a rapidly growing table that is using almost all of its assigned space, you can add more containers. You would not be able to do this with an SMS table space.

You may want to use a DMS table space if:

- You have an array of drives with different speeds and you wish to assign the fastest drives to the most often-accessed data for optimal performance.
- You have a wide variety of data in your table space, including large objects, with different access frequencies, and you wish to include these considerations in your backup scheme.
- You anticipate a lot of growth in your tables in the future.
- Your tables hold large objects.
- You know the maximum size of your database.

For example, suppose that you have a table called EMPLOYEE. The table contains an employee's name, phone number, and a photo. Assume that an employee's photograph is not frequently accessed or updated, and that it's only used when creating or replacing an employee's access card while other data gets accessed more frequently (such as employees querying the database for another employee's name or phone number, for example). An administrator is therefore likely to place the photos for all employees in a separate table space, most likely on a container that uses a slower drive, since they are accessed less often than other information. Most of the updates and queries involve columns other than the column that has the employee's photo.

In examples such as this, placing the index on the fastest drives on your system is advantageous because the index is used often. Because photos are only used when an access card is created, this data can be placed on a slower drive. The remaining data is placed in another table space for data.

If the previously mentioned EMPLOYEE table was created in an SMS table space, all the data (including the photographs, indexes, and data) would have to reside on the same drive. In an SMS table space, you are unable to leverage the performance of different disk speeds for commonly accessed data. A DMS table space also prohibits you from wasting resources on backing up an entire table. Remember that in the EMPLOYEE example, the photos of the different employee rarely change. You don't want to continually back up data that doesn't change. You can avoid this with a DMS table space.

Another advantage to separating data like in the previous example is with your backup/recovery scheme. Because you don't frequently update or alter photographs of an employee, you may not want to include them for nightly backups of your mission critical data. Using a DMS table space, you can take nightly backups without the wasted resource spent backing up the photographs.

Although you can separate large object data and indexes in different table spaces, the remaining data must belong to the same table space. For example, you can't assign the Name column to a different table space than the Phone Number column.

Do not store any non-DB2 data on physical drives that you define as a DMS container. DB2 doesn't like it. Trust me on this one!

Creating a Table Space

In this section we show you how to create an SMS table space and a DMS table space for a database. In order to create a table space, you must log in to the system as a user with SYSADM or SYSCTRL authority on the database. (See Chapter 2 for more information on authorities.)

We recommend that you log on to your system with the user account that you used to perform the installation; this user by default has SYSADM authority.

Creating an SMS table space

You can use the Table Space SmartGuide, the Table Space notebook, or a DB2 command to create a table space. The upcoming steps guide you through creating a table space with the Table Space SmartGuide.

Before you start, you need to make sure that you have an empty directory to use as a container. If a directory that you want to assign as a container to a table space isn't empty, you receive an error saying that the container is already in use. You can ensure that there is nothing in the directory that you want to use as a container for you table space by typing the `dir <directory name>` command.

An SMS table space on Windows can only take the form of a directory.

To create an SMS table space with a container using the Create Table Space SmartGuide, follow these steps:

1. **Create a directory for the container for this table space by typing the** md *<directory name including path>* **command at a command prompt.**

   where *<directory name including path>* is the fully qualified path name of the directory that you want to use as a container. For example, if you want to use the *SMSA* directory as a container, but it is located in the `c:\temp` directory, you would specify this variable as `c:\temp\smsa`.

   Repeat the preceding step as many times as you want containers.

2. **In the Control Center, expand the System, Instances, and Databases views by clicking the plus sign [+] to the left of each object until you locate the database you want to create a table space for.**

3. **Right-click the Table Spaces folder in the tree of the database that you want to work with and choose Create⇨Table Space Using SmartGuide from the pop-up menu that appears.**

   The Create Table Space SmartGuide appears, as shown in Figure 9-4.

Figure 9-4: The Create Table Space SmartGuide.

   The Create Table Space SmartGuide guides you through the creation of a table space, as well as making recommendations for some of the parameters that you can set.

4. **Type a name for your table space in the Table Space Name text box.**

5. **Click Next.**

The Type tab appears. This tab enables you to choose the type of data that you want to store in your table space. You want to create a table space that holds all types of data (regular, temporary, and long-field data). If you aren't sure about the different types of data in DB2, see Chapter 2 for the lowdown.

6. **Click the Regular option.**
7. **Click Next.**

   The Management tab appears.
8. **Click the Low Maintenance option.**
9. **Click Next.**

   If you want to create a DMS table space, you select the High Performance option. You find out how to create a DMS table space in the next section, "Creating a DMS table space."

   The Containers tab appears, as shown in Figure 9-5.

   Because this is an SMS table space, you must define as many containers as you think you need before it is created. You cannot add containers at a future date. In this example, we only create one.

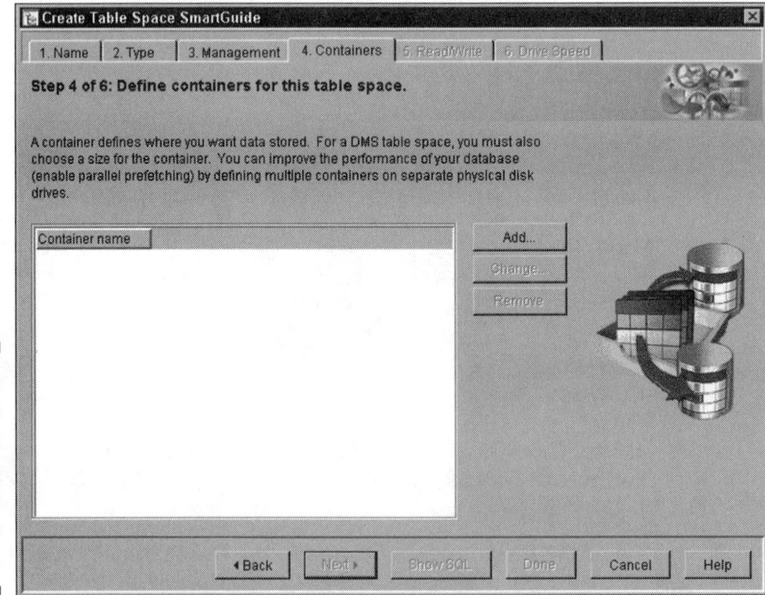

Figure 9-5: The Containers tab in the Create Table Space SmartGuide.

10. **Click Add.**

    The Add Container window appears, as shown in Figure 9-6.

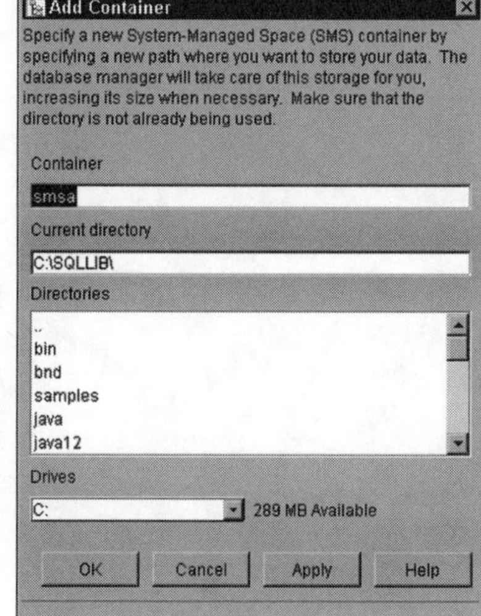

Figure 9-6: The Add Container window is used to add containers to an SMS table space.

11. **Double-click the directory that you want to use for a container from the Current Directory, Directories, and Drives fields.**

    The Add Container window behaves in a mischievous way. If you only select the container that you want to use by clicking it once in the Directories box, the Current Directory field does not change; only the Container field changes. If you click OK now, the name of the container is SMSA. But notice that the directory for the container is `C:\`, not the intended `C:\SMSA` (of course, we are assuming here that the directory name of the container is `c:\SMSA`). You can now expect to receive an error noting that the container (which is just a directory) is already in use. Chances are that you have files on the `C:\` drive. Remember, you must create the table space in an empty directory.

12. **Type a name for this container in the Container field and click OK.**

    You return to the Containers tab.

13. **Click Next.**

    The Read/Write tab appears, as shown in Figure 9-7.

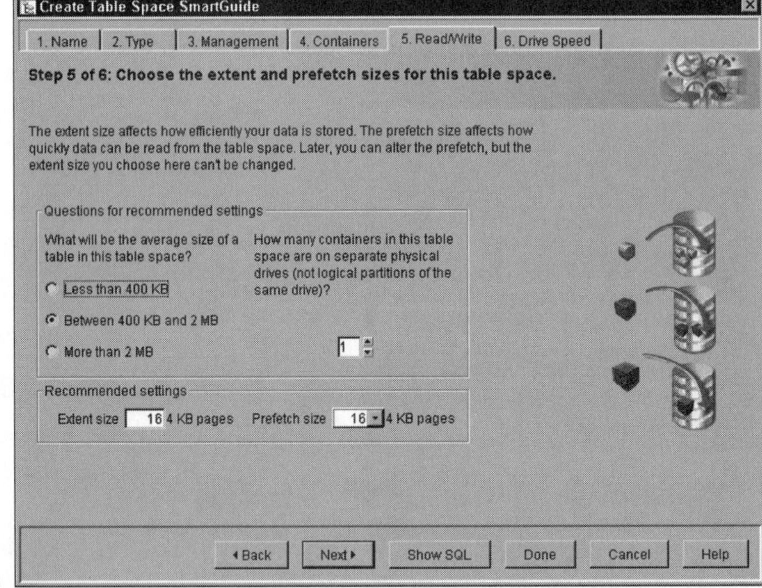

Figure 9-7: The Read/Write tab in the Create Table Space SmartGuide.

14. **The SmartGuide asks you questions about your database and makes recommendations for the settings of the Extent Size and Prefetch Size table space parameters.**

    Answer these questions. Then you can review the recommendations the SmartGuide makes and accept them. Or, you can input your own values.

    For example, if you created an SMS table space with two containers on the same drive, you would have to pay close attention to this SmartGuide. Notice that one of the questions asks you how many containers are on different physical drives? Click the spin button and change this value to the number of containers you have.

    Extent size refers to the size of the extent for your containers, which we discussed earlier in the chapter. *Prefetch size* refers to the number of pages that are loaded into memory (because memory access is faster than disk access) from the table space in anticipation of access. For example, if you think you are going to access parts of a table, you may want the database manager to load it into memory so that when that data is requested, the database manager does not have to go to the disk to get it. This is an advanced performance issue; check out the *DB2 Administration Guide* for more information.

15. **Click Next.**

    The Drive Speed tab appears, as shown in Figure 9-8.

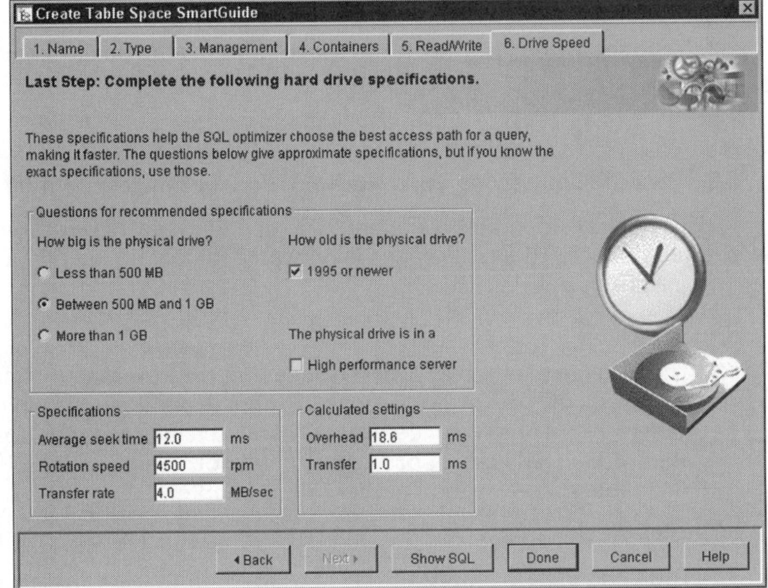

Figure 9-8: The Drive Speed tab in the Create Table Space SmartGuide.

The SmartGuide asks questions and makes recommendations about your hard drive.

16. **Answer the questions and accept whatever recommendations the SmartGuide makes (unless you have some compelling reason not to).**
17. **Click Done.**

    The Control Center creates an SMS table space.

Creating a DMS table space

You can create a DMS table space for regular data, index data, and for large object-based data. You use these table spaces for a table that has large-object or index data, as well as regular data.

To create a DMS table space for long field data by using the SmartGuide, perform the following steps in the Control Center:

1 **Click the plus sign [+] to expand the System, Instances, and Databases views until you locate the database that you want to create the DMS table space for.**

2. **Right-click Table Spaces within the database that you want to work with, choose Create⇨Table Space Using Smart Guide from the pop-up menu.**

The Create Table Space Smart Guide appears (see Figure 9-4).

3. **Type the name for your table space in the Table Space Name text box.**
4. **Click Next.**

   The Type tab appears.
5. **Click the Long (Long Text, Audio, Video, or Images) option.**

   This option identifies a specific type of data that will be stored in this table space. This table space is only able to contain long data if you select this option.
6. **Click Next.**

   The Management tab appears. Notice that the Low Maintenance option is grayed out? This is because you cannot separate long-field or index data in an SMS table space. The Low Maintenance radio button is associated with an SMS table space. For more information, see the "Creating an SMS table space" section earlier in this chapter.
7. **Click Next.**

   The Containers tab appears.
8. **Click Add.**

   The Add Container window appears, as shown in Figure 9-9.

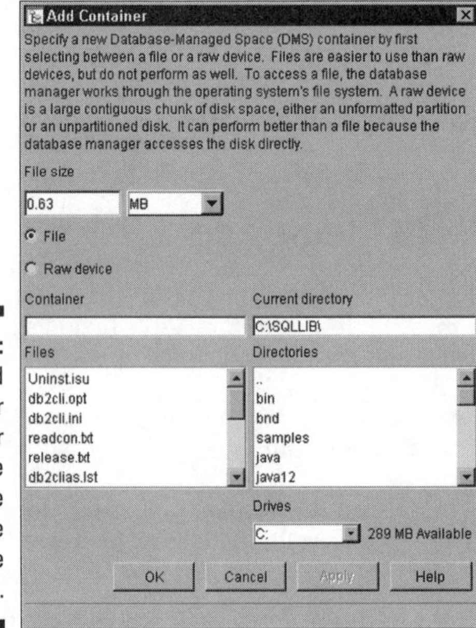

Figure 9-9: The Add Container window for a DMS table space in the Create Table Space SmartGuide.

The Add Container window when creating a DMS table space looks different than when you're creating an SMS table space. Besides the fields that you see in an SMS Add Container window, you also have a File Size text box and File and Raw Device options.

You must preallocate the size of a DMS table space. You don't have to do this for an SMS table space because the operating system allocates storage as needed.

So what if you want to use a raw device (or a *logical volume* as those tech-heads call them)? If you click the Raw Device option, the Add Container window appears as shown in Figure 9-10.

Because a raw device is a partition (which could be represented as a drive) in Windows, two other options appear that give you the option of creating the table space container on an unformatted partition or an unpartitioned drive.

9. **Click the option that corresponds to the type of container that you want to use for this table space.**

   For our example, we selected the File option. This tells DB2 that you want to use a file as a container for this table space. If you need more information, click Help.

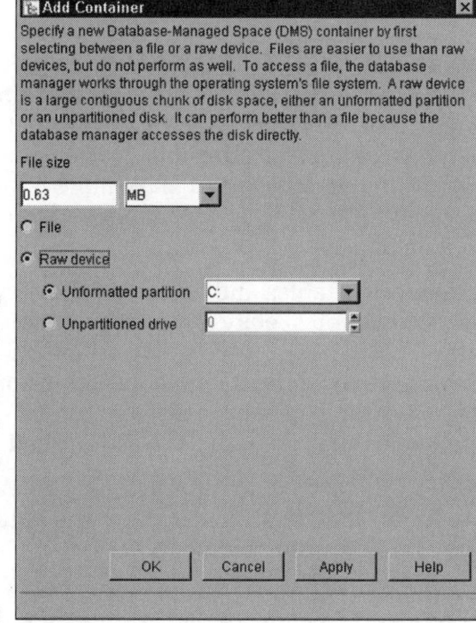

Figure 9-10: The Add Container window for raw devices in the Create Table Space SmartGuide.

10. **Type the size of this container in the File Size text box.**

    You can enter this value in MB or 4KB pages. Use the drop-down list box to select the unit of measurement you want to use.

    For now, we suggest you make this container about 20MB.

11. **In the Current Directory field, select the directory where you want the container for this table space to reside.**

    The default directory for the container is `c:\sqllib`, where `c:\` is the drive where you install DB2. You probably don't want to use this directory to store your containers because it is used by DB2. You always want to ensure that no other applications write to the directory that you use as a container for a table space.

12. **Type the name of the container in the Container text box.**

13. **Click OK.**

The Default Table Spaces

There are three default table spaces that are created whenever you create a database using the default method:

- **SYSCATSPACE**: Stores the system catalog tables that are created when the database is created. Unless you specify otherwise during database creation, DB2 creates the SYSCATSPACE table space as an SMS table space. The system catalog table contains all kinds of information that DB2 uses to run the database. Administrators can use some of these tables to learn more about their database and make more informed decisions on performance issues. This table space cannot be altered or dropped after creating a database.
- **TEMPSPACE1:** Stores temporary tables and objects that are created during DB2 processing. Unless you specify otherwise during database creation, DB2 creates the TEMPSPACE1 table space as an SMS table space. For example, if your request for data included some sorting or joining of tables, a temporary table may be created in the TEMPSPACE1 table space and dropped when the resultant set was returned.
- You can alter the TEMPSPACE1 table space after creating a database, but you cannot drop it if another TEMPSPACE doesn't exist. A database must always have a temporary table space assigned to it.
- If a database uses more than one temporary table space, temporary objects are allocated among the temporary table spaces in a round-robin fashion in order to balance the workload. We don't recommend using more than one temporary table space. The only reason for having two temporary table spaces is that you want to change the definition for TEMPSPACE1.

- **USERSPACE1**: Stores a user's table data and indexes. This is the table space where by default all of your user's data and indexes will be stored. Unless you specify otherwise during database creation, DB2 creates the USERSPACE1 table space as an SMS table space. You can drop or alter the USERSPACE1 table space after creating the database. USERSPACE1 is the table space where all table data resides unless you create another user table space or explicitly specify a table space in which to place a table's data. If you create another user table space, the new user table space becomes the default table space.

You can specify if these table spaces are to be managed by the system or database, as well as other characteristics, by using some of the advanced options when you create a database. For more information on creating databases, see Chapter 8. If you do not specify any options for table spaces when you create a database, they will all be created as SMS table spaces.

In the Control Center, click the Table Spaces folder in the tree for the database with which you want to work. The Name column shows all the default table spaces. The Types of Data column describes the type of data that you can store in the associated table space. The Managed By column details what type of table space (SMS or DMS) the corresponding table space is. Look at your table spaces for your database in the Control Center. Did you notice the default table spaces?

Chapter 10

Working with Tables

In This Chapter

- Understanding the parts of a table
- Slapping together a new table
- Dropping a table (later, dude!)
- Altering a table

You can begin the exciting steps of implementing your database design (see Chapter 3) by creating tables. After you create your tables, you can fill them up with data (*populate* them), and then start working with that data. In this chapter, you find out how to create a table, how to change a table after it's created, and how to get rid of a table (drop it) if necessary.

Building Tables

You can create a table with DB2 in several ways. You can enter the `create table` command at a DB2 command prompt or run a script file that includes a `create table` command. If you're not too keen on operating system prompts, you can use the Command Center or the Script Center. And if that's still too geeky for you, you can use the Control Center to create a table using the Create Table notebook or the Create Table SmartGuide. In this section, we show you how to create a table with the SmartGuide and how to create SQL statements that allow you to automate table creation later.

To create a table, you must log in to the system as a user with SYSADM or DBADM authority. (For more info on authorities and other table basics, see Chapter 2.) To make things easier, just log on to the system with the same user account that you used to install your DB2 server; by default, this user has SYSADM authority.

You can choose to create a simple table with many of the default settings, or choose to specify advanced options, such as constraints. If you want to know more about these advanced options, see the *IBM DB2 SQL Reference*.

Creating a table the easy way

You can quickly create a table by using the Create Table SmartGuide. To do so, follow these steps:

1. **Open the Control Center by clicking the Start button and choosing Programs⇨DB2 for Windows NT⇨Control Center.**
2. **Open the Create Table SmartGuide by right-clicking the Tables folder for your database in the DB2TEST instance and then choosing Create⇨Table Using SmartGuide.**

   The Create Table SmartGuide window appears, as shown in Figure 10-1.
3. **In the Table Name text box, type a name for the table that you want to create and click Next.**

   Leave the Table Schema drop-down list box as the default.

   The Columns tab appears, as shown in Figure 10-2.
4. **Click an appropriate column lists entry in the Column Lists scroll box.**

   In Figure 10-2 we selected the ID Numbers list. If the list of available columns does not include the column name that you want to use, you must define a new column.

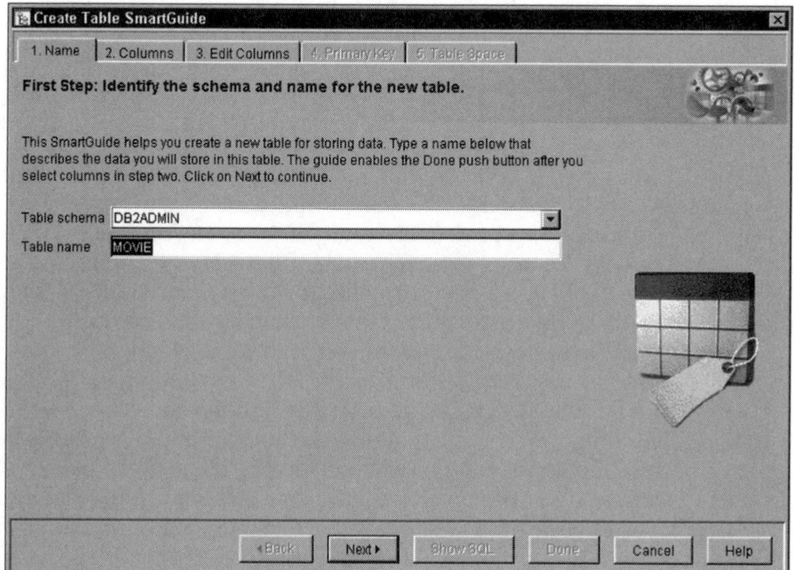

Figure 10-1: Specifying a name for the new table.

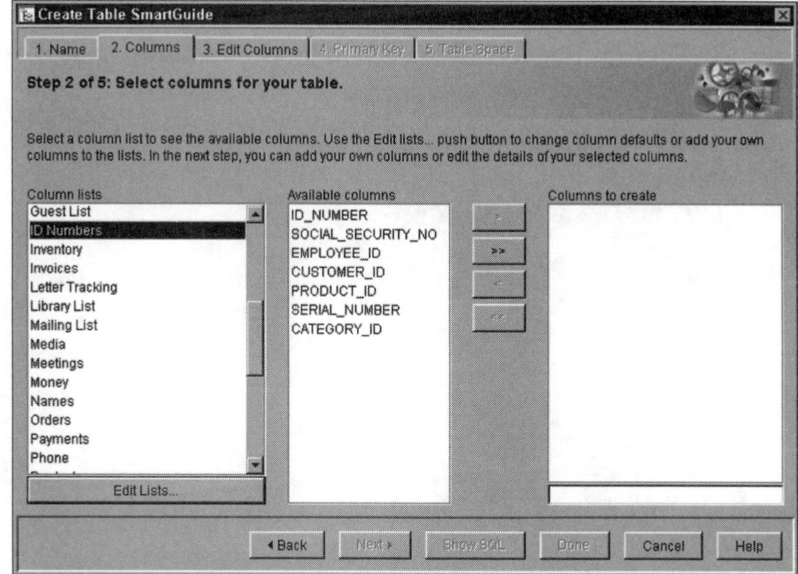

Figure 10-2: Selecting columns for the new table.

5. **Click the Edit Lists button.**

 The Edit Column Lists window appears, as shown in Figure 10-3.

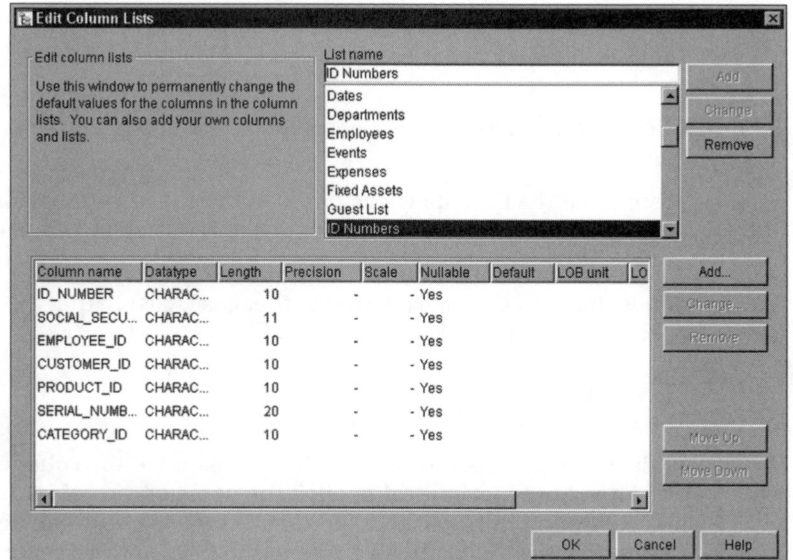

Figure 10-3: Customizing the column lists.

6. **Click ID Numbers in the List Name box.**
7. **Click the Add button in the middle of the window to add a column definition.**

   The Add Column window appears, as shown in Figure 10-4.

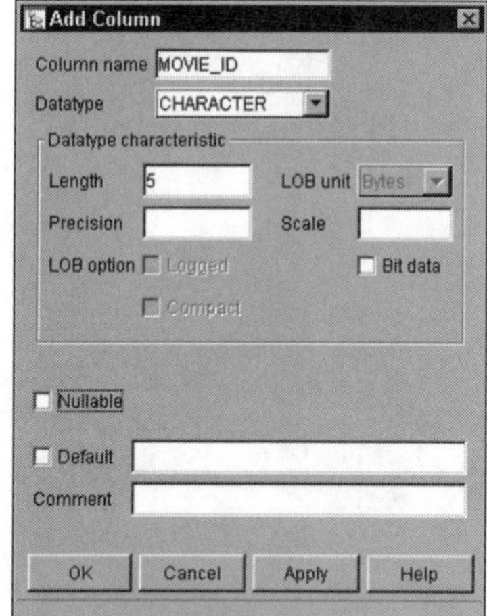

Figure 10-4: Adding a new column definition.

8. **Type a name for the column in the Column Name text box.**

   The default data type is CHARACTER, so you don't have to change the value in this field, but you can change the length value from 10 bytes to 5 bytes.

9. **Click in the Length text box and type in a number for the column length.**

   Ensure that the Bit Data check box is not checked, or the data in the column will be treated as binary data and returned in hexadecimal form.

   REMEMBER

   If your new column serves as the primary key column for the table, then it must have a value in each row. In that case, ensure that the Nullable check box is not checked.

10. **Click OK.**

    You return to the Columns tab.

11. **In the Column Lists scroll box, click the name of the column list that you have been working with, click the name of the column that you just defined in the Available Columns scroll box, and then click the [>] button to move that column name to the Columns to Create box.**

    In our example, we have been working with the ID Numbers column list.

12. **Repeat Steps 3 through 10 to define and select any other columns that you want.**

    In Figure 10-5, for example, we created a TITLE column (of data type VARCHAR and maximum length 30) and a YR_RELEASED column (of data type SMALLINT). Unlike the MOVIE_ID column, these columns are nullable.

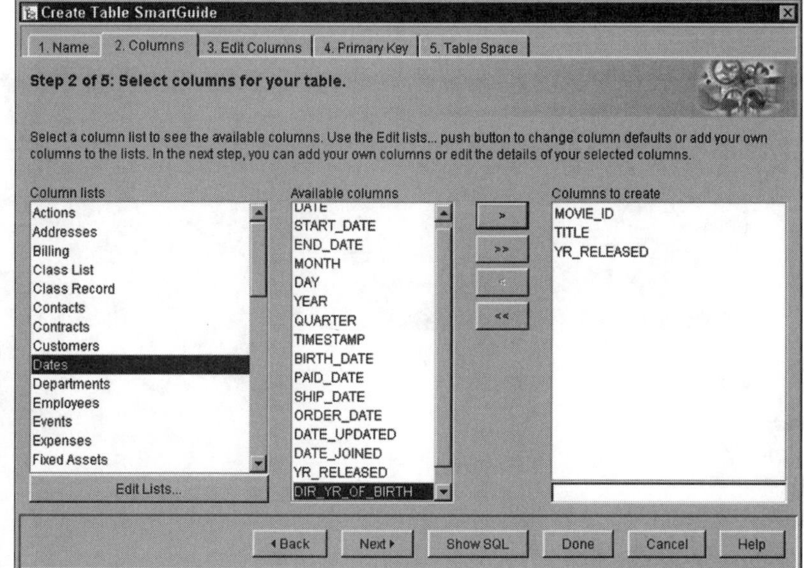

Figure 10-5: Selecting additional columns for the new table.

13. **(Optional) Click the Show SQL button to verify that your resulting table definition is as you expected. Click Close when you have finished looking at the SQL statement.**

    Figure 10-6 shows the generated SQL for the new table. It confirms that the character column data isn't stored in binary form, and that null values aren't permitted in the primary key column.

14. **Click Next.**

    The Edit Columns tab appears, as shown in Figure 10-7. Here is your opportunity to make any necessary changes. If everything looks fine, pat yourself on the back.

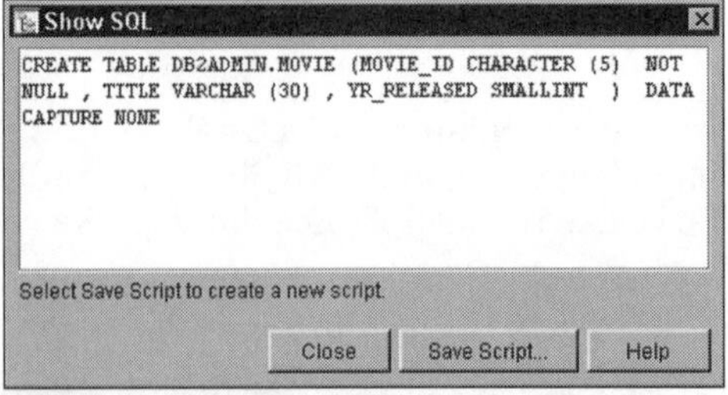

Figure 10-6: An SQL CREATE TABLE statement.

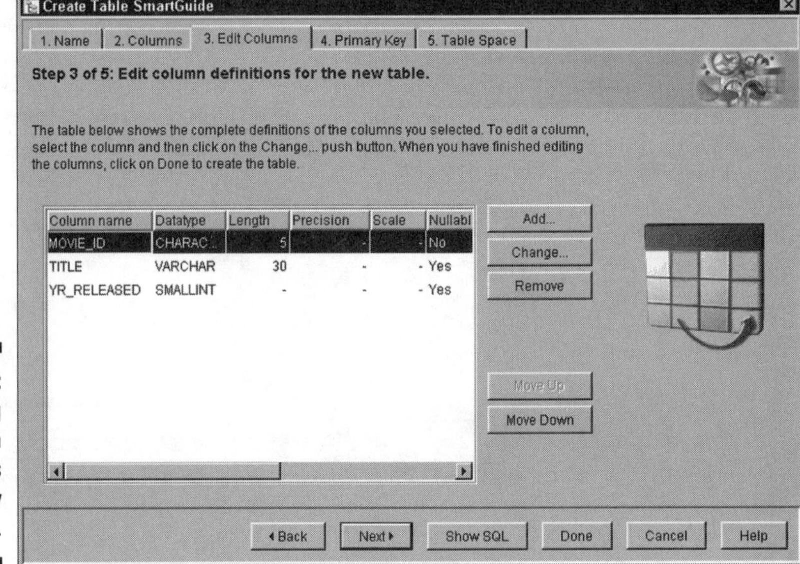

Figure 10-7: Editing column definitions for the new table.

15. **Click Next.**

    The Primary Key tab appears, as shown in Figure 10-8.

16. **Click one or more columns that you want to define as the primary key in the Available Columns list, and then click the [>] button to move them to the Primary Key Columns box.**

17. **Click Next.**

    The Table Space tab appears, as shown in Figure 10-9. This tab enables you to customize the table spaces in which the table data is stored. To keep things simple, you can leave the Table space text box blank and DB2 uses the default table space USERSPACE1. We discuss creating table spaces in Chapter 9.

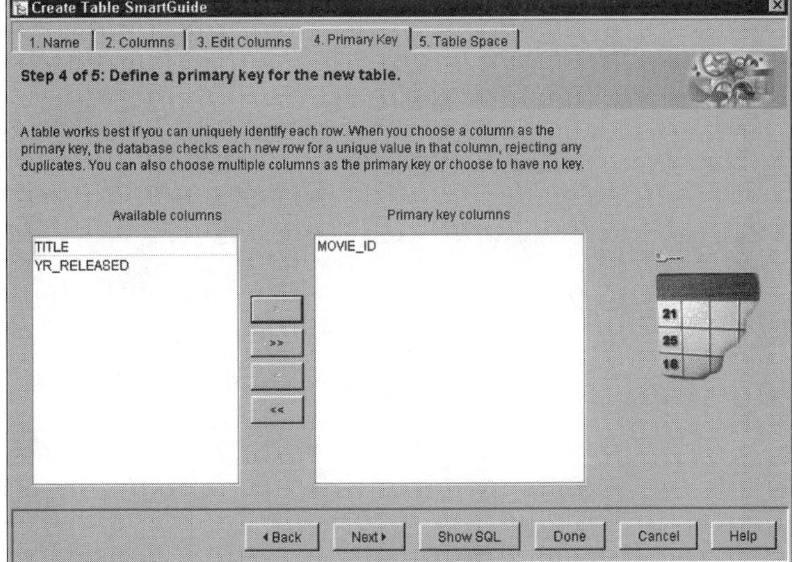

Figure 10-8: Defining a primary key for the new table.

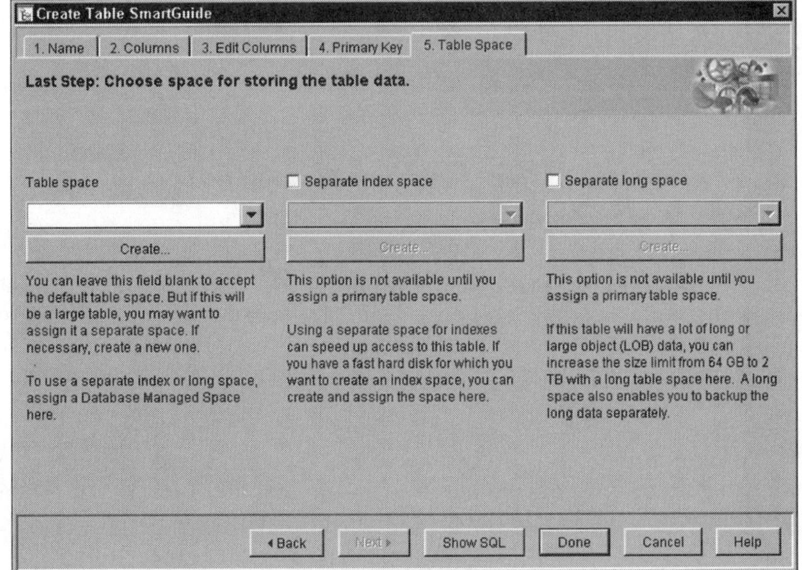

Figure 10-9: Choosing space for storing the table data.

18. **Click Done.**

    The SmartGuide creates the table.

You can now look at the Control Center view of your database again. The table you created appears in the Control Center. Figure 10-10 shows the Control Center with a new MOVIE table.

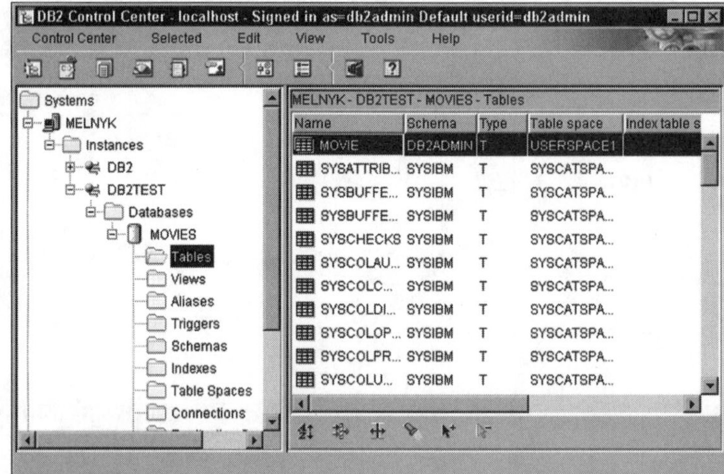

Figure 10-10: A new table appears in the Table object tree view of the database.

Creating new tables automatically with db2look

After you've gone through all the hard work of creating tables, would you want to start all over and do it again, if you had to, say, create these tables in a different database, or on a different system? No? Well, of course you wouldn't, and you don't have to if you used a nifty shortcut command called `db2look`.

You can use the `db2look` command to generate a table definition script, which is a series of commands in a plain text file. You can run a table definition script to recreate the user tables for a database.

To use the `db2look` command to create a table definition script, follow these steps:

1. **From a command prompt, set the DB2INSTANCE environment variable so that the instance that you want to create a table definition script for is the current instance by typing the following command:**

   ```
   set DB2INSTANCE=<instance name>
   ```

   where <*instance name*> is the name of the instance that you want to be the current instance.

2. **Start a DB2 command window by typing** db2cmd **at a command prompt**.

   Use the `cd` command to change the current directory to your working directory to help you find the `db2look` output file.

3. **Start** `db2look` **by typing the following command at a command prompt:**

   ```
   db2look -d <name of database to be queried> -u <name of
            creator ID> -e -o <name of the file to which the
            output will be written>
   ```

   where `d` specifies the alias name of the database that is to be queried; `-u` specifies the creator ID (`db2admin`); `-e` generates a command line processor (CLP) script containing data definition language (DDL) statements to recreate the tables; and `-o` specifies the name of the file to which the output is to be written. So, for example, our MOVIES database example with the `db2admin` creator ID would be as follows:

   ```
   db2look -d MOVIES -u db2admin -e -o db2look.sql
   ```

   and would output to the file `db2look.sql`.

   If you want, you can look at the output by opening the file in your favorite text editor or word processor. You can find the file in the same directory or folder from where you issued the `db2look` command.

To recreate the tables by using the script created by `db2look`, follow these steps:

1. **Type the following command at the prompt in a DB2 command window:**

   ```
   db2 -tf <name of the .sql file that db2look created when
            you ran the db2look command>
   ```

2. **In the Control Center, select the Tables folder in the appropriate database. Right-click the Tables folder and choose Refresh to restore your tables to the list.**

   Wow, wasn't that easy?

Dropping a Table

You may sometimes need to drop (get rid of) a table. The table may no longer be needed after adjustments to a new database design, or you may need to change some aspect of the table's definition that cannot be changed after the table is created. In the latter case, it is best to drop the table and then to recreate it with new specifications. To drop a table, you need to log on to the system with the same set of user rights that you use to create a table.

To drop a table, follow these steps:

1. **From the Tables folder for your database in the Control Center, select one or more tables that you want to drop.**
2. **Right-click the selected tables and choose Drop from the pop-up menu.**

   For this example, drop the tables that you created earlier in this chapter. A Confirmation window appears (see Figure 10-11) asking you to confirm the tables that you want to drop.

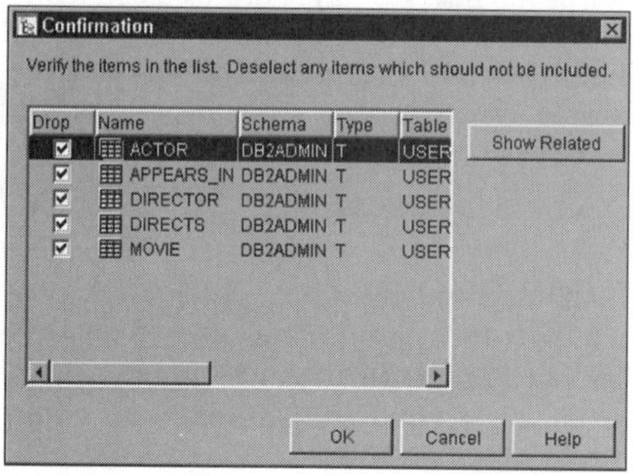

Figure 10-11: A Confirmation window ensures that the correct tables are dropped.

3. **Click OK.**

   The selected tables are dropped from the database, and are removed from the list of tables in the Control Center.

Altering a Table

After you create a table, you can alter some, but not all, of its characteristics. To alter a table, you need to log on to the system with the same set of user rights that you use to create a table.

When altering a table, you can:

- Change table properties
- Change the comment
- Add columns
- Change column comments
- Change the length of an existing VARCHAR column
- Define the primary key
- Change the primary key
- Add foreign keys
- Change foreign keys
- Add check constraints
- Change check constraints
- Select a lock size
- Specify the percentage of free space that is to be left on each page
- Request data capture for propagation
- Extend data capture to include long variable length columns
- Indicate whether data is to be appended to the end of the table data

To alter a table, follow these steps:

1. **From the Tables folder for your database in the Control Center, right-click the table icon for the table that you want to alter and choose Alter.**

   The Alter Table notebook appears.

2. **Make any necessary changes and then click OK.**

Chapter 11

Views, Aliases, and Other Stuff in Mother Hubbard's Cupboard

In This Chapter

- Checking out the view
- An alias by any other name
- Looking it up in the index
- Scheming with schemas
- Pulling the trigger
- Swimming in buffer pools

Picture yourself selecting a vacation spot (settle back — this is a relaxing analogy). Your travel agent shows you ten different brochures. All ten locales look good, but you're only interested in looking at hotels that are in Mexico, are right on the beach, and have at least two swimming pools. The travel agent can then narrow down the options and show you a different view of what's available. Better yet, your travel agent now knows what you look for in a vacation, and next time only shows you the options that meet your requirements.

You can narrow down the types of information you want to look at in a database in a similar way. This chapter covers how you can modify what information you see in a table. You also find out about using aliases, or nicknames, and accessing DB2 data faster.

Haggling with Views

DB2 defines a *view* as a logical table that consists of data that is generated by a query. A query is an SQL statement that accesses data.

Basically, views are just another way of looking at data in database tables. The data that you see through a view is not actually stored on disk — only the query is stored. A view keeps you from poring over several tables individually and piecing out each tidbit of info that you need from hundreds of rows and columns. You can create or drop views; you can also insert data through views.

Creating a View

This section shows you how to go about creating a view. Creating a view is useful if you want to look at only a subset of rows in a table or multiple rows from a combination of tables.

To create a view, follow these steps:

1. **Open the Control Center by clicking the Start button and choosing Programs⇨DB2 for Windows NT⇨Control Center.**
2. **Right-click Views and choose Create from the pop-up menu.**

   The Create View window appears, as shown in Figure 11-1. You see a sample SQL statement that is meant to guide you in creating a view.

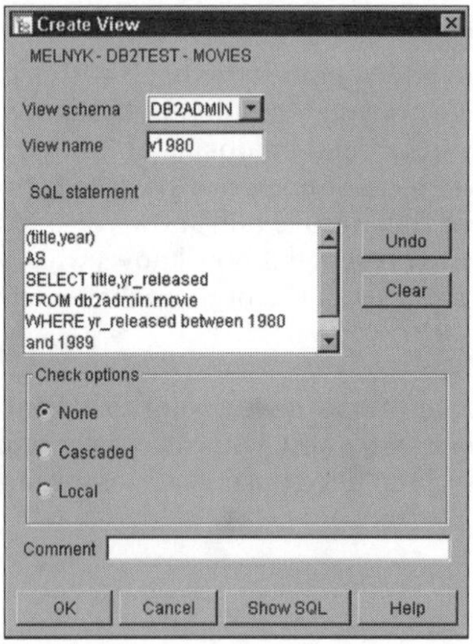

Figure 11-1: Creating a view with the Create View dialog box.

3. **Fill in the fields for the information you want to retrieve.**

Leave the default in the View Schema drop-down list box. (We explain schemas later in this chapter.) Name your view (preferably something indicative of its contents) by typing a name in the View Name field. You must then alter the default SQL statement to create a query that will extract info from one or many tables and define your view, as follows:

```
(<view column 1>, <view column 2>, <view column 3>)
AS
SELECT <table column 1>, <table column 2>,
       <table column 3>
FROM <table name>
WHERE <some condition>
```

where:

<view column 1>, *<view column 2>*, and *<view column 3>* are the column names that you will have in your view (you don't need to have three columns, you can have as many or few as you want).

<table column 1>, *<table column 2>*, and *<table column 3>* in the SELECT clause are the columns from the table that you want to extract. The number of table columns must match the number of view column names you specify.

<table name> is the name of the table you are selecting from.

<some condition> in the WHERE clause is optional, but it lets you narrow down the results you get back. The condition can be any arithmetic or text comparison. An arithmetic condition such as *<table column1 >* > 0 checks all the values in *<table column 1>* and returns only those rows where the number stored in *<table column 1>* is greater than 0. A text comparison such as *<table column 2>*='KANSAS', for example, checks all the values in *<table column 2>* and only returns those rows where the value in *<table column 2>* is set to KANSAS.

4. **(Optional) Click the Check Options you want and enter a comment that describes this view in the Comment text box.**

   The Check Options are useful for creating views that are used in more complex ways (see the next section for more on check options or refer to the online help).

5. **Click OK.**

   Your new view appears in the Views folder. Figure 11-2 shows the contents of a view folder (in the right pane).

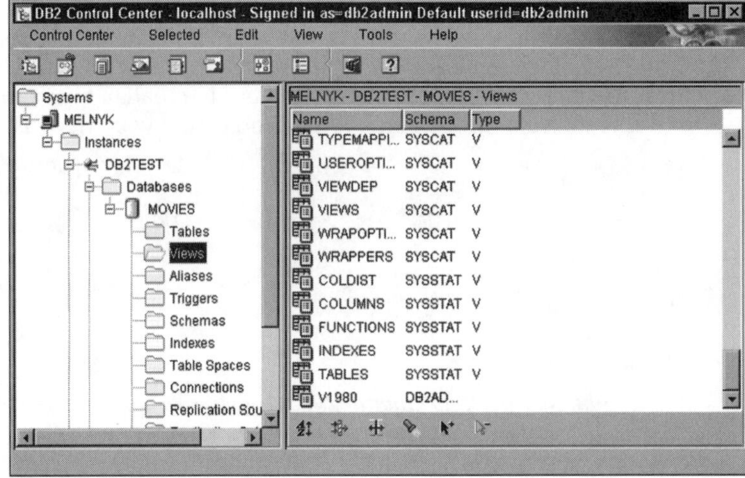

Figure 11-2: The contents of a sample Views folder in the DB2 Control Center.

6. **To see the contents of a view, right-click the view name and choose Sample Contents from the pop-up menu.**

Inserting rows through a view

You can use regular SQL `insert` statements to insert rows through a view and into a table. These rows can, but are not required to, meet the conditions of the view. But in the Create View window (refer to Figure 11-1), clicking a Check Option other than None enables you to only insert rows that meet the conditions of the view into the underlying table. Each time that you try to insert a row into a view, DB2 checks to see that the <some condition> clause you specified when creating the view is met.

Dropping a view

You can drop the view from the listing of views in the Control Center. To drop a view, follow these steps:

1. **Open the Control Center by clicking the Start button and choosing Programs⇨DB2 for Windows NT⇨Control Center.**
2. **Right-click a view name and choose Drop from the pop-up menu.**

   A confirmation dialog box appears, as shown in Figure 11-3.
3. **Click OK to drop the view.**

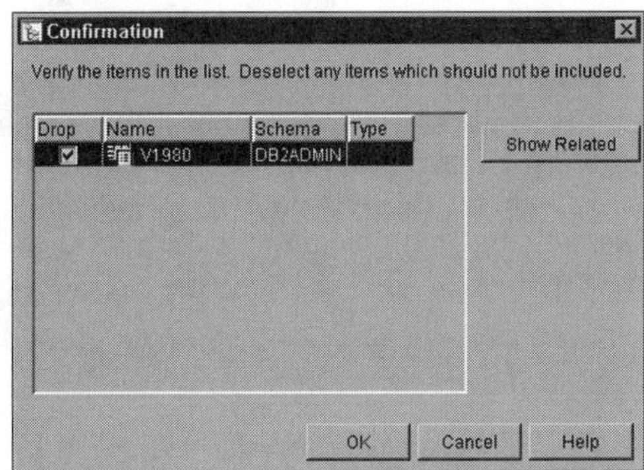

Figure 11-3: The Confirmation dialog box appears when you choose to drop a view.

Don't worry, the underlying tables are there. You're only deleting the query that you saved when the view was created.

Giving a View an Alias

Chapter 8 discusses how you can use aliases as nicknames for your database. DB2 also lets you create nicknames for your tables and views. In DB2, a nickname for a table or view is also called an alias.

To give a view an alias, follow these steps:

1. **Open the Control Center by clicking the Start button and choosing Programs⇨DB2 for Windows NT⇨Control Center.**
2. **Right-click the Aliases folder and choose Create.**

   The Create Alias dialog box appears, as shown in Figure 11-4.

Figure 11-4: Creating an alias details.

3. **Fill in the fields.**

   Select the alias schema from the Alias Schema drop-down list box (more on schemas shortly). Name your alias (preferably something indicative of its contents) by typing a name in the Alias Name field. Select an object schema from the Object Schema drop-down list box and fill in the Object Name field. The object schema and object name identify the table or view for which you're creating an alias.

4. **Click OK.**

   You've just created an alias!

Looking It Up in the Index

Everyone knows that if you are looking for information in a book, the first place you go is the index in the back. Imagine buying a travel guide about the United States, but without an index (no Table of Contents either!), and then needing information for Chicago. You would have to flip through the entire book searching for references about Chicago! You could certainly find information about Chicago much faster with an index.

Similarly, if you query DB2 tables that don't have an index, DB2 must look through the entire table to find the data that you are requesting. But if you define an index on a table, you're enabling DB2 to point itself in the right direction to get the information faster.

An index in DB2 is defined as pointers that are logically ordered by the values of a key. Indexes provide quick access to data and can enforce uniqueness on the rows in the table. The first part of this definition is like the index of a book, but the second part about enforcing uniqueness gets a little trickier.

Suppose that you are looking at a dictionary and want to look for the definition of the word architect. You find the word, but right below it architect appears again with a different definition! There isn't a unique definition for the word. In DB2, you can create an index that enforces that each word appears with only a single definition. Fortunately, DB2 provides a SmartGuide for creating indexes.

To create an index, follow these steps:

1. **Open the Control Center by clicking the Start button and choosing Programs⇨DB2 for Windows NT⇨Control Center.**

2. **Right-click the Indexes folder and choose Create Index Using SmartGuide from the pop-up menu.**

   The Introduction tab of the Index SmartGuide appears, as shown in Figure 11-5.

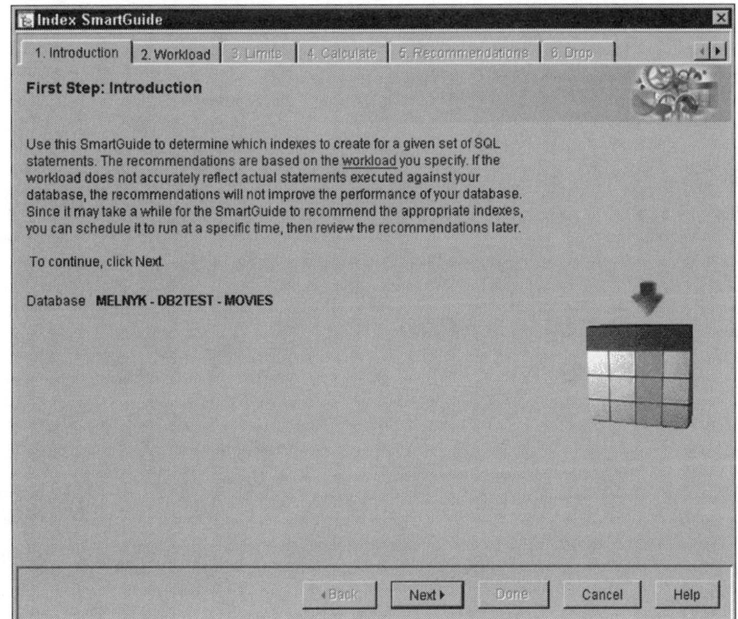

Figure 11-5: The DB2 Index SmartGuide.

3. **Click Next.**

   You use the Next key to move from tab to tab. You don't, however, have to fill in information on all the tabs. When the SmartGuide has determined that you have enough of the basic fields filled it, it enables the Done button that you can click to create your index.

   Clicking Next on the Introduction tab takes you to the Workload tab, as shown in Figure 11-6.

4. **On the Workload tab, click Add.**

   The Create Workload dialog box appears. A *workload* is a set of SQL queries. DB2 needs to know what kinds of queries you plan on running before it can advise you on the type of index to create.

   An example of a workload is a simple SQL statement:

```
select * from <schema name><table name> where <some
        condition>
```

   For example, to look at a MOVIES database that was created by the `db2admin` user and query it for movies from the eighties, you could use the following SQL:

```
select title from db2admin.movie where yr_released
        between 1980 and 1989
```

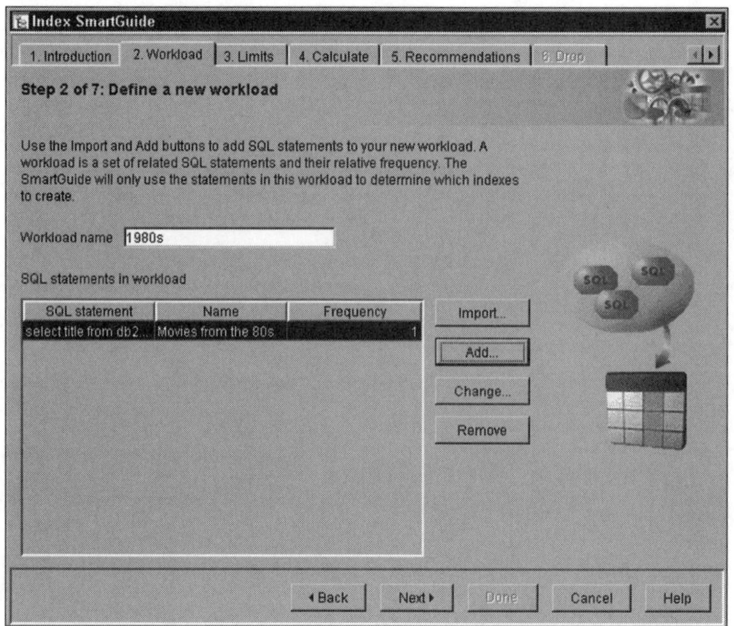

Figure 11-6: Creating a workload.

5. **In the Workload Name field of the Create Workload window, type a name for your workload.**

   The name should be descriptive enough for you to find it when you need it again.

6. **Click Add.**

   The Add SQL Statement window appears.

7. **Type the SQL statement that's your workload.**
8. **Click OK.**
9. **Click the Recommendations tab.**

   You see DB2 do some thinking. (You know it's thinking because the message, `Determining optimal indexes — please wait`, appears in the window.) The DB2 Index SmartGuide recommendations appear, as shown in Figure 11-7. DB2 recommends that you create an index on a table. You're shown whether the index already exists, what columns it should be defined on, and its size.

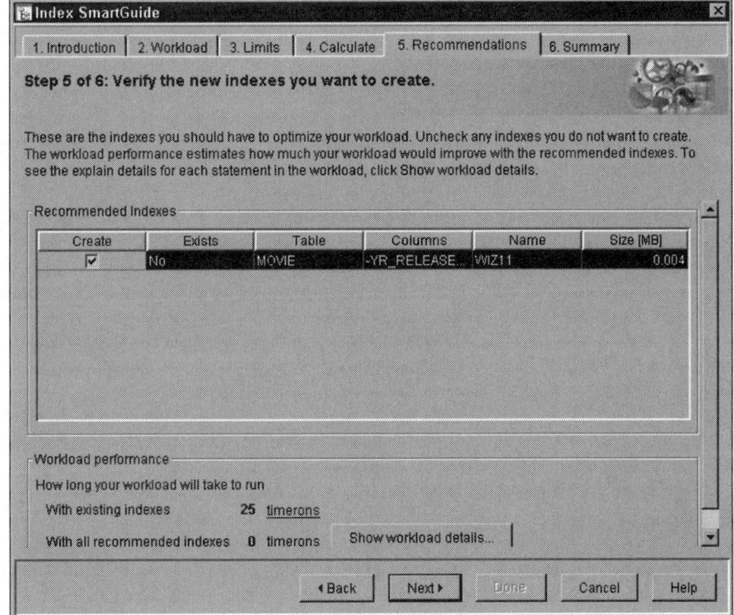

Figure 11-7: DB2 Index SmartGuide recommendations.

At the bottom of the Recommendations tab in Figure 11-7, you see the measured improvement that this index will have on the workload that was specified. In this case, the improvement is fabulous; from 25 timerons to 0 timerons! (*Timerons* are a unit of measurement used to give a rough estimate of how much it costs to run a DB2 query.)

Notice that between Figure 11-6 and clicking the Recommendations tab to get Figure 11-7, the Drop tab has disappeared. This is because at the time we captured the screenshot for 11-6, we did not have any indexes defined in the table that we are using for our workload. If there were indexes already defined on this table, the Drop tab would still be active. In the tab, you would see a list of all the current indexes defined on the table. You would then have the option of dropping some indexes from the table because they are not improving the performance of this workload.

10. **Click the Summary tab, as shown in Figure 11-8.**

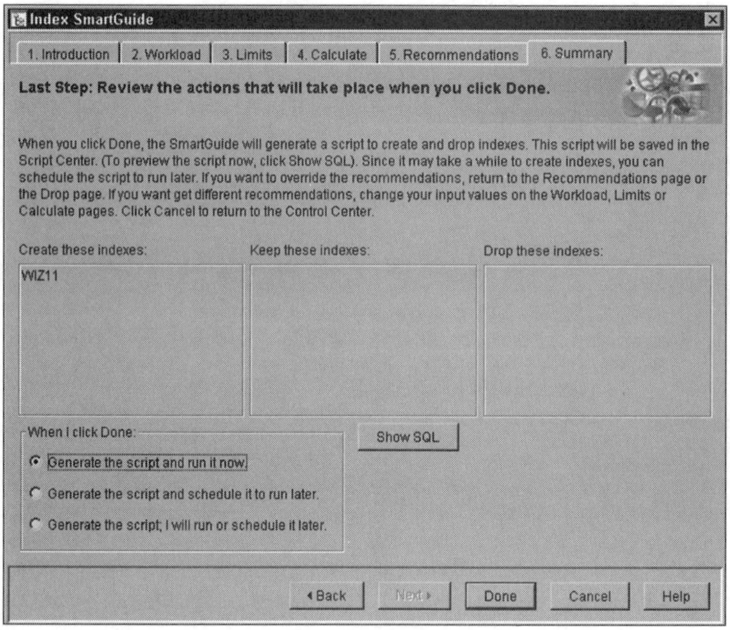

Figure 11-8: The Index SmartGuide Summary tab.

The Summary tab summarizes the index operation and gives you the following three choices:

- **Generate a script to create indexes and run the script right away.** The preferred and quickest option.
- **Generate a script to create indexes and schedule it to run at a specific time.** This option is useful if you run the Index SmartGuide during a time when there are many users on the system and you want to avoid placing extra load on the system. For example, you may want to schedule the creation of the index during the night when there aren't many users.
- **Generate a script to create indexes but don't schedule it yet.** Allows you to generate the script of necessary command, but lets you choose to run it whenever you wish instead of scheduling it.

11. **Click the Generate the Script and Run it Now option.**
12. **Click Done.**

    The Edit Command Script dialog box appears (see Figure 11-9), asking you to name the script that is generated.

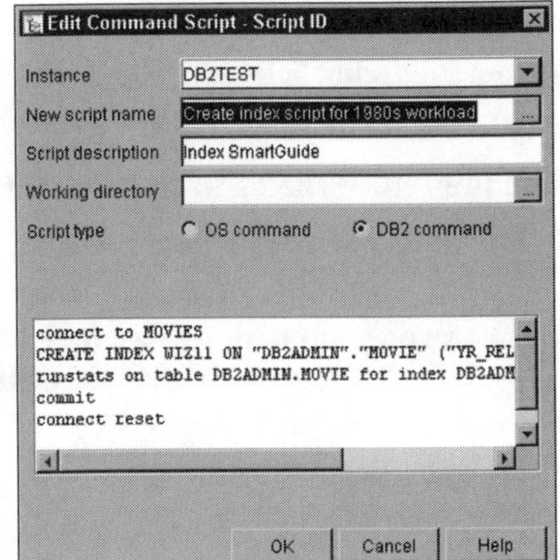

Figure 11-9: Generating a create index script.

13. **Fill in the fields to create a Create Index script.**

    Fill in a name for the script in the New Script Name field.

    The script is stored in the Script Center, enabling you to look at it later and rerun it if necessary. You can launch the Script Center from the icon menu in the Control Center.

14. **Click OK to run the script and create the index.**
15. **Click the Indexes folder to show all indexes in the database.**

    The new index appears in the list.

Creating a unique index

You can use unique indexes to dictate uniqueness on a set of columns in a table.

Don't forget that a primary key on a table is also a unique index on that table. Refer to Chapter 2 for more information on primary keys.

To create a unique index on a table, follow these steps.

1. **Open the Control Center by clicking the Start button and choosing Programs⇨DB2 for Windows NT⇨Control Center.**
2. **Right-click the Indexes folder and choose Create Index from the pop-up menu.**

The Create Index dialog box appears as shown in Figure 11-10.

3. **Select an Index Schema from the Index Schema drop-down list box.**
4. **Type a name for the index in the Index Name field.**
5. **Select a table schema from the Table Schema drop-down list box.**
6. **In the Table Name field, type the name of the table on which you plan to create an index.**
7. **Select the columns from which you want to define an index from those listed in the Available Columns box on the left side of the Create Index window.**
8. **Click the Unique check box.**
9. **Click OK.**

To drop an index, right-click it in the index listing and choose Drop from the pop-up menu.

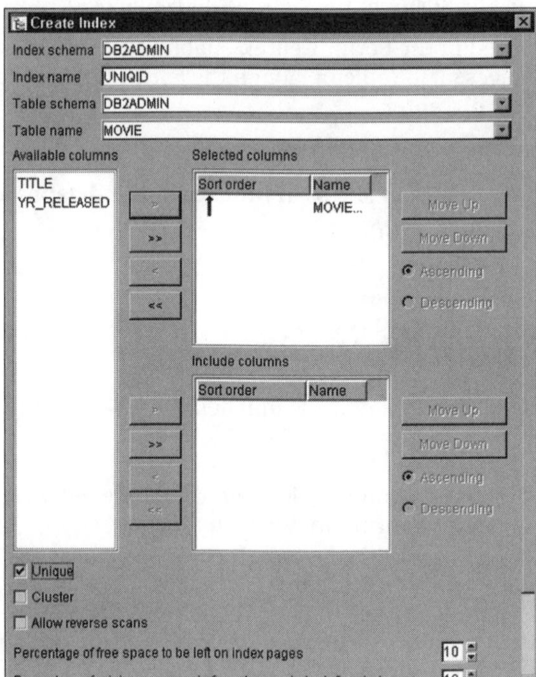

Figure 11-10: Creating a unique index.

Schema with a Purpose

You use *schemas* to classify the following types of DB2 objects in a database: tables, views, aliases, indexes, user-defined data types, user-defined functions, packages, and triggers. If you are a lone DB2 user, then creating new schemas may be unnecessary. But if you have hundreds of users on your database, and every one of them wants to create a table named ADDRESS_BOOK, then schemas are an important tool.

Every object, such as tables or views, has another characteristic associated with it. This is the schema of the object, and by default it is named after the person who creates the object. Suppose you have a user named ANNIE. If ANNIE creates a table named ADDRESS_BOOK, the table ADDRESS_BOOK belongs to the schema ANNIE. So, Annie's ADDRESS_BOOK table would be known to DB2 as ANNIE.ADDRESSBOOK. You can also create schemas that don't necessarily correspond with user names.

To create a schema, follow these steps:

1. **Open the Control Center by clicking the Start button and choosing Programs⇨DB2 for Windows NT⇨Control Center.**
2. **Right-click the Schemas folder and choose Create from the pop-up menu.**

   The Create Schema dialog box appears, as shown in Figure 11-11.

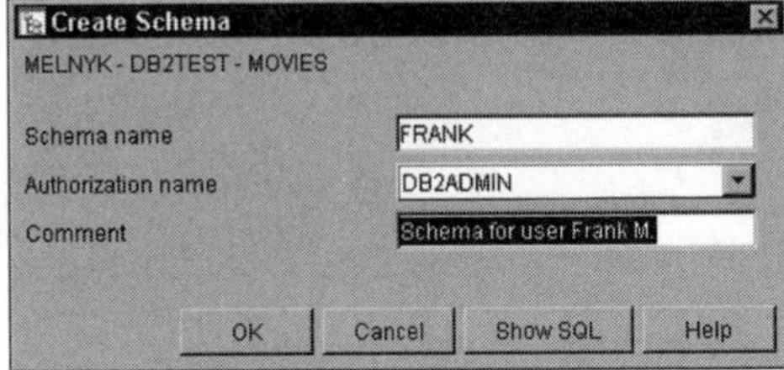

Figure 11-11: Creating a schema.

DB2 doesn't allow you to create a schema that is more than eight characters and begins with the letters *SYS*. We can't really say much about this other than that this is a limitation of DB2.

Pull the Trigger

In DB2, a trigger is another type of DB2 object containing an action that is invoked by DB2 when a particular SQL statement is run. A *trigger* enables you to define actions that get executed every time a particular insert, update, or delete statement is done. For example, say that each time a movie was rented from a video rental store, a row was inserted into the RENTED table. A trigger could be used to have DB2 send a customer satisfaction e-mail to the person that rented the movie based on the fact that their name was inserted into the RENTED table.

To create a trigger, follow these steps:

1. **Open the Control Center by clicking the Start button and choosing Programs⇨DB2 for Windows NT⇨Control Center.**
2. **Right-click Triggers and choose Create from the pop-up menu.**

   The Create Trigger dialog box appears, as shown in Figure 11-12.

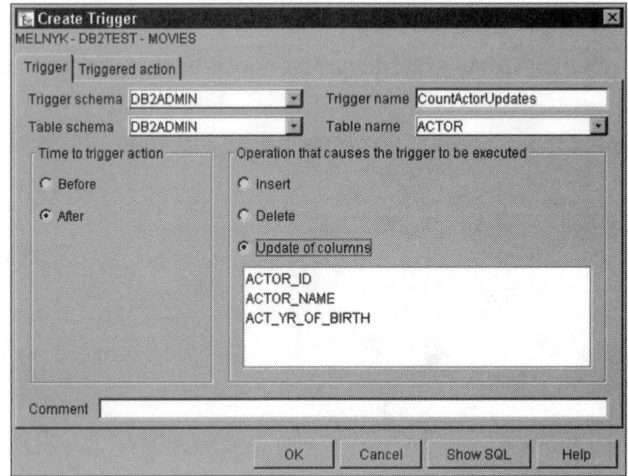

Figure 11-12: Creating a trigger.

3. **Type a name for your trigger in the Trigger Name field.**
4. **Click the Update of Columns option.**
5. **Click the After option.**
6. **(Optional) Enter a comment that describes this trigger in the Comment text box.**
7. **Click the Triggered Action tab.**

   The Triggered Action tab appears, as shown in Figure 11-13.

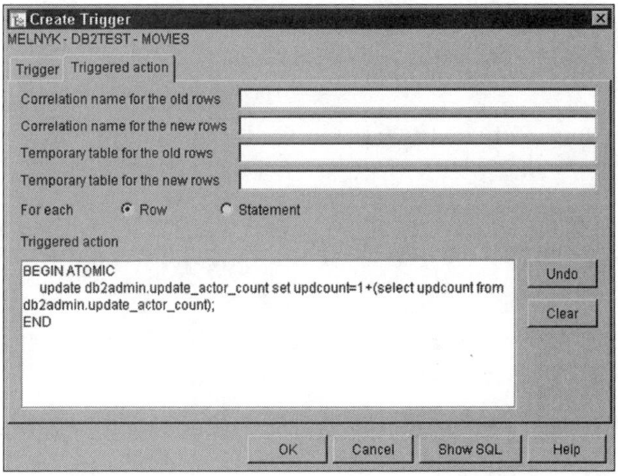

Figure 11-13: The Triggered Action tab.

8. **In the Triggered Action box, type in the script you want to trigger when the action occurs.**
9. **Click OK.**

   You created your trigger!

Swimming in Buffer Pools

Reading information from disk is costly, but reading from memory is relatively cheap. DB2, therefore, sets up areas in memory where it temporarily reads from and writes to your data. These areas are the buffer pools. In DB2, a *buffer pool* is memory storage where database information is temporarily read and changed before it is written out to disk.

The purpose of a buffer pool is to improve DB2 performance. The fewer times that DB2 needs to read from or write to disk, the better.

You have one default buffer pool — IBMDEFAULTBP — when you create a database. A simple way to describe what happens is if you connect to a database and start looking at any tables. DB2 loads the table, or parts of it, into the default buffer pool. This results in disk access for the information in that table. When another user comes along and starts looking at the same table, DB2 first checks the buffer pool and sees that the data is already there. So, DB2 avoids reading off of disk (expensive) and just looks at it in the table in the buffer pool (cheap).

When DB2 puts information from disk into the IBMDEFAULTBP buffer pool, it does so by reading the data in chunks of 4KB. This is what the geeks refer to as the default 4K page size of buffer pools.

DB2 also lets you create multiple buffer pools to fine-tune your database system. New buffer pools can have 4K, 8K, or 16K page sizes.

Each buffer pool also has a collection of table spaces for which it's responsible. Only data from that list of table spaces is read into a particular buffer pool.

Before this gets too technical, we'll guide you through some examples to make sense of it all.

To create a buffer pool, follow these steps:

1. **Open the Control Center by clicking the Start button and choosing Programs⇨DB2 for Windows NT⇨Control Center.**
2. **Right-click Buffer Pools and select Create.**

   The Create Buffer Pool dialog box appears, as shown in Figure 11-14.

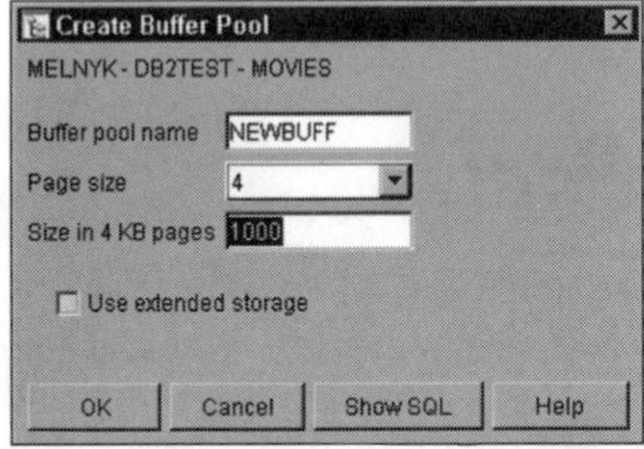

Figure 11-14: Creating a buffer pool.

3. **Type a name for the buffer in the Buffer Pool Name field.**
4. **Select 4 from the Page Size drop-down list box.**
5. **Type** 1000 **in the Size in 4KB Pages field.**
6. **Click OK.**

   The new buffer pool only becomes active after you restart the database (you can restart a database by using the RESTART option in the Control Center — see Chapter 8 for more information). Until then, all operations on existing table spaces use the old buffer pool. Similarly, any new table spaces are assigned to the default buffer pool.

Now you have to assign table spaces to this buffer pool. This ensures that data read from the assigned table spaces is placed in your new buffer.

To assign table spaces to your new buffer pool, follow these steps:

1. **Open the Control Center by clicking the Start button and choosing Programs⇨DB2 for Windows NT⇨Control Center.**
2. **Click the Table Spaces folder.**
3. **Right-click a table space that you want this buffer pool to be associated with and choose Alter from the pop-up menu.**

   The Alter Table Space dialog box appears, as shown in Figure 11-15.

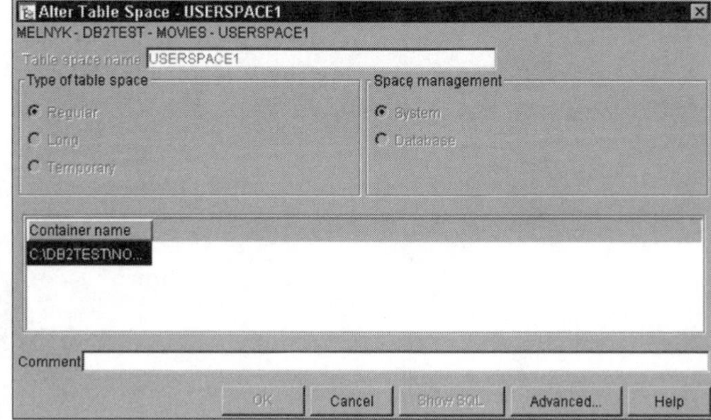

Figure 11-15: The Alter Table Space dialog box.

4. **Click the Advanced button.**

   The Advanced dialog box appears, as shown in Figure 11-16.

Figure 11-16: Advanced options for altering a table space.

5. **In the Buffer Pool drop-down list box, select the name of your new buffer pool and leave the other options as they appear.**
6. **Click OK.**

You have successfully created a buffer pool and assigned it a table space.

Part IV

DB2 Tasks That Every Good Geek (err . . . Administrator) Should Know

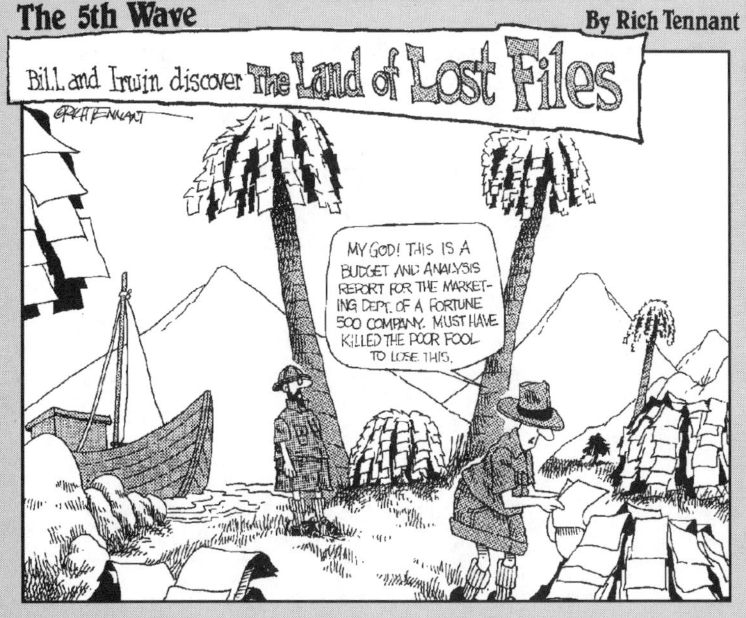

The 5th Wave
By Rich Tennant
BILL and Irwin discover The Land of Lost Files
MY GOD! THIS IS A BUDGET AND ANALYSIS REPORT FOR THE MARKETING DEPT. OF A FORTUNE 500 COMPANY. MUST HAVE KILLED THE POOR FOOL TO LOSE THIS.

In this part . . .

Now it's time to show you basic day-to-day tasks that each database administrator (DBA is their nickname, though it may just be "geek" to you) needs to know. Here we show you how to get data into your database or move it to another, and how to create a backup of a server so that when you make a mistake (and you will) all is not lost. We also touch on the topic of replication, which is just a photocopier for databases. If you ever have had a problem with DB2, or want to know how to handle the ones that may come up, this part will also help you out with some troubleshooting tips as well.

So, are you ready for a transformation? "Transformation into what?" you ask. Why, a nerd . . . I mean DBA . . . of course.

Chapter 12

Loading, Importing, and Exporting Data In and Out of Tables

In This Chapter

- Importing data into tables
- Loading data into tables
- Exporting data from tables

Now it's time to put some data into those tables that you work so hard to create (see Chapter 10 for info on creating and working with tables). After adding data to a table, you can *query* (or search) the data for useful information or update the data.

You can put data into a DB2 table in two ways: data importing and data loading. A separate DB2 utility controls each of these operations. (Of course, you can also put data into a table by issuing SQL insert statements, one for each row being inserted, but that stops being fun after about the fifth row!)

Importing Data into Tables

The DB2 Universal Database import utility uses SQL `insert` statements to write data from an input file into a table or updateable view. If the target table or view already contains data, you can either replace the existing data or append to it.

To replace data in an existing table or view, you must have SYSADM authority, DBADM authority, or CONTROL privilege on the table or view. To append data to an existing table or view, you must have SELECT and INSERT privileges on the table or view. To make things easier, just log on to the system with the same user account that you used to install your DB2 server; by default, this user has SYSADM authority.

You can enter the `import` command from a command prompt, or you can run a script file that has an `import` command in it. You can also import data through the Command Center, the Script Center, or the Control Center (using the Import notebook).

Importing data from the Windows command prompt

This section introduces you to the required syntax for the DB2 `import` command; that is, all the parts of the command that you *must* specify to get it to do some useful work for you.

The basic format of the `import` command is:

```
db2 import from <file name> of <file type> <mode> into <table
         name>
```

where:

<file name> is the path and the name of the input file.

<file type> is the format of the data in the input file. This format can be:

- **DEL (delimited ASCII format):** This is the format you're most likely to use. Each line in the input file contains data items that are separated by some delimiter, such as a comma. DB2 knows to put the first data item into the first column of the target table, the second data item into the second column of the target table, and so on. The delimiter tells DB2 where one data item stops, and the next one begins.
- **ASC (non-delimited ASCII format):** Each line in the input file contains data items that are located in a specific position and that are not separated by some delimiter. DB2 knows to put the first data item into the first column of the target table, the second data item into the second column of the target table, and so on. DB2 figures out where one data item stops, and the next one begins, on the basis of specific byte positions within the row. You can specify these byte positions through the optional METHOD L parameter on the `import` command (use DB2's online help facility for information on how to do this).
- **IXF (integrated exchange format):** This is a generic relational database exchange format that you will probably never use, so don't worry about what the beginning of this sentence means!
- **WSF (work sheet format):** This is a format used by some earlier types of spreadsheet programs. You may find it useful for importing some of your older legacy data.

<mode> specifies whether the input data is to be inserted into the table or view, or whether existing data in the table or view is to be updated or replaced by the input data. This mode can be:

- INSERT. Adds rows of data to the table without changing the existing table data.
- INSERT_UPDATE. Adds rows of data to the table, or updates existing table data.
- REPLACE. Deletes all existing data from the table, and inserts the imported data.
- REPLACE_CREATE. This mode is only valid with IXF files. If the table exists, deletes all existing data from the table, and inserts the imported data. If the table does not exist, creates the table and index definitions, and inserts the imported data.

<table name> is the name or alias of the target table or view.

You must specify a value for these parameters when you invoke the `import` command. All of them are required.

Many other `import` options are available, but we won't cover them in this book because you'll probably never need to use them! If, however, you really do want to find out more, check out the *DB2 Data Movement Utilities Guide and Reference*.

Importing data using the Control Center

The easiest way to import data, in our collectively humble opinions, is with the Import notebook in the Control Center, which guides you through the process of specifying values for the import parameters. After you run an import operation, you can use the Control Center to view sample contents of the table into which you imported data, examine the import command that is created based on your specifications, and even copy it into scripts that you can schedule to run later.

To import data into a table using the Control Center, follow these steps:

1. **Make sure the current instance is the instance containing the table you want to import data into.**

   To change the current instance from a command prompt, for the duration of its session, type the following command in a command prompt:

   ```
   set DB2INSTANCE=<instance name>
   ```

   where *<instance name>* is the name of the instance you want to set as default.

2. **Open the Control Center by clicking the Start button and choosing Programs⇨DB2 for Windows NT⇨Control Center.**
3. **Open the Import notebook by right-clicking a table icon in the Tables folder and then choosing Import from the pop-up menu.**

   The Import notebook opens, as shown in Figure 12-1.
4. **In the Import File text box, type the fully qualified name of the file that you want to import.**

   A *fully qualified* name contains the complete path. In figure 12-1, the input `movie.TXT` file is in the `WorkDir` working directory on the `C:` drive, so you would type **C:\WorkDir\movie.TXT**.
5. **Click the Delimited ASCII Format (DEL) option to specify this input file format.**
6. **In the Message File text box, type the fully qualified name of the file to which warning and error messages that occur during an import operation are written.**

   If you leave this field blank, the messages are written to standard output, which usually means the display.

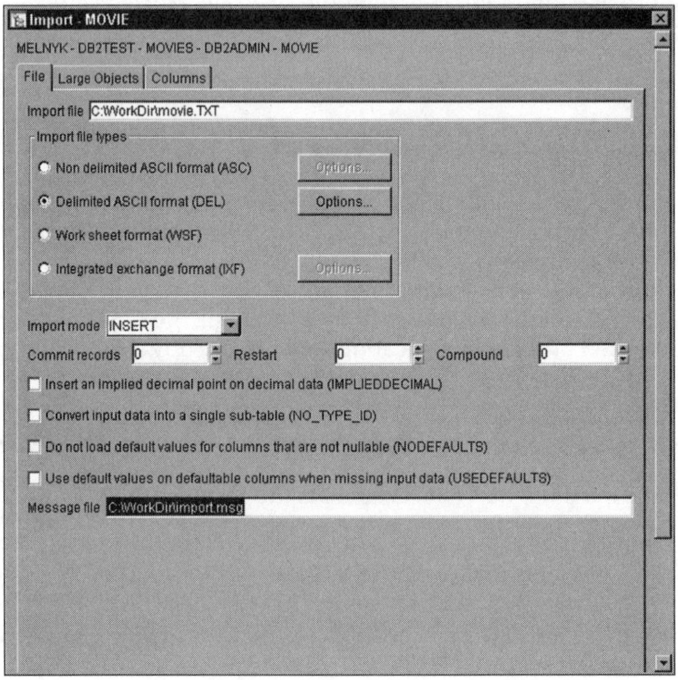

Figure 12-1: Importing data into a table.

7. **Click OK.**

   A DB2 Message window appears, reporting a successful import operation.

To view sample contents from a table, right-click the table icon in the Tables folder, and then click Sample Contents from the pop-up menu that appears.

The Sample Contents window appears, as shown in Figure 12-2.

Sample Contents - MOVIE

MELNYK - DB2TEST - MOVIES - DB2ADMIN - MOVIE

MOVIE_ID	TITLE	YR_RELEASED
23154	Carousel	1956
44524	El Cid	1961
78456	Giant	1956
45692	African Queen	1951
67845	Casablanca	1942
77773	Dr. No	1962
56872	The Graduate	1967
95123	Rear Window	1954
67349	La Strada	1954
76188	Singin' in the Rain	1952
88445	Psycho	1960
91673	Picnic	1955
88562	The Lost Weekend	1945
92234	The Sound of Music	1965
85412	Viva Las Vegas	1963
55573	Zorba the Greek	1965
90451	The West Side Story	1961
66432	What Ever Happened to Baby J...	1962

Close Help

Figure 12-2: Displaying sample contents from a DB2 table.

Figure 12-3 shows a CLP command that was generated from the information specified in the Import notebook.

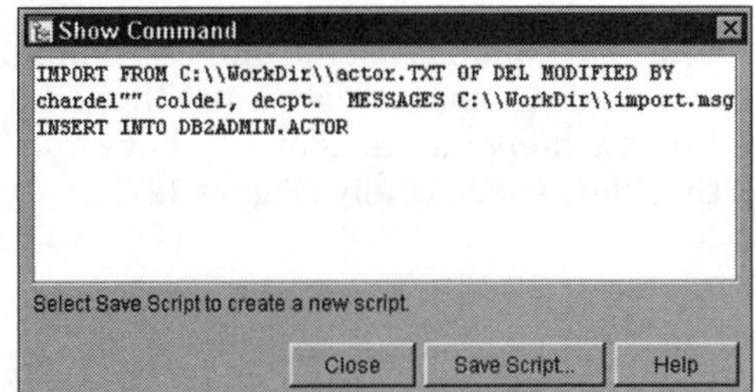
Show Command
IMPORT FROM C:\\WorkDir\\actor.TXT OF DEL MODIFIED BY
chardel"" coldel, decpt. MESSAGES C:\\WorkDir\\import.msg
INSERT INTO DB2ADMIN.ACTOR
Select Save Script to create a new script.
Close
Save Script...
Help

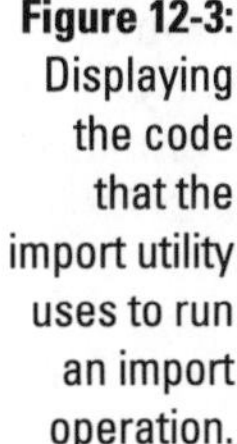

Figure 12-3: Displaying the code that the import utility uses to run an import operation.

You can open the Show Command window by clicking the Show Command button in the Import notebook. If you click the Save Script button in this window, the Edit Command Script window opens. An example of the command to import data into a table is shown in Figure 12-4. To save this code as a script that you can run later, follow these steps:

1. **Type a fully qualified script name in the New script name text box.**
2. **(Optional) Type a brief but meaningful description for this script in the Script Description text box.**
3. **Type the fully qualified name of your working directory in the Working Directory text box.**
4. **Click OK.**

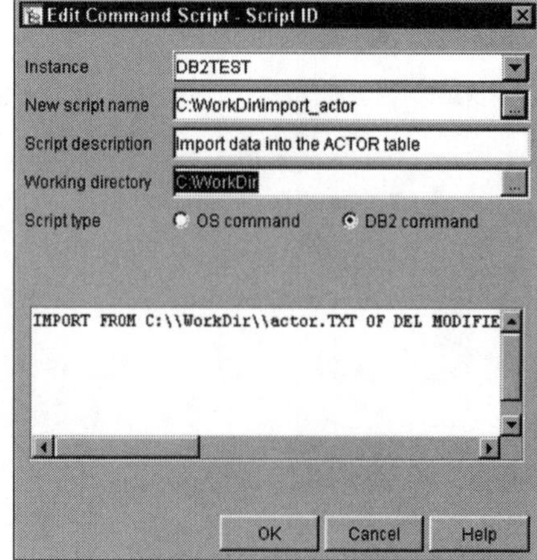

Figure 12-4: Saving an import command as a script that can be run later.

Your new script is accessible through the Script Center. From there, you can run it, schedule it to run later, change it, or copy it.

To make the script that you just saved more useful, you can edit it through the Script Center, adding commands to import data into other tables. By adding the CONNECT TO <*database name*> statement, you have a self-contained script (saved as "Import") that runs successfully (Figure 12-5).

Importing data from spreadsheets: A tale of triumph

Romchyk had been collecting movies on video for a long time. This was a serious hobby for him: meticulously recording information about movies in a Lotus 1-2-3 spreadsheet. (What fun!)

Eventually Romchyk decided it was time to graduate to a relational database management system, and he wisely chose DB2. Faced with the task of moving his spreadsheet data into the MOVIES database that he designed for himself one Saturday morning, he winced at the thought of retyping all that information. "There must be a better way!" he thought. Conscripting his wife, Tree, and his daughters, Rosita and Jo-Jo, briefly crossed his mind. But the stony silence that greeted this suggestion convinced him not to pursue the idea.

When Romchyk read that the DB2 import utility could move WSF data into relational tables, he thought that this would solve his problem. He tried it. It didn't work. His spreadsheet files were all in WK1 format! What to do? Being a nerd of great depth and girth, he quickly devised a plan. As ingenius as his plan was, we've included it here for your use.

To turn your spreadsheet files into acceptable format for DB2, follow these steps:

1. **Open the spreadsheet that you want to import into DB2 (or a copy of it) and insert new columns between each of the existing columns.**
2. **Copy a comma into each cell of those columns.**

   These commas are your column delimiters, as shown in the accompanying figure.
3. **Save the spreadsheet file in text (.txt) format.**

   The resulting text files are quite acceptable to the DB2 import utility.

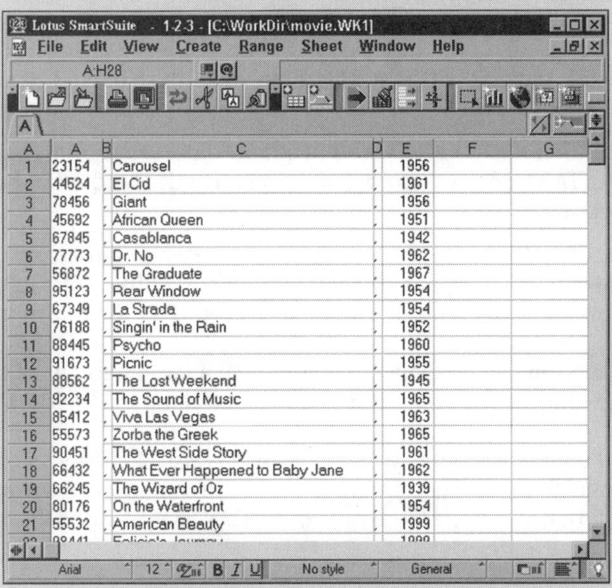

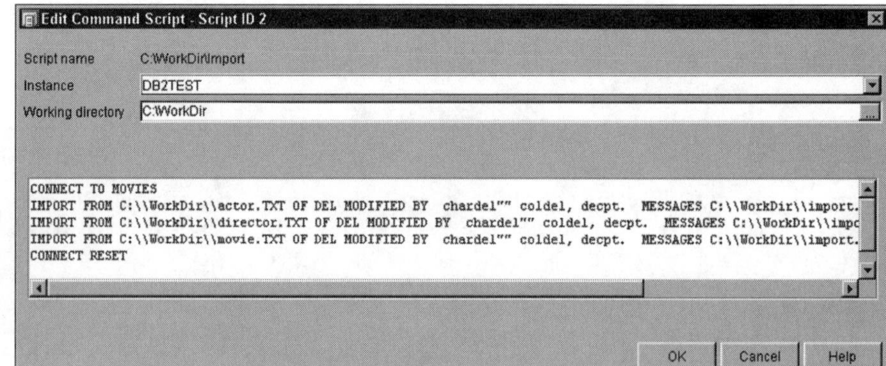
Edit Command Script - Script ID 2
Script name
C:\WorkDir\Import
Instance
DB2TEST
Working directory
C:\WorkDir
CONNECT TO MOVIES
IMPORT FROM C:\\WorkDir\\actor.TXT OF DEL MODIFIED BY chardel"" coldel, decpt. MESSAGES C:\\WorkDir\\import.
IMPORT FROM C:\\WorkDir\\director.TXT OF DEL MODIFIED BY chardel"" coldel, decpt. MESSAGES C:\\WorkDir\\impc
IMPORT FROM C:\\WorkDir\\movie.TXT OF DEL MODIFIED BY chardel"" coldel, decpt. MESSAGES C:\\WorkDir\\import.
CONNECT RESET
OK
Cancel
Help

Figure 12-5: Editing a command script.

Loading Data into Tables

The DB2 Universal Database `load` utility can move large quantities of data into newly created tables, or into tables that already contain data and can handle all data types. The `load` utility is faster than the `import` utility because it writes formatted pages directly into the database; the `import` utility uses SQL insert statements. The `load` utility does not fire triggers, and does not perform referential or table constraints checking (other than validating the uniqueness of the indexes). The data being loaded must be local to the server.

The load process consists of three distinct phases:

- **Load:** Data is written to the table. If a failure occurs, you can restart the load operation.
- **Build:** Indexes are created. If a failure occurs during the build phase, the RESTART option automatically restarts the load operation at the appropriate point.
- **Delete:** The rows that cause a unique key violation are removed from the table. If a failure occurs during the delete phase, the RESTART option automatically restarts the load operation at the appropriate point.

REMEMBER

Each deletion event is logged. If you have a large number of records that violate the uniqueness condition, the log can fill up during the delete phase.

REMEMBER

To load data into a table, you must have SYSADM authority or DBADM authority. To make things easier, just log on to the system with the same user account that you used to install your DB2 server; by default, this user has SYSADM authority.

Do not attempt to delete or to modify any temporary files created by the `load` utility. Some temporary files are critical to the delete phase.

Because all load processes (and all DB2 server processes, in general), are owned by the instance owner, and all of these processes use the identification of the instance owner to access needed files, the instance owner must have read access to input data files. These input data files must be readable by the instance owner, regardless of who invokes the command.

You can enter the `load` command from the command prompt, or you can run a script file that has a `load` command in it. You can also load data through the Command Center, the Script Center, or the Control Center (using the Load notebook).

Loading data from the Windows command prompt

This section introduces you to the required syntax for the DB2 `load` command; that is, all the parts of the command that you *must* specify to get it to do some useful work for you.

The basic format of the `load` command is:

```
db2 load from <file name, named pipe, or device> of <file
          type> <mode> into <table name>
```

where:

<*file name, named pipe, or device*> is the path and the name of the input file, named pipe, or device that you wish to load data from.

<*file type*> is the format of the data in the input file. This format can be:

- DEL (delimited ASCII format)
- ASC (nondelimited ASCII format)
- IXF (integrated exchange format)

See the "Importing data from the Windows command prompt" section earlier in this chapter for descriptions of these formats.

<*mode*> specifies whether the input data is to be appended to the table, or whether existing data in the table is to be replaced by the input data. This mode can be:

- INSERT. Adds rows of data to the table without changing the existing table data.
- REPLACE. Deletes all existing data from the table, and inserts the loaded data.

If an error occurs during a LOAD REPLACE operation, or if you load the wrong data by mistake, the original data in the table is lost. Retain a copy of the input data to allow the load operation to be restarted.

- RESTART. Restarts a previously interrupted load operation.
- TERMINATE. Terminates a previously interrupted load operation, and removes data that was loaded during this operation.

<table name> is the name or alias of the target table.

You must specify a value for these parameters when you invoke the `load` command. All of them are required.

Many other `load` options are available, but we won't cover them in this book because you'll probably never need to use them! If, however, you really do want to find out more, check out the *DB2 Data Movement Utilities Guide and Reference*.

Loading data using the Control Center

This section introduces you to the *easy* way of loading data, using the Load notebook in the Control Center. The Load notebook guides you through the process of specifying values for the load parameters. Once you run a load operation, you can use the Control Center to view sample contents of the table into which you loaded the data. You can examine the load command that is created based on your specifications, or copy it into scripts that you can schedule to run later.

To load data into a table, follow these steps:

1. **Make sure the current instance is the instance containing the table from which you want to export data.**
2. **Start the Control Center by clicking the Start button and choosing Programs⇨DB2 for Windows NT⇨Control Center.**
3. **Open the Load notebook by right-clicking the desired table in the Tables folder and then choosing Load from the pop-up menu.**

   The Load notebook appears, as shown in Figure 12-6.
4. **Click Add.**

   The Add window opens.
5. **In the File, Pipe, or Device text box, type the fully qualified name of the file that you want to load.**

In this example, the input file (appears_in.TXT) is in the WorkDir directory on the C: drive — so you would type in **c:\workdir\appears_in.txt** (the figure shows .TXT in all caps but there's no reason to type it in that way).

6. **Click Add.**

   Back in the Load notebook, note that the file name that you just specified now appears in the Files, Pipes, or Devices Containing the Data box. You can specify multiple files, if necessary.

7. **Click the Delimited ASCII Format (DEL) option to specify this input file format.**

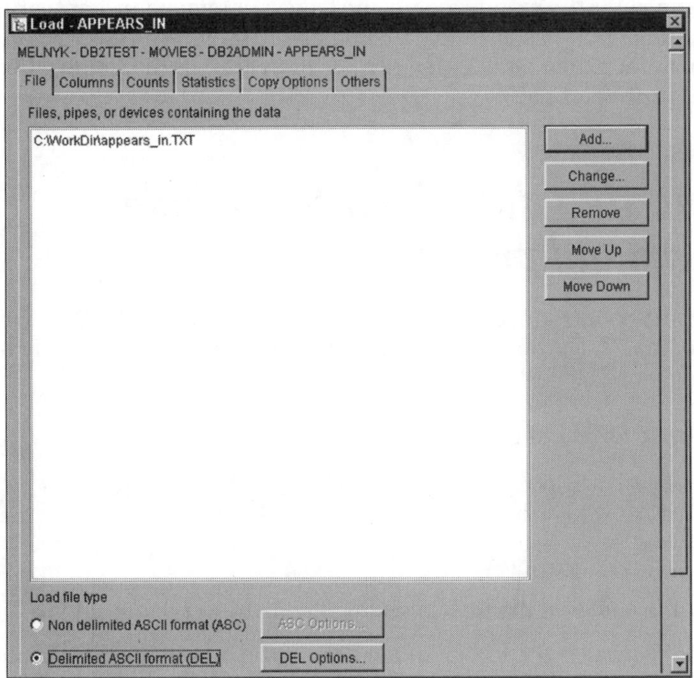

Figure 12-6: Loading data into a table.

8. **Click OK.**

   A DB2 Message window appears, reporting a successful load operation.

Notice that you did not specify a message file where load-related messages were to be written. The notebook specified a message file for us called db2load.msg.

Exporting Data from Tables

You use the DB2 `export` utility to move data from a database into operating system files to create files containing data that you can import or load into *another* database or application (for example, moving DB2 data from a table to Lotus 1-2-3).

You must have SYSADM or DBADM authority, or CONTROL or SELECT privilege for each table participating in the `export` operation. To make things easier, just log on to the system with the same user account that you used to install your DB2 server; by default, this user has SYSADM authority.

You can enter the `export` command from a command prompt, or you can run a script file that has an `export` command in it. You can also export data through the Command Center, the Script Center, or the Control Center (using the Export notebook).

Exporting data from the Windows command prompt

This section introduces you to the required syntax for the DB2 `export` command; that is, all the parts of the command that you *must* specify to get it to do some useful work for you.

The basic format of the `export` command is:

```
db2 export to <filename> of <file type> <select statement>
```

where:

<file name> is the path including the name of the output file.

<file type> is the format of the data in the output file. This format can be:

- DEL (delimited ASCII format)
- IXF (integrated exchange format)
- WSF (work sheet format)

  See the "Importing data from the Windows command prompt" section earlier in this chapter for descriptions of these formats.

<select statement> is the SQL select statement that returns the data to be exported.

- You must specify a value for these parameters when you invoke the `export` command. All of them are required.

Many other `export` options are available, but we won't cover them in this book because you'll probably never need to use them! If, however, you really do want to find out more, check out the *DB2 Data Movement Utilities Guide and Reference*.

The export utility fails if the data you want to export exceeds the space available on the file system on which you're going to create the exported file. In this case, limit the amount of data selected by specifying conditions on the WHERE clause, so that the export file fits on the target file system. You can invoke the export utility multiple times to export all of the data.

Exporting data using the Control Center

The Export Table notebook in the Control Center guides you through the process of specifying values for the export parameters. You can examine the export command that is created based on your specifications, or copy it into scripts that you can schedule to run later.

To export table data into a delimited ASCII (DEL) file, follow these steps:

1. **Make sure the current instance is the instance containing the table you want to import data into.**
2. **Start the Control Center by clicking the Start button and choosing Programs⇨DB2 for Windows NT⇨Control Center.**
3. **Open the Export Table notebook by right-clicking the table icon in the Tables folder and then choosing Export from the pop-up menu.**

   Figure 12-7 shows the open Export Table notebook.
4. **In the Output File text box, type the fully qualified name of the file to which you want to export the data.**

   In this example, the output file (`movie.BKP`) is being created in the `WorkDir` working directory on the `C:` drive — so you type in **c:\workdir\movie.bkp** (the figure shows .BKP in all caps but there's no reason to type it in that way).
5. **Click the Delimited ASCII Format (DEL) option to specify this output file format.**
6. **In the Message File text box, type the fully qualified name of the file to which warning and error messages that occur during an export operation are written.**
7. **(Optional) To export a subset of the table data, change the default statement in the SELECT Statement box.**
8. **Click OK.**

   A DB2 message window appears, reporting a successful export operation.

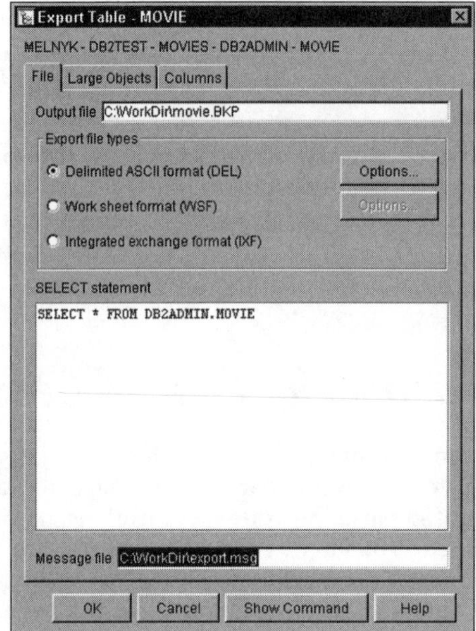

Figure 12-7: Exporting table data into a file.

Chapter 13

Backing Up and Recovering Data

In This Chapter

- Backing up your data
- Recovering a database

Once you've designed a database, created some tables, put data into those tables, and worked with that data, everything's great, right? Maybe not. What about backing up your precious data so that, in the event that something bad happens, you don't lose everything? Or what about restoring data in the event that you lose it all?

Backing up data is a good idea when you have important stuff stored on a computer, but it is even more important in the case of databases. A database that you use regularly becomes more valuable with time. A large database that stores significant amounts of information is difficult to recreate if something goes wrong — unless, that is, you have a good backup and recovery strategy. This chapter shows you how to back up your data, and how to recover that data from a backup.

Backing Up Your Data

A *database backup* is the same as any other data backup: you take a copy of the data and store it in a different place in case something bad happens to the original. The simplest example of a backup is when you shut down a database to ensure that no further transactions occur, and then simply back it up. To back up a database from the Control Center, follow these steps:

1. **Make sure the current instance is the instance containing the database you want to back up.**

To change the current instance from a command prompt, type the following command:

```
set DB2INSTANCE=<instance name>
```

where *<instance name>* is the name of the instance you want to be the current instance.

2. **Open the Control Center by clicking the Start button and choosing Programs⇨DB2 for Windows NT⇨Control Center.**
3. **Open the Backup Database notebook by right-clicking the icon representing the database that you want to back up in the instance's Databases folder and then choosing Backup⇨Database.**

   Figure 13-1 shows the open Backup Database notebook.

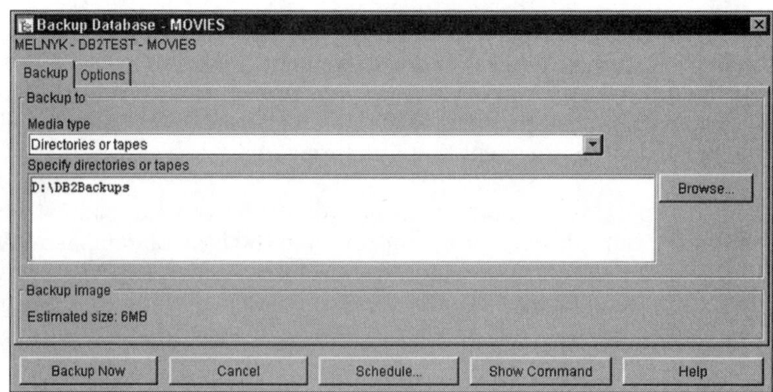

Figure 13-1: Backing up a database with the Backup Database notebook.

4. **In the Media Type drop-down list, select Directories or Tapes.**
5. **In the Specify Directories or Tapes area, type in the pathname where you want to back up your database.**

   You can click the Browse button to see a list of available directories or tape devices.

   You can specify several backup locations here, if you don't expect the first location to be large enough to hold the entire backup image.

   Make sure that the backup location that you select exists before proceeding. Also make sure that there is enough space in the backup location for the backup image. DB2 gives you an estimate of the space required; in Figure 13-1, the estimated size is 6MB.

6. **Click the Backup Now button.**

   Your database backup operation begins immediately.

Scheduling a backup

If you don't want to run your database backup now, you can schedule your backup to automatically run later. By using the nifty Schedule button, you don't have to worry about forgetting to back up your data. To schedule the backup operation, follow these steps:

1. **Open the Backup Database notebook for the database you want to back up, as shown in Steps 1 through 3 in the preceding section.**
2. **Click the Schedule button.**

   The Schedule — Backup Database window opens, as shown in Figure 13-2.

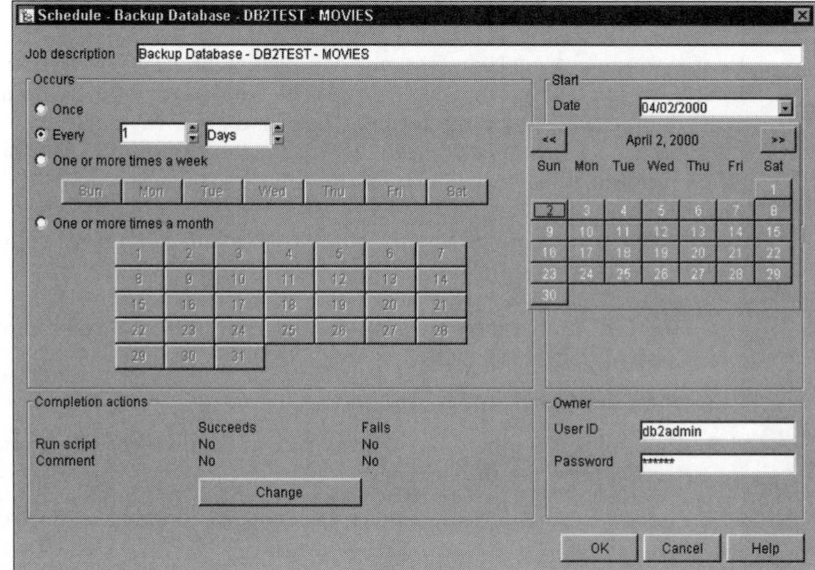

Figure 13-2: Scheduling a regularly occurring database backup operation.

3. **In the Occurs section, click the option corresponding to how often you want the backup to occur.**

   For example, you can request that a full database backup operation run once every day. You can schedule your backup to run as often as you like — your scheduling options are nearly unlimited.
4. **Click the down arrow to the right of the Date text box in the Start section.**

   A monthly calendar appears.

5. **Click a date to specify the date on which the backups are to begin.**

   You can use the double left or right arrows at the top of the calendar to change the month.

6. **In the Owner section, type your user ID and password in the User ID and Password text boxes and click OK.**

   A DB2 Message window appears, reporting a successful job creation. The job is given a number, and you're told that you can view the status and output of the job in the Journal.

Scanning the Journal

The Journal is a Control Center component that keeps track of jobs. You can open the Journal by clicking the Journal icon near the top of the Control Center window. A *job* is an instance of a particular script or system-driven operation, such as a database backup. The Jobs page of the Journal provides a Pending Jobs view, a Running Jobs view, and a Job History view. A scheduled job has a Journal entry in the Pending Jobs view. After your job is finished running, it leaves an entry in the Job History view.

To view the results of one of your database backup operations, follow these steps:

1. **Open the Journal by clicking the Journal button at the top of the Control Center window.**
2. **Open the Job History view on the Jobs page.**
3. **Right-click the job whose results you want to view and choose Show Results from the pop-up menu.**

   The Job Results window opens, showing the job output (Figure 13-3).

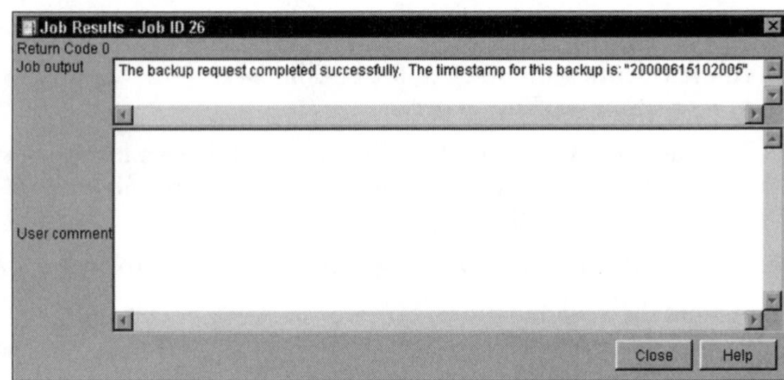

Figure 13-3: Viewing the job results for a database backup operation.

Introducing Database Recovery

The term *disaster recovery* describes what needs to be done to restore a database in the event of a catastrophic event, such as fire, vandalism, or hardware or software failure — it needs to be rebuilt. The following two sections discuss the two main methods of recovery: version recovery and roll-forward recovery.

Version recovery

Version recovery is the restoration of a previous version of a database by using a copy that was created during an offline, full database backup operation. (An offline backup means that no other application can use the database when the backup operation is in progress.) Using the version recovery method, you must schedule and perform full backups of the database on a regular basis.

Although a database backup allows you to restore a database to the state it was in when the backup was made, every unit of work from the time of the backup to the time of the failure is lost. With version recovery, the recovered database is only as current as the backup copy that was restored. For instance, if you make a backup copy at the end of each day, and you lose the database midway through the next day, you lose a half-day of changes.

The version recovery method requires space to hold the backup copy of the database and the restored database.

Version recovery, by using offline backups, is the primary means of recovery for a nonrecoverable database. Nonrecoverable databases only keep logs that are required for crash recovery. These logs are known as *active logs,* and they contain current transaction data. Logs, you ask?

All databases have logs associated with them. These logs keep records of database changes. Version recovery uses *circular logging.* Only full, offline backups of a database are valid with circular logging. As the name suggests, circular logging uses a ring of online logs to provide recovery from transaction failures and system crashes, as depicted in Figure 13-4. The logs are used and retained only to the point of ensuring the integrity of current transactions.

Restoring a database requires that you rebuild the entire database by using the most recent backup image.

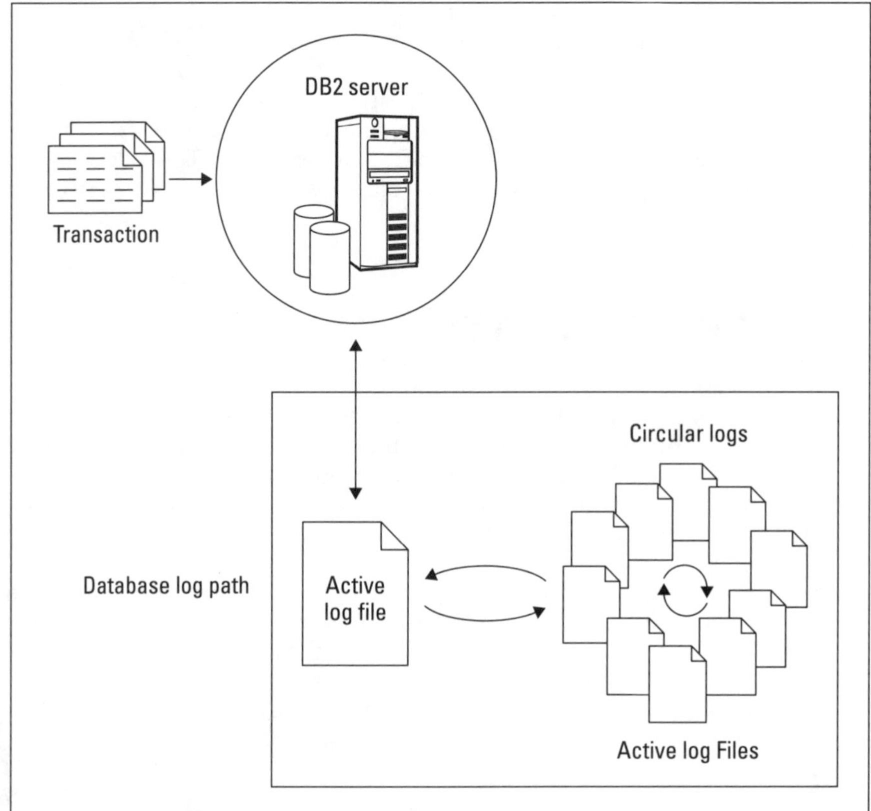

Figure 13-4: The active log uses a ring of log files during circular logging.

Roll-forward recovery

Roll-forward recovery uses both archived logs and active logs to rebuild a database or individual table spaces. The roll-forward function achieves this by reapplying committed changes found in the archived and active logs.

You use *archived logging* specifically for roll-forward recovery. When changes in the active log are no longer needed for current transactions, the log is closed, and becomes an archived log. An archived log is *online* when it is stored in the database log path directory (see Figure 13-5), and *offline* when it is no longer found in the database log path directory (see Figure 13-6).

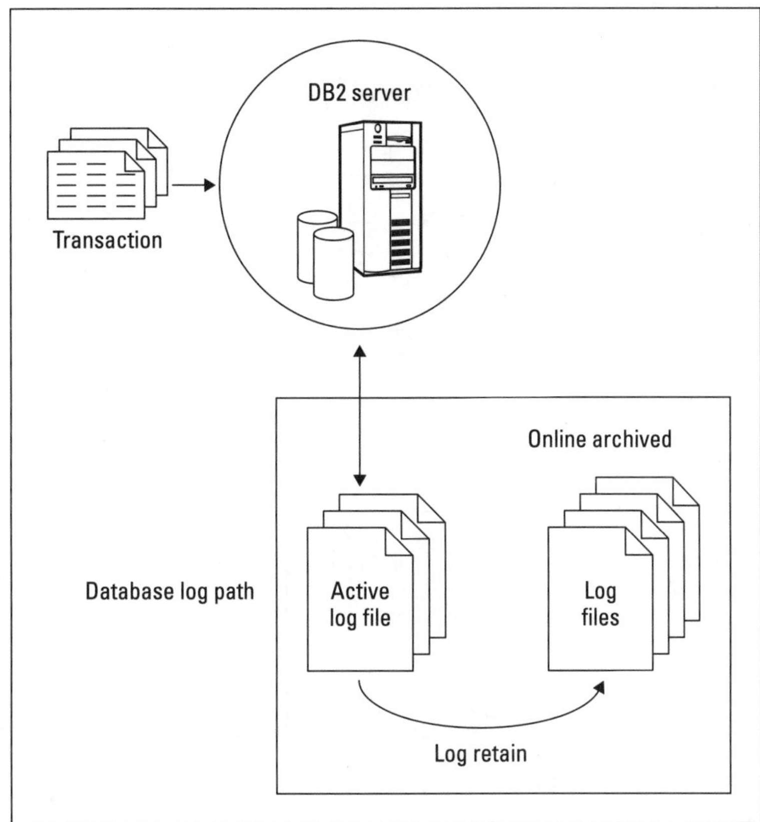

Figure 13-5: Online archived logs are stored in the database log path directory.

The roll-forward recovery method requires space to hold the backup copy of the database, the restored database, and the archived database logs.

To use roll-forward recovery, you must take a backup of the database and archive the logs (by setting the *logretain* database configuration parameter to RECOVERY, enabling the *userexit* database configuration parameter, or both).

The *logretain* database configuration parameter specifies whether the active log files are to be retained for use during roll-forward recovery. The *userexit* database configuration parameter specifies whether DB2 can call a user exit program (called `db2uexit`) to archive or retrieve log files the next time the database is opened. You can update these parameters by using the `update database configuration` (or `update db cfg`) command.

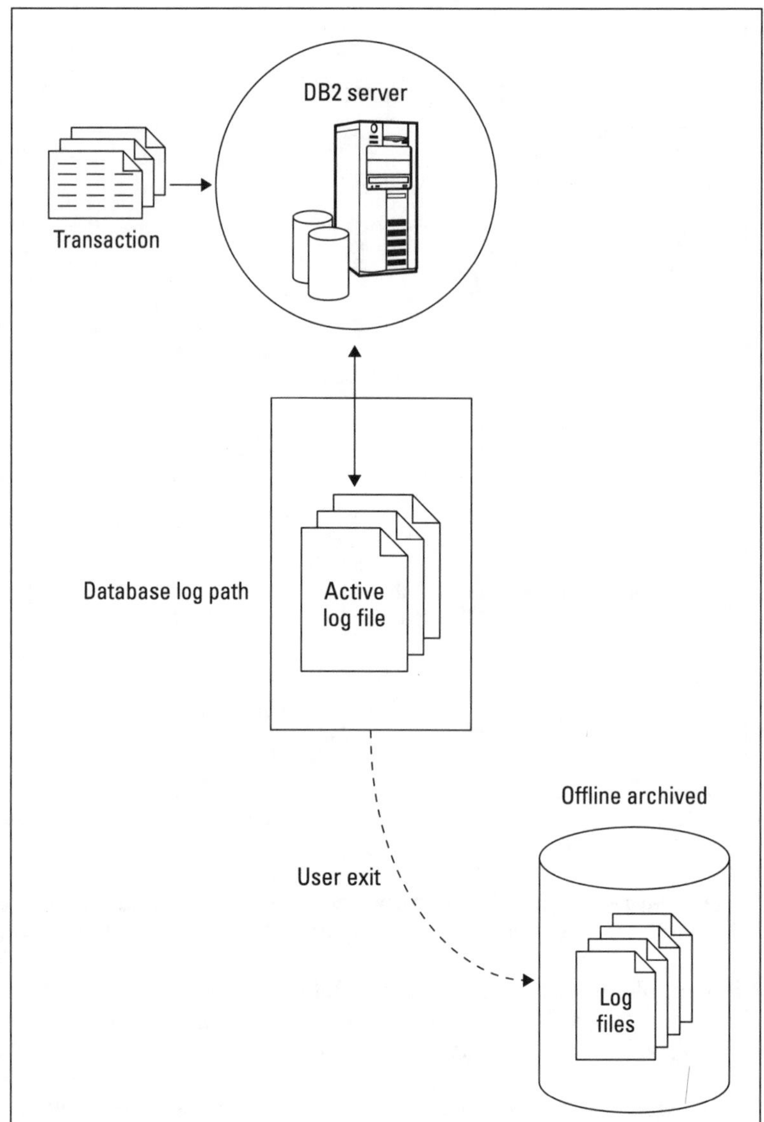

Figure 13-6: Offline archived logs cannot be found in the database log path directory.

To prevent media failure from destroying a database and your ability to rebuild it, keep the database backups, the database logs, and the database itself on different devices. For this reason, it is recommended that you use the *newlogpath* database configuration parameter to put database logs on a separate device once the database is created. You can update this parameter by using the `update db cfg` command.

Restoring Your Database with the Control Center

You can restore a database by using the Control Center. To start the Control Center to work with the DB2TEST instance, for example, perform the following steps:

1. **Make sure the current instance is the instance containing the database you want to restore.**
2. **Open the Control Center by clicking the Start button and choosing Programs➪DB2 for Windows NT➪Control Center.**
3. **Open the Journal by clicking the Journal icon near the top of the Control Center window.**
4. **Click the History tab.**
5. **Click the Select button.**

   The Database selection window opens.
6. **Click to select the appropriate system and instance names in the System and Instance fields (that is, those which contain the database you want to restore) and the name of the database you want to restore from the Database field; then click OK.**

   Figure 13-7 shows a user selecting the MOVIES database from the DB2TEST instance on system MELNYK.

Figure 13-7: Selecting a database whose operations history is to be displayed in the Journal.

Database selection
System | Instance | Database
MELNYK | DB2TEST, DB2 | MOVIES
OK | Cancel | Help

7. **Right-click a database backup entry on the History page of the Journal and then choose Restore from the pop-up menu.**

   Figure 13-8 shows the open Restore Database notebook.

8. **Click the Select an Entry From the List option.**
9. **Select the desired backup image.**

   Most times the backup image you want is the most recent, but use your own judgement.

10. **Click OK.**

    The backup is restored. Figure 13-9 shows a directory listing of the backup images for the MOVIES database.

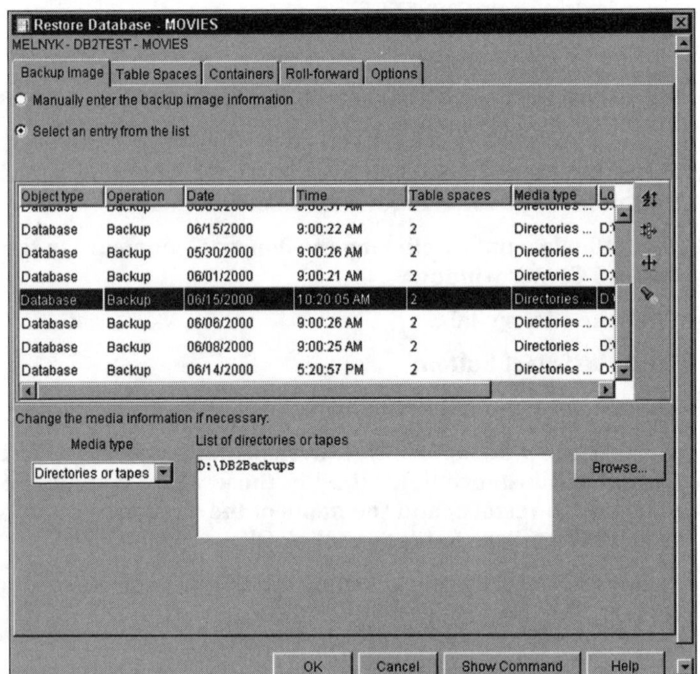

Figure 13-8: Restoring a database.

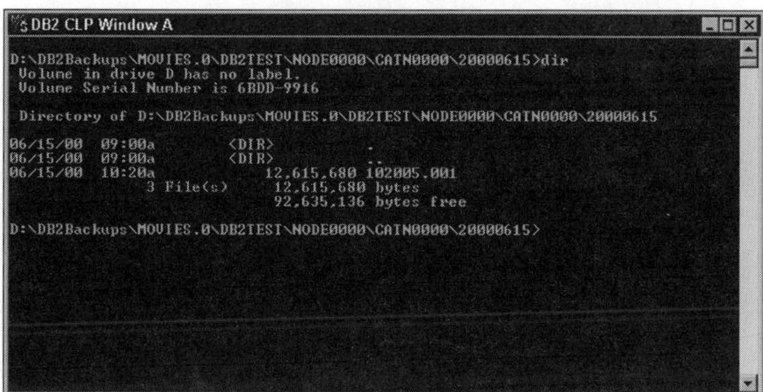

Figure 13-9: A directory listing showing the storage location of a database backup image.

Chapter 14

DB2 Data Replication

In This Chapter

- Boggling your mind with data replication
- Checking out the different concepts and components of data replication
- Checking data replication configurations
- Being brave and replicating your data

Think of data replication as a process that enables you to maintain multiple copies of the same data in more than one location. Data replication involves copying a defined set of data from one location (source) to another (target), and keeping the data in both locations synchronized.

In this chapter, we take a look at the exciting world of data replication (well, it's exciting if you're a geek, at least!). Data replication is too large a topic to discuss in detail within the pages of a single chapter. But by the end of this chapter you should have a good grasp of the concepts and be familiar enough with the tools to easily pick up the more in-depth aspects of DB2 replication you may come across in the future.

The following information is a general overview of common replication configurations. Specific instructions are not provided in this chapter. IBM has a 500-page book on replication, the *IBM DB2 Data Replication Guide and Reference* that is available through the information center (if you installed it). You can also download it from the DB2 Technical Library Web site:

```
www-4.ibm.com/software/data/db2/library/
```

Understanding Data Replication

Suppose that you're a traveling salesperson working for a company that stores all of its inventory information on a database server located at corporate headquarters. Without data replication, you have two ways of accessing the company's inventory. You can travel to company headquarters and use a company workstation to access the database server locally, or you can connect remotely, using your laptop and an Internet connection. But what happens if you're not anywhere near company headquarters, and a remote connection isn't possible? What if your remote connection can't provide you with the information you need fast enough? This is where data replication saves the day. Data replication enables you to have a local copy of the data available on your laptop for fast and easy access. Making multiple copies of the same data, and keeping those copies synchronized, is what data replication is all about.

The preceding is just one example of how you can use data replication. We discuss other examples in the "Data Replication Configurations" section later in this chapter.

Data Replication Components

Three main data replication components exist: The Control Center, the Capture program, and the Apply program.

- **DB2 Control Center:** The central administration tool for DB2, and also the interface to administer data replication. You can use the DB2 Control Center to define data replication sources, targets, and other data replication criteria.
- **Capture Program:** After you set up a data replication environment by using the Control Center, your job is to keep source and target data synchronized. Two tools help you to do this; the first of which is the Capture program. When you run the Capture program, any updates or changes that you have made to your source data are identified, gathered, and stored temporarily in DB2 tables.
- **Apply Program:** The Apply program picks up where the Capture program leaves off. When you run the Apply program, the data source updates and changes that are stored in temporary DB2 tables by the Capture program are copied (applied) to the target data source. After the Apply program is run, your source and target data is synchronized. Running both the Capture and Apply programs are tasks that you must perform to keep your multiple copies up to date. The Apply program can also copy data directly from a source to a target (this is called a *full-refresh copy*).

Data Replication Concepts

In this section we discuss a few of the more essential data replication concepts. You also find out about data replication sources, targets, and subscription sets. We also take a look at different operations that you can perform on the data you replicate.

Data replication sources

A *data replication source* is any DB2 table or view. When you publish a DB2 table or view as a data replication source, you define things such as:

- Which table columns you want to replicate.
- Whether you want before image values for a column. This is explained in the "Data Manipulation" section of this chapter.
- Whether you want to completely refresh the data (full-refresh).
- What level of conflict detection to use for update-anywhere. We discuss update-anywhere replication in the "Data Replication Configurations" section.

The process of publishing a DB2 table or view as a data replication source is referred to as *registration*.

Subscription sets and subscription set members

Before you can replicate data from a replication source, you must associate the replication source with a replication target. The attributes of this association, which you specify, are defined by using subscription sets and subscription set members. Think of the *subscription set* as the package, and the *subscription set members* as the contents.

For the subscription set, you define information such as:

- The subscription set name.
- The Apply qualifier. This is explained in the "Jumping in and Replicating Your Data" section later in this chapter.
- When to start replication, how often replication occurs, and whether to use interval or event-based timing.

A subscription set must have a subscription set member for each target table or view. When you define a subscription set member, you specify the following attributes:

- The relationship between a source table or view and a target table or view.
- The structure of the target table or view.
- The columns that you want replicated.
- The rows that you want replicated.

Why have subscription sets? Subscription sets ensure that all subscription set members (tables or views) are treated alike. When using the Apply program to copy changes from replication sources to replication targets, the changed data for all subscription members in a subscription set are applied in a single transaction, or unit of work. This means that when changes are replicated to the target tables, either all of the updates occur or none of them occur.

Why is it important that changed data for all members of a subscription set be applied in a single transaction? Source tables are often linked to one another with referential integrity constraints. This simply means that certain actions, if performed on one table, can have an effect on other tables. Subscription sets allow you to copy changes that have occurred to multiple related source tables and apply the changes to the target in a single transaction. Applying these changes together in a single transaction ensures the integrity of the data at the target.

The following example further explains this concept:

You run a company database that includes an Employee table, a Department table, and a Salary table. The database is defined in such a way that an employee must belong to a department, and must have a salary. Suppose that you hire a new employee and add information for this employee to each of the three tables. Now suppose that you have a replication target where these three tables also exist. If you replicate only the Employee table to the target, your data's integrity is compromised — the target Employee table contains an entry for a new employee, but the target Department table and target Salary table remain unchanged. In this example, you're breaking the rules that you have outlined for your database, and thereby compromising the integrity of the data at the target.

Using a subscription set and defining each of the three tables as subscription set members enables you to copy changes that have occurred to all three tables in a single transaction, thereby preserving the integrity of the target data.

Data manipulation

When replicating data, you may only want to replicate a subset of a source table. Or, maybe you want to create a simple view of the source data and have the view replicated to the target. The following are some ways that you can manipulate your data:

- **Subsets of Source Tables:** You have the option of selecting specific columns or rows for replication. The process of selecting certain rows is called *row subsetting.* The process of selecting certain columns for replication is called *column subsetting.*

  Column subsetting is useful when you only want to replicate certain columns from a replication source. You may consider using column subsetting in situations where specific columns contain particularly large amounts of data, such as columns with a large object data type (LOB), or in a situation where a specific column contains sensitive information. A large object data type (LOB) can be a binary image file, such as a photograph, for example. A table named Employee Salary may contain a column with confidential salary information.

  Row subsetting is useful when you only want to replicate specific rows of data from a replication source. You may use this type of subsetting to weed out irrelevant information. For example, you may want to replicate data recorded only within a specific time frame, or the sales records for a specific item in your inventory.

- **Run-Time Processing the Data:** You may need to massage or manipulate your source and/or target data. DB2 replication enables you to manipulate data at different stages of the replication process by using SQL statements or stored procedures. The ability to do run-time processing on the data gives you a lot of flexibility and control over how your data is replicated. We don't get into this aspect of data replication in this chapter, but run-time processing is a powerful feature of data replication that you may want to explore further after you understand the basics.

Renaming columns

The column names at the replication target can be different from the column names of the replication source. You have the option of renaming columns when you define a subscription. Maybe the column name at the source is too long, or maybe another name makes better sense in the context where your replicated data is used — who knows? The point is that this option is there for you to use.

Computing columns

DB2 data replication enables you to create new columns in your target table, and to populate those columns with data derived from SQL expressions. You can use any valid SQL arithmetic expression or aggregate function, such as AVG or SUM. For example, suppose that you have a source table that contains a bunch of columns with different sales statistics. During replication, you can use SQL to create a new column and populate that column with a new statistic derived from existing information in other columns.

For more information on SQL, you can refer to *SQL For Dummies* by Allen G. Taylor (IDG Books Worldwide, Inc.).

Replicating before- and after-image data

Before-image data is the data that exists at the target before updates or changes are applied. *After-image data* is the updated target data. When you replicate data from the source to the target (update the target data), you have the option of preserving an image (copy) of what the target data looked like before changes were applied. Replicating before and after-image data is useful where applications require rollback or auditing capability. To put it simply, this utility is useful in situations where you need to keep track of what a value was before you made changes.

If you choose to replicate both before and after-image data, additional columns are created at the replication target to store the column data values that existed at the replication target before you applied changes. This means that for a single column of data that exists at the replication source, you will have two columns at the replication target — one column containing before-image data, and another containing after-image data. You have the option to select the columns for which you want both before and after-image data.

Defining a table join as a replication source

At some point, you may want to replicate data from more than one source to a single target, or structure your data in a different way. For example, suppose that you want to take three rows of data from source table A and three rows of data from source table B and replicate (copy) this data to a single target table. To do this, you would perform a join on source table A and source table B. DB2 data replication provides you with the functionality to create and maintain target tables that contain data from joins of existing source tables. You may use this feature of DB2 replication if you need to restructure your data, or define a target table that contains columns from different source tables. For more information on SQL, you can refer to the *SQL For Dummies* by Allen G. Taylor (IDG Books Worldwide, Inc.).

Replication targets

A data replication target is always in the form of a table. You define a target table and its structure when you define a subscription set member. Much of what we cover in the "Data manipulation" section earlier in this chapter affects the characteristics of your replication target table.

When you define a subscription set member, you also define the type of target table that is used. Several types of targets exist. Table 14-1 contains a brief explanation of a few of the tables you can choose from.

Table 14-1: Target Table Types

Table Type	*Characteristics*
User copy	Exact, read-only copies of the replication source. No columns are added during replication and they look like regular source tables. User copy tables are a good starting point for someone new to data replication.
Point-in-time	Exactly the same as a user copy table, except that a time stamp column is added. You use this type of table if you want to keep track of the last time that changes were made to your data.
Aggregate Tables	Read-only tables that use SQL column functions (such as SUM and AVG) to compute summaries of the entire contents of source tables or of recent changes made to the source table. Rows are appended to the aggregate tables over a period of time.
Replica	You can make a target table a replica table. Replica tables are the only read-write target table type. This means that you can change the data at the target and replicate those changes back to the source. You can use this type of table if you're setting up update-anywhere replication. We discuss update-anywhere replication in the next section.

Data Replication Configurations

This section covers four data replication configurations — four different ways that you can use data replication in the real world. Many more data replication configurations exist, and new configurations are always being created to service a variety of new business environments. But we cannot discuss all of them here, nor do we want to try. The configurations covered here can give you an idea of what you can do with data replication.

Data distribution configuration

In this configuration, the source data resides on a source server. Changes made to the source data are replicated to one or more read-only target tables in a distributed network. Because the target tables are read-only, you don't have multiple copies of the same data being updated simultaneously. You have no potential for conflicting updates in this data replication configuration. Figure 14-1 illustrates a data distribution configuration in which changes made to a source table are replicated to read-only target tables.

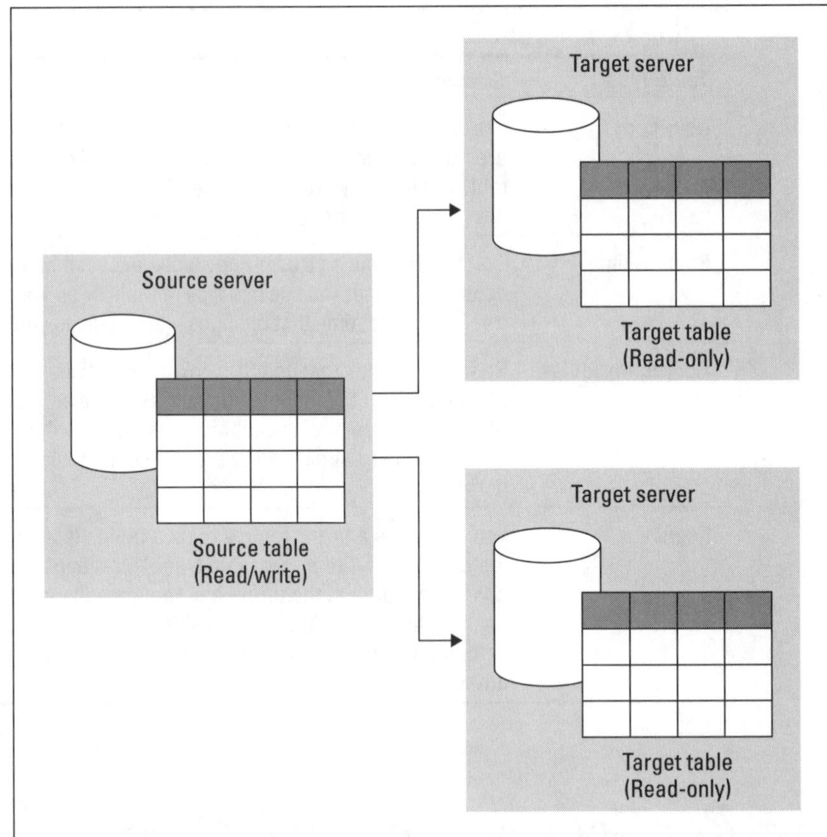

Figure 14-1: A data distribution configuration.

Where can you use data distribution configuration? Suppose that you own a company that has several sites. You want to share data among the sites, but you don't want to reduce the performance of your business applications that require access to the data. A data distribution configuration enables each site to have a local copy of the data on a target database server. The network remains unclogged, and complaints that data access is too slow are kept to a minimum.

Data consolidation configuration

In this configuration, a central database server acts as a repository for data that comes from several data sources. In other words, many source tables exist, but the result is only one read-only target table with many subset views. Changes made to the multiple data sources are replicated to the central server containing the target table and subset views. Figure 14-2 illustrates a data consolidation configuration in which each source provides unique rows of data to the target table.

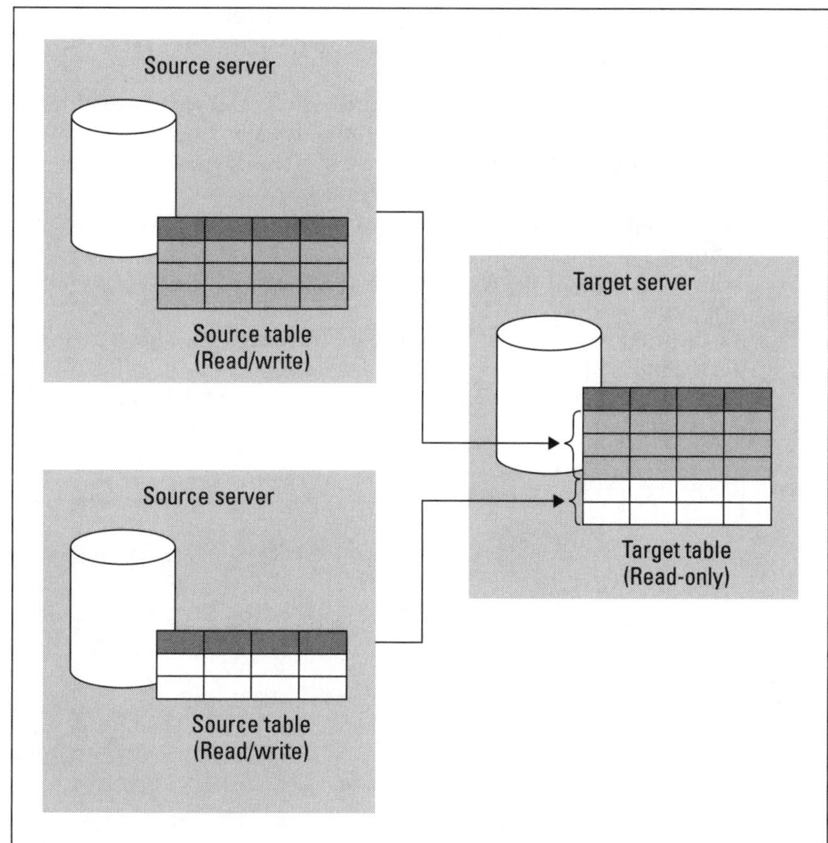

Figure 14-2: A data consolidation configuration.

A data consolidation configuration may be useful in a decision support system (DSS) environment where you want to analyze data without having to compete for database resources. Data access is centered on the target server, thereby relieving the stress on the actual source databases.

Update anywhere configuration

In an update anywhere configuration, replication targets are read-write tables. This means that you can make changes to copies and then those changes are replicated back to the replication source. The changes made to the replication source are then replicated back to all the target tables. Updates to the data can occur at either the source or the target tables. As you can imagine, making changes to multiple copies of the same data can lead to conflicting data. If you decide to use this type of replication, you must first decide how you plan to handle conflicts in your environment. DB2 data replication has different levels of conflict detection that you can choose from. A solution to the conflict problem is to design your system so that conflicts cannot occur. Figure 14-3 illustrates an update anywhere configuration without the risk of conflicts. In this figure, each read-write target table has a unique set of rows that can be updated locally. Conflicts are avoided because no target can update the same rows of data.

For example, an update anywhere configuration can be used by a financial company that supports a mobile computing environment for its many agents who travel to do business. The agents require the most up-to-date data and are more productive if they don't have to deal with slow network connections or the inconvenience of having to be connected to serve their clients' needs. To maintain up-to-date company data, each agent must be able to send updated data back to company headquarters, which is then replicated out to each agent.

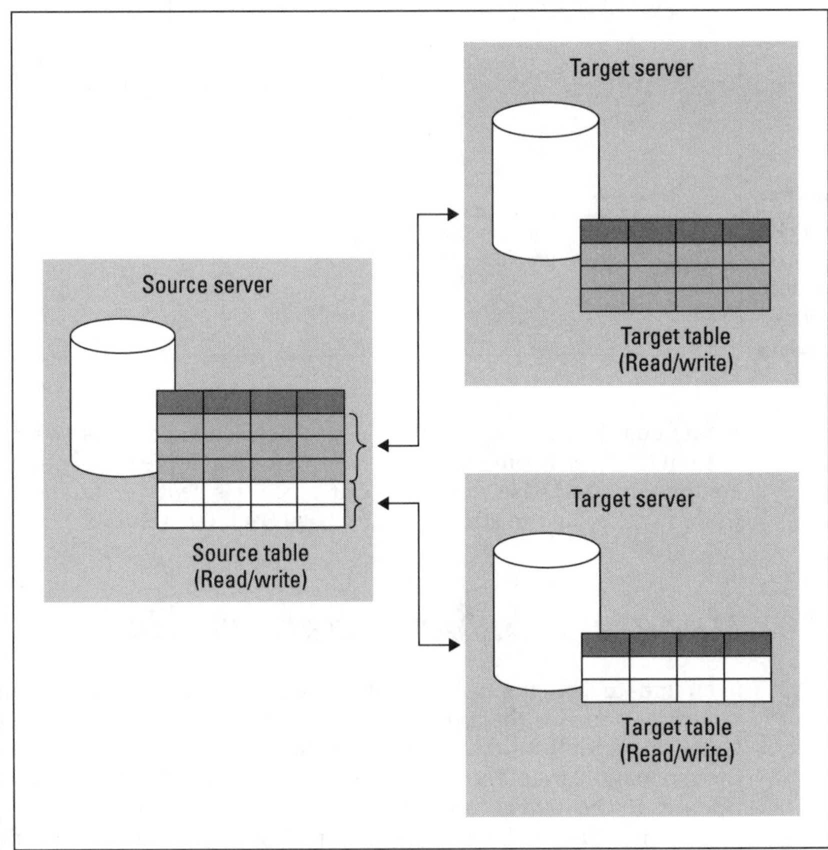

Figure 14-3: An update anywhere configuration.

Occasionally connected configuration

In this configuration, users can connect to and transfer data on demand. These types of configurations enable users to connect to the source servers long enough to synchronize their local copy of data. After a connection between a source server and a target is established, changes that have occurred to the data are replicated and the connection is terminated. An occasionally connected configuration can reduce communication costs in a mobile computing environment by keeping connection time to a minimum. This configuration can also be used for on-site computers that are not always connected to the source server. A good example of this is an employee that works only three days a week. Figure 14-4 illustrates an occasionally connected configuration in which the target servers aren't continually connected to the source server. Changes that are made to the source are replicated when the target servers make a connection.

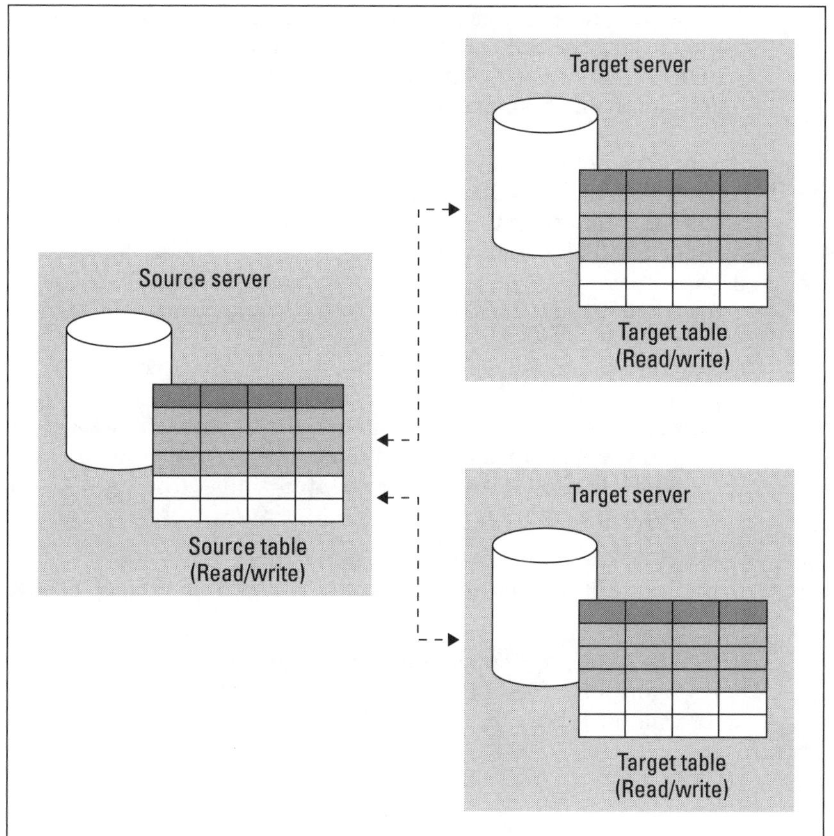

Figure 14-4: An occasionally connected configuration.

Jumping in and Replicating Your Data

In this section, we take you through a simple replication example. We also show you the administration interfaces available through the Control Center, many of the data replication options you can choose from, and you get a first look at the Capture and Apply programs.

STEP 1: Defining a replication source and creating a replication subscription

Make sure your Control Center is set to the default settings. If not, some steps in this example may not match what you see on your screen.

Use the DB2 Control Center to create a database with the default options. You will use this database as the replication target database. You can do this by right clicking the Databases folder in the Control Center and choosing Create⇨Database using SmartGuide from the pop-up menu. See Chapter 8 for information on creating databases.

If you have not done so already, use the First Steps icon in the IBM DB2 program group to create the DB2 SAMPLE database. We use a table from the SAMPLE database as the replication source in this example. We suggest you use the SAMPLE database if you've created it in First Steps (discussed in Chapter 4). Otherwise you need to find and use a database that has data in it (newly created databases do not have data in them).

Next you need to define a replication source. To do so, follow these steps:

1. **In the Control Center, right-click the Tables folder for the database you want to work with and then select it to display the database's tables in the Control Center contents pane (the right pane) of the Control Center.**

2. **Right-click a database table and choose Define as a Replication Source⇨Custom from the pop-up menu that appears.**

   The Define as Replication Source window appears, as shown in Figure 14-5. (See Table 14-2 for a list of options in the Replication Source window.)

Table 14-2: Replication Source Window Options

Option	*Definition*
Data Capture is Full Refresh Only	Changes are not captured. Selecting this option indicates that you want to copy the entire source table to the target table whenever you replicate data from this source. Data is transferred directly from the source to the target. The Capture process is bypassed in this case because you're replicating the entire source table. By default, this setting is not selected.
Define as Source	By selecting or deselecting the check boxes under the Define as Source heading, you can choose which columns you want replicated.
Capture Before Image	By selecting or deselecting the check boxes under the Capture Before Image heading, you can choose to include or exclude a column's before image. Selecting this option adds a before image column to your target table when you replicate changes. The before image column contains the value of the column data before the update occurred.
Changed Data for Partitioned Key Columns Captured as Delete and Insert	If you select this option, an update to a partition key is captured as a delete and insert.
Table will be Used for Update Anywhere	Select this option if you operate in an update anywhere replication environment. If you select this option, you can choose from three different levels of conflict detection. Refer to the "Data Configuration" section of this chapter for more information on update-anywhere replication configurations.

3. **In the Define as a Replication Source window, make sure that all source table columns are selected and that no before images are captured for any of the columns.**
4. **Make sure that the Data Capture is Full Refresh Only option and the options available at the bottom of the window are not selected.**
5. **Click OK.**

   The Run Now or Save SQL window opens.
6. **Click Run Now and then click OK.**

   A message pops in and tells you that the replication source was defined successfully.

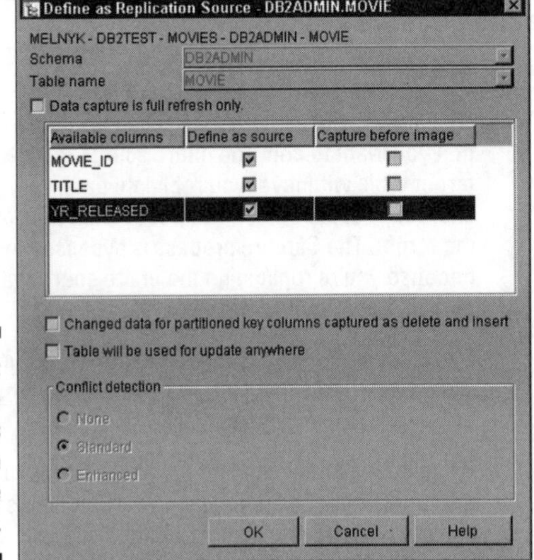

Figure 14-5: The Define as Replication Source window.

7. **To view the replication source you created, right-click the Replication Sources folder in the left pane of the Control Center window and choose Refresh from the pop-up menu.**

   The table you defined as a replication source should appear to the right of the Control Center in the contents pane.

8. **In the right pane of the Control Center, right-click the table you have defined as a replication source and choose Define Subscription.**

   The Define Subscription window opens, as shown in Figure 14-6. (See Table 14-3 for a list of options in the Define Subscription window.)

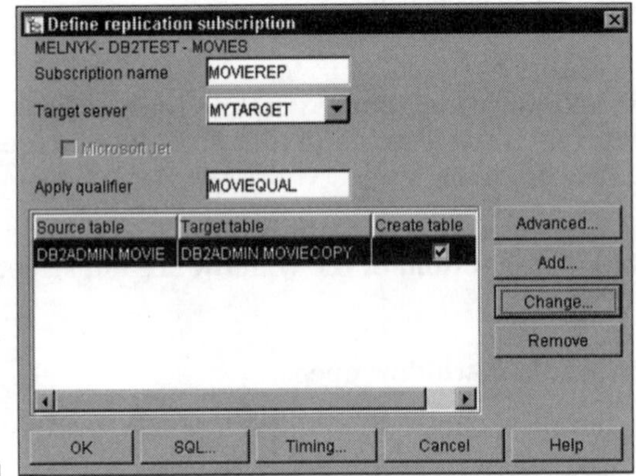

Figure 14-6: The Define Subscription window.

Table 14-3: Define Subscription Window Options

Option	*What It's For*
Subscription Name	An identifier for the subscription set.
Target Server	You select a database for the target server that holds or will hold the target table. This can be the same database that contains the replication source or a different database. In order to select a database, you must have access to it through the Control Center. Refer to Chapter 6 for information on adding databases to your system.
Apply Qualifier	The apply qualifier associates an Apply program with one or more subscription sets. When the Apply program starts, this qualifier is used as a parameter. You can use one apply qualifier for all subscriptions you define, or you can use several different apply qualifiers, which allow you to run more than one instance of the Apply program.
Target Table	The column names for the target table are found beneath this heading. By default, the target table name is the same as the source table name. You can change the name of the target table column by clicking this field and editing the name.
Create Table	The check box under the create table heading must be selected for the target table to be created in the target database. If you do not select this check box, you must create the target table yourself.
Advanced button	Clicking the Advanced button opens the Advanced Subscription Definition window where you can specify advanced options for your subscription. These advance options include selecting a target table type and selecting specific columns and rows for replication.
Add button	You can use the Add button to add additional replication sources (tables or views) to your subscription set as a new subscription set member. The Add button brings up a window where you can choose from any of the replication sources that are defined.
Remove button	Where the add button allowed you to add a subscription set member (replication source), the remove button allows you to get rid of one.
SQL button	The SQL button opens the SQL window, where you can add, change, or remove run-time SQL processing statements that are submitted either before or after the subscription is processed. This is covered in the "Data Manipulation" section of this chapter.
Timing button	The Timing button opens the Subscription Timing window, which is where you define the replication schedule for a particular subscription.

9. **Type a name for the subscription in the Subscription Name text box.**

   You can provide whatever name you like for the subscription. Usually, you would provide a name that is easy to remember and descriptive of the table you have chosen to replicate.

10. **In the Target Server drop-down list box, select the name of the target database you created (that is, the database you are replicating data to).**

11. **Type a name for the Apply Qualifier in the Apply Qualifier text box.**

   You can provide whatever name you like for the apply qualifier. You need this name later when using the Apply program, so it is a good idea to provide a name that is easy to remember.

12. **Click the Create Table check box.**

13. **Click the Advanced button.**

   The Advanced Subscription Definition window opens, as shown in Figure 14-7.

Figure 14-7: The Advanced Subscription Definition window.

   The Advanced Subscription Definition window has three tabs. Each tab contains advanced options that you can use when defining your subscription.

14. **Click the Target Type tab and select both the Target Table is Read-Only and User Copy options.**

   This tab enables you to choose the Target Table type (refer to the "Data Replication Concepts" section earlier in this chapter).

15. **Click the Target Columns tab.**

    This tab enables you to specify which columns you want replicated, to create new columns using an SQL expression, to change or rename a column, or to display the source table's primary key(s) or unique indexes.

    Make sure that all the columns are selected under the Subscribe column.

16. **Click the Rows tab.**

    This tab enables you to select which rows you want replicated or define the arrangement of rows. This is done by using a WHERE predicate or GROUP BY clause. We're not going to perform any actions on this tab, but it is good to take a look through!

17. **Accept the default value for all other options and click OK.**

    You return to the Define Replication Subscription window.

18. **Click the Timing button.**

    The Subscription Timing window appears.

19. **On the Source to Target tab, set the relative timing interval to every two minutes.**

    This will be the replication frequency (how often replication of data from the source to the target occurs). The Time-Based option and Using Relative Timing option should be selected by default.

    For more detailed information on replication timing, click the panel's Help button.

20. **Click OK to close the Timing window, and then click OK in the Define Replication Subscription window.**

    The Run Now or Save SQL window appears.

21. **Select the name of the target database you created earlier from the drop-down box as the Control Server, click the Run Now option, and then click OK to Create the Subscription.**

    A message pops up proudly announcing that the replication subscription was completed successfully.

DB2 uses control tables to run the database system. Replication has its own control tables that are created during the replication process.

Congratulations! You have defined a replication source and created a replication subscription telling DB2 how the source data should be replicated, and where it will go.

STEP 2: Starting the Capture program

You're now ready to replicate data. First, you run the Capture program. As discussed earlier in this chapter, the Capture program identifies, gathers, and stores changes that have occurred to the source data in temporary DB2 tables. If this is the first time that the Capture program is being run against your source data, all the source data is considered an update or a change. For this reason, all the data from the source is gathered and stored in temporary DB2 tables, waiting to be applied to the target.

From a DB2 command window type **asnccp *<source database name>*** and press Enter, where *<source database name>* is the name of the database you're replicating data from. In this replication example, we suggest that you use the SAMPLE database that we show you how to set up in Chapter 4. You know the Capture program has run successfully if the command prompt returns and no error messages are received.

To capture future changes to your source data and apply those changes to your target data, your source database has to be enabled for roll-forward recovery, either by enabling Log Retain for Recovery or User Exit for Logging. Enabling either ensures that database logs are kept for all database transactions. The Capture program uses the database logs to keep track of changes that occur to the source data. You can find out how to enable Log Retain or User Exit in the *IBM DB2 Universal Database Administration Guide* (available from the DB2 information center).

STEP 3: Starting the Apply program

After the Capture program finishes processing, you are ready to run the Apply program. The Apply program takes the data gathered and stored in temporary DB2 tables by the Capture program and applies (copies) the data to the replication target.

From a DB2 command window type **asnapply *<apply qualifier name>* *<target database name>*** and press Enter, where *<apply qualifier name>* is the name you gave to the Apply qualifier in Step 11 in the preceding numbered list, and *<target database name>* is the name that you gave to the target database you're replicating data to. The Apply program successfully starts if it begins to run and no command prompt appears.

When the Apply program processing completes, you have successfully replicated data. You can now go back to the Control Center and examine your fine work. The table you defined as a replication source in the database is now viewable in the database you defined as a target.

In the Control Center, expand the objects tree (left side of the Control Center) to display the Tables folder for the target database. After you have found the Tables folder for the target database, click it to display the target database tables in the contents pane (the left pane) of the Control Center. If you followed the steps correctly, the table you defined as a replication source appears there among a number of DB2 control (system) tables.

Chapter 15

Monitoring the Performance of Your Database

In This Chapter

- Recognizing database users
- Mingling with DB2 monitors
- Setting up the Windows NT/2000 Performance Monitor
- Understanding the optimizer
- Establishing levels of optimization and access plans
- Figuring out access plans
- Keeping stats

The more you use your database, the more curious you're going to be about what is going on behind the scenes. You may already wonder how you can monitor who uses the database and how you can improve the performance of accessing the data. In this chapter we show you how to identify who uses your database, how to monitor what they are doing, and how to look at DB2 optimizer plans.

Identifying Who Uses Your Database

You may find yourself wondering who's connected to your database — how many users there are, where they're connecting from, and what applications they're using to connect to the database. To start looking at this information, open the Control Center by clicking the Start button and choosing Programs⇨DB2 for Windows NT⇨ControlCenter. Then click the Connections folder in the Control Center. You see an output similar to Figure 15-1, which shows all the users on the database.

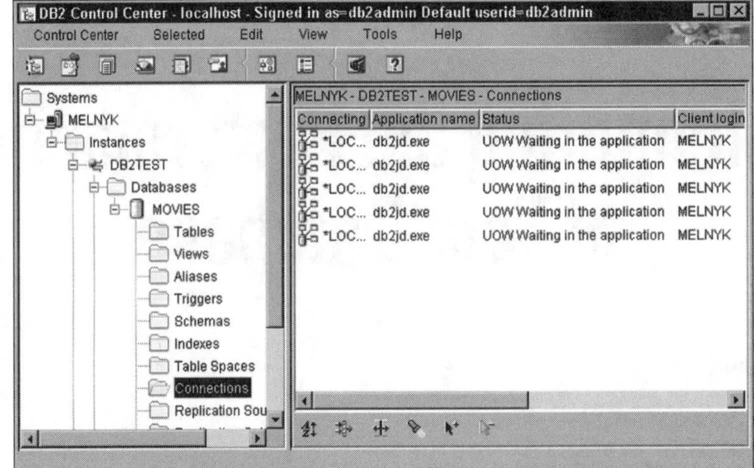

Figure 15-1: A listing of users connected to your database.

The first column in that output tells you whether the connection is local or remote. In the figure, there are five local connections, which you can tell because the first column shows "LOC..." in all the rows.

The next column tells you the application name that is connecting. This is useful information because it gives you a sense of how users are utilizing your database. In this case, it looks like all of the users are accessing the database through an application named `db2jd.exe`.

If you click the column name at the top of the output, this sorts the output alphabetically using that column.

The next column is the status of that particular application. Table 15-1 shows the output values you may see under the Status heading in the Connections output.

Table 15-1: Possible Application Status

Status	*Translation*
Connect Pending	An application or user has initiated a database connection but the request hasn't completed.
Connect Completed	An application has initiated a database connection and the request has completed.
UOW Executing	DB2 is executing requests for an application's unit of work.

Status	*Translation*
UOW Waiting	DB2 is waiting for requests from an application. This usually means that the system is executing in the application's code.
Lock Wait	The unit of work is waiting for a lock in order to proceed.
Commit Active	The application is committing changes to the database.
Rollback Active	The application is rolling back any changes it made to the database.
Request Interrupted	The application is being interrupted. This is usually due to a user interrupt (like a Ctrl+Break) or if an application is forced using a `db2 force` command.
Creating Database	The application is creating a database.
Restoring Database	The application is restoring a backup image to the database.
Backing Up Database	The application is performing a backup of the database.

In Figure 15-1 you can see that there is further output to the right, which you can scroll to see. The Connection output contains the following additional columns:

- **Client Login ID:** Identifies the user connected to your database.
- **Application Handle:** This is a number decided on by DB2 that uniquely identifies that particular application.
- **Authorization ID:** Shows the ID with which that application was authorized to connect to the database
- **Status Change Time:** Keeps track of the last time that the Status column changed.

If you're not happy with an application that is connected to your database, you can easily force it off your system by following these steps:

1. **In the Connections output, right-click the application you want to force off, and select Force from the pop-up menu that appears.**
2. **Refresh the listing of Connections to your database by right-clicking the Connections folder and choosing Refresh.**

   Ta da . . . the application you forced off is no longer connected to the database.

The preceding operation is very useful for getting those pesky users that shouldn't be connected to the database off the system. One tip, however, is that the force request is asynchronous. This means that once you send the force request, the application doesn't always disappear instantaneously. Whatever that application was doing may need to be rolled back, and this can take some time.

Monitoring DB2

DB2 comes with extensive capabilities to monitor the usage of your database. The Performance Monitor is your one-stop shop for monitoring activities on your database. Monitoring your database is an important part of database administration because you should keep track of what users are doing: who's running long queries that hog the CPU, who's being sneaky and running Napster, and who's trying to run backups.

The Performance Monitor is useful when you need to look at database activity or monitor an existing performance problem, such as users complaining that their SQL doesn't work fast enough. The Performance Monitor enables you to:

- Tune your database for better performance
- Analyze performance trends
- Detect performance problems or prevent problems from occurring

To open the Performance Monitor, right-click a database name in the Control Center, click Performance Monitoring, and then click Show Monitor Activity.

Figure 15-2 shows what the Performance Monitor looks like when you first open it. The Performance Monitor creates visual representations (charts and graphs) of database information, such as how buffer pools are being used, how much disk I/O exists, or how locks are being used in the database. All these items can help you narrow down bottlenecks in your database system. Perhaps the buffer pools are too small and this is causing queries to run slow, or maybe it's taking too much time waiting for I/O and you need faster disks, and so on.

One of the things that the Performance Monitor enables you to do is to select different built in monitors to watch for specific database events. The Monitor Name drop-down list box contains the predefined monitors included with DB2. You can choose a monitor from the list, modify a monitor, or even create your own monitors.

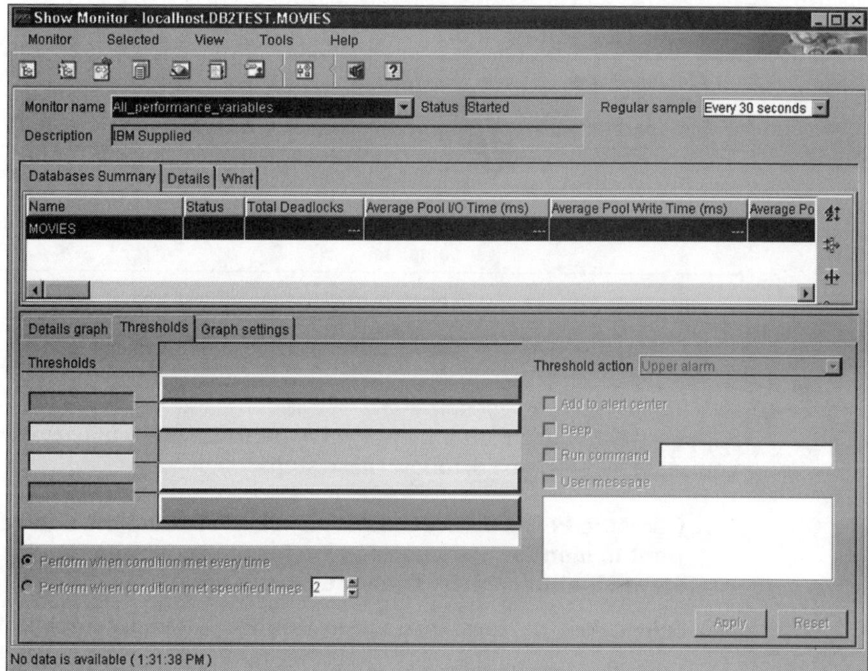

Figure 15-2: The Performance Monitor.

Table 15-2 lists the predefined monitors that come with DB2.

Table 15-2: Predefined DB2 Monitors

Monitor Name	***Function***
Locking	Shows how much the applications on a system are competing for access to the same objects.
Cache	Shows information on cache configuration parameters and whether they are set properly.
Deadlocks	Shows if applications are getting into situations where one application is waiting for a second in order to access the same object, while the second application is waiting for the first. In the end, neither application will budge since they are both waiting for locks.
Sort	Shows information pertaining to sort heaps (parts of memory that DB2 uses for sorting).

(continued)

Table 15-2 *(continued)*

Monitor Name	*Function*
Disk_performance	Shows information on disk I/O.
Global_memory	Shows information on how DB2 is using memory.
Long_running_query	Shows information on SQL that's taking a long time to complete.
Capacity	Shows overall usage of the system.
Bufferpool	Shows information on buffer pool usage.

Suppose that you want to monitor drive performance while users are using your database. To do so, follow these steps:

1. **Open the Performance Monitor by right-clicking the database you want to monitor and choosing Performance Monitor⇨Show Monitor Activity from the pop-up menu.**
2. **Select Disk_performance in the Monitor Name drop-down list box.**
3. **Click the Details tab.**

   The information in the Details tab shows you all the elements that the Disk_performance monitor tracks. For example, the monitor is tracking total synchronous I/O time and its value. At the bottom of the screen you see the graphical representation of the total synchronous I/O time.
4. **Click the What tab.**

   The information in the What tab shows all the database elements being monitored and tracked by the Disk_performance monitor. The elements being monitored are the total pool writes (the number of times DB2 writes pages to the buffer pool), the total pool reads (the number of times DB2 reads pages from the buffer pool), and the total physical I/O.

   You can see how buffer pools are used by looking at the DB2 Performance Monitor outputs for the Disk_performance monitor. DB2 uses buffer pools as areas in memory where it reads and updates all data. Data is read from disk into a buffer pool as it is required by queries or applications. After changes are made in the buffer pool, the data is written out to disk. From here, we have the concept of buffer pool reads (reading information from the buffer pool, cheap because it's in memory), buffer pool writes (writing information to the buffer pool, again cheap because it's in memory), disk reads (reading a page from disk, which is more costly), and disk writes (writing a page to disk).

You want the buffer pool to be sufficiently large (without knocking the system to its knees!) so that as many pages as possible fit in the buffer pool. To figure out if a buffer pool is big enough, you need to look at the buffer pool hit ratio. The buffer pool hit ratio indicates the percentage of time DB2 is able to reference a page in the buffer pool instead of having to read it from disk. The greater the buffer pool hit ratio, the lower the frequency of disk I/O.

Normally, you have to calculate the buffer pool hit ratio by looking at various DB2 snapshots. But with the Performance Monitor, the buffer pool hit ratio appears as a Performance Variable in the What tab.

Activating your Windows Performance Monitor

Windows NT/2000 comes with its own performance monitor. This monitor can help you to track CPU usage, memory utilization, disk activity, and network activity. DB2 comes with a special utility to register DB2 with the NT Performance monitor, which enables you to track your DB2 instance.

To register DB2 with the Windows NT/2000 Performance Monitor, type **db2perfi –i** at a command prompt and press Enter.

To start the Windows Performance Monitor and monitor aspects of DB2, follow these steps:

1. **Click the Start button and choose Programs⇨Administrative Tools⇨ Performance Monitor.**

   The Performance Monitor appears.

2. **Choose Edit⇨Add to Chart.**

   The Add to Chart dialog box appears, as shown in Figure 15-3.

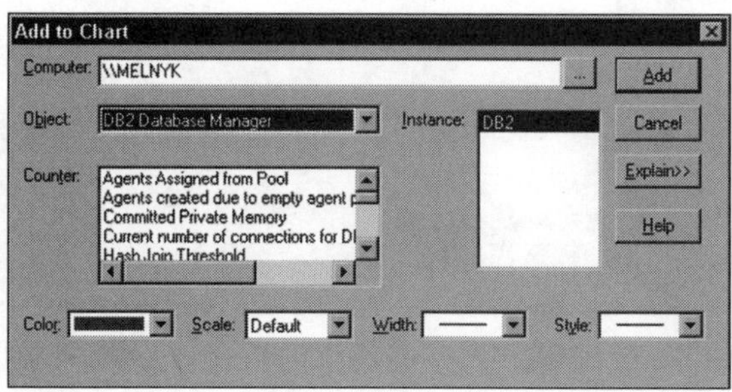

Figure 15-3: Using the Add to Chart dialog box to monitor the DB2 Database Manager in the Windows NT Performance Monitor.

3. **Choose DB2 Database Manager in the Object drop-down list box.**
4. **Click Agents Assigned from Pool in the Counter list box.**

   The Counter list box contains many elements that you can monitor. After selecting a counter, you can click the Explain button to bring up the definition for that particular counter.
5. **Click Add.**
6. **Click Agents Created Due to Empty Agent Pool, Local Connection, and Local Connection Executing in Database, clicking Add after each selection.**

   The Performance Monitor adds these elements to its chart, enabling you to track them. The result looks something like Figure 15-4.

Choosing to monitor the DB2 Database Manager through the Windows NT/2000 Performance Monitor enables you to monitor elements of DB2 that are at the instance level. This includes items such as total number of active databases and amount of memory being used for sorts. In the Add to Chart dialog box, however, you can also choose to monitor DB2 Databases. Monitoring databases as opposed to the database manager provides information for a particular database. For example, you can track the number of rows deleted, inserted, or selected in a particular database.

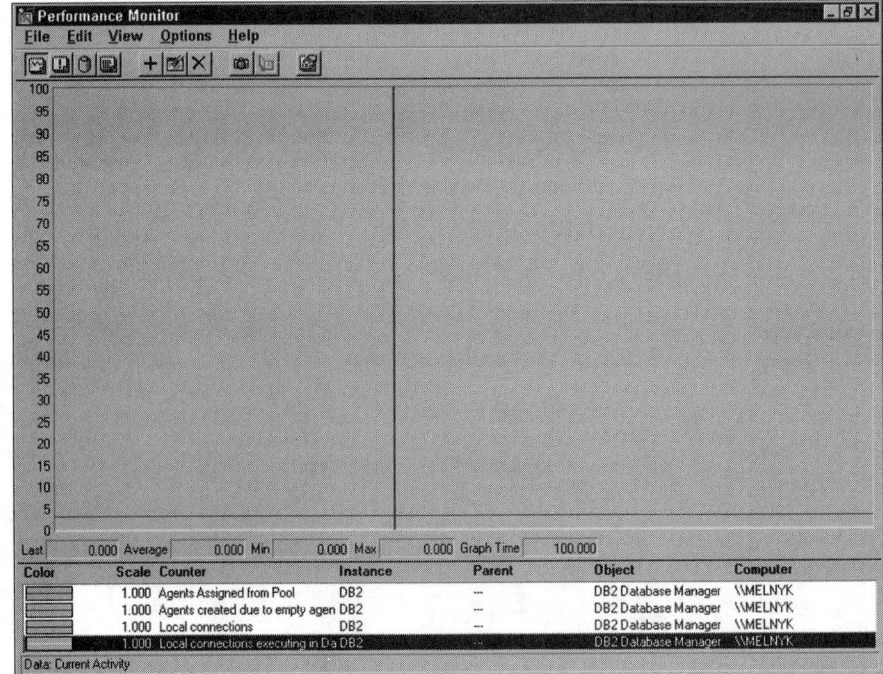

Figure 15-4: Tracking connections to the database with Windows NT Performance Monitor.

Working with the optimizer

One of the best features of DB2 is its optimizer. Consider this example: You're administering a large database that is accessed by many users — from the managers looking at reports to the application programmers writing their tools. Each user forms their queries for data differently. If the database accepted all queries as is, there would be a free-for-all for data, without any controlled access to the information.

DB2 can rewrite any SQL submitted to it, and then optimize it to run faster. You can access data in tables in several ways, including scanning through a whole table or looking through an index. The optimizer looks at a particular SQL query and decides how to get the data.

The optimizer decides how to get that data by looking at statistical information. What's that, you say? Well, when you create a database, views exist in the system catalog table space that hold information about all the other tables in the database. Some of these views contain statistical information about the data that is in the other tables. DB2 keeps tabs on all the data in the database and feeds this information to its optimizer, enabling it to access data as fast as possible.

The optimizer acquires information from three important views.

- **SYSSTAT.TABLES:** This view contains a row for each table in the database. The most important information it tracks is the total number of rows in a particular table (CARD column) and the total number of pages on which rows of this table exist (NPAGES column).
- **SYSSTAT.INDEXES:** This view contains one row for each index that exists in a database.
- **SYSSTAT.COLUMNS:** This view contains one row for each column defined in the database and keeps track of various types of information, including the number of distinct values in a column in the database. It also tracks the second highest and second lowest value in a column, in the HIGH2KEY and LOW2KEY columns, respectively.

All three views are created as part of the `create database` command and reside in the SYSCATSPACE table space (which we discuss in Chapter 9).

Levels of optimization and access plans

Now that the techno mumbo-jumbo is out of the way, we can discuss what the optimizer means to you.

DB2 has seven levels of optimization. These levels specify how hard the optimizer is going to work to get you the best plan (or road map) to your data possible. Table 15-3 is a rundown of the different optimization levels.

The higher the optimization level, the more time the optimizer is going to spend rewriting the query. So, even though the query may run faster, it may take longer for the optimizer to complete! The default optimization level is set in the DB2 Database Configuration File, which is defined by the parameter named DFT_QUERYOPT (see Chapter 8).

After doing its stuff, the optimizer generates an access plan.

Table 15-3: Optimization Levels

Level	*Result*
0	Tells the optimizer to use minimal optimization. You're basically telling the optimizer, "I'm smarter than you. I've written my SQL efficiently and all my tables have outstanding indexes." Level 0 is used only in special cases — I don't recommend you use it.
1	Tells the optimizer to use optimization comparable to the old version of DB2. The old optimizer was not as developed as it is now, and the optimizer at level 0 may not use all the fancy stuff developed in later versions.
2	Better than level 1, but still not the greatest.
3	Uses what DB2 calls a "moderate amount of optimization." This level comes closest to imitating optimization by DB2 for the MVS host operating system.
5	The default level — best for most cases. Here the optimizer uses all available statistics to come up with the best way to get at the data.
Level 7	The optimizer spends more time analyzing the statistics to figure out the best way to access the information that an SQL query is trying to retrieve.
Level 9	The optimizer spends even more time analyzing the statistics to figure out the best way to access the information. This is great, but the cost may outweigh the benefits because the optimizer may take a very very long time to analyze the statistics at this optimization level. So, it's not true that you should always run with optimization level 9 to get the best results. The best idea is to start with the default and evaluate the cost and benefit of incrementing or decrementing the optimization level.

Checking out access plans

The *access plan* is a road map to the data. DB2 enables you to see what the optimizer has done by allowing you to look at the access plan that the optimizer selected to perform a particular SQL query. You can do this in several ways, but the best way is by using a tool called Visual Explain.

To see how Visual Explain works, follow these steps:

1. **Open the Command Center by clicking the Start button and choosing Programs⇨DB2 for Windows NT⇨Performance Monitor.**
2. **In the command window type** select * from db2admin.movie**.**
3. **Click the Run button to run the SQL script.**

   The Results tab of the Command Center becomes active. The output of the command appears, similar to that shown in Figure 15-5.

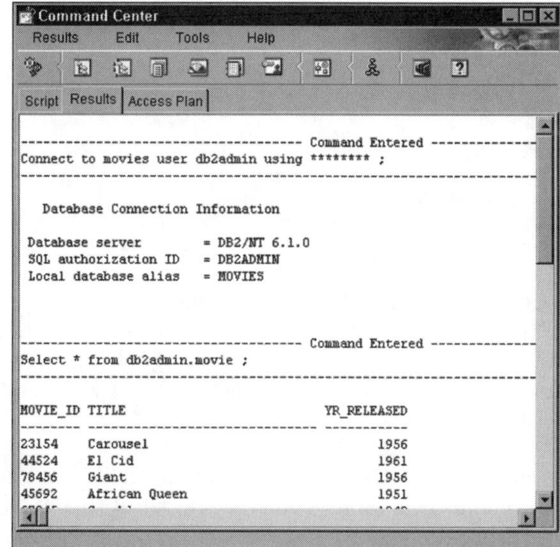

Figure 15-5: Results of an SQL query.

4. **Click the Access Plan tab.**

   An *access plan* is a graphical representation of how DB2 accesses data. In Figure 15-6 you can see that the access plan is doing a TBSCAN for the DB2ADMIN.MOVIE table. TBSCAN means that it will scan each row in the table in order to return results for the SQL. In another situation it could do an INXSCAN, for example, which is an index scan for some other SQL query.

Keeping stats

You need to know one last, important thing about the statistical values that the optimizer uses to generate access plans. These statistics don't just pop out of nowhere. You must help DB2 gather them but running the `runstats` utility on a regular basis.

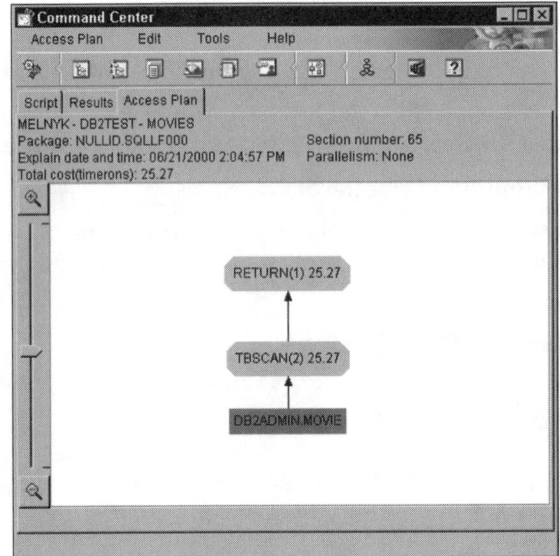

Figure 15-6: An access plan using Visual Explain.

`runstats` is a DB2 utility that collects statistics based on both table and index data so that the optimizer can have accurate information to generate access plans. If the information in the system catalog tables is incorrect or out of date, the optimizer can make a decision that costs you hours of execution time.

We recommend running `runstats` any time you make a large number of inserts, updates, or deletes to a table. You can check out the *DB2 Command Reference* online for more details, but the basic way to run `runstats` is as follows:

```
db2 runstats on table <table name>
```

You can also include indexes in `runstats` by adding **and detailed indexes all** to the end of the above command.

Another important utility that DB2 comes with that helps performance is `reorg`, which reorganizes the way a table is stored by reconstructing the rows to eliminate fragmented data and by compacting information. For example, if you have a table with 1,000,000 rows, and you delete 300,000 rows, then you have all these empty spaces on your disk. `reorg` eliminates these free spaces by moving the rows around.

To run `reorg` on a table, the command syntax is:

```
db2 reorg table <table name>
```

Chapter 16

Troubleshooting DB2

In This Chapter

- Knowing where to start when you have a problem
- Determining whether your problem is DB2's fault or not
- Pondering cryptic, spiteful error messages
- Interpreting messages in the diagnostic log
- Looking at other files in the diagnostic path
- Knowing the different types of problems
- Impressing the heck out of DB2 support staff
- Checking out some tricks of the trade

Support geeks can be know-it-alls, always expecting or wishing for the perfect user. This chapter shows you how to save yourself valuable time that you may otherwise spend on hold if you call for support, or helps you avoid ending up on hold or having to call back (and then from holding some more!).

The Web site for any kind of DB2 support is `www.ibm.com/software/data`. Here you can search for known problems in DB2 as well as see Technotes that support analysts and developers have made available. Technotes describe common DB2 errors and how to deal with them.

Where Do I Start?

The best way to minimize any troubleshooting that you may need to do is to keep a detailed record of everything you do. I know that this is a pain, but trust me, if you ever call for support, the first thing they ask you is, "What have you changed recently in your system?"

Always make sure that you record events, such as:

- Upgrading the operating system
- Upgrading DB2
- Changing database manager configuration parameters
- Changing database configuration parameters

Also try to keep a record of any table spaces, tables, and indexes that are created or dropped.

Fortunately, you don't have to keep track of everything yourself. The recovery history file (which we discuss in Chapter 13) stores tasks, such as when you ran the last `backup`, `restore`, `load` job, or `reorg` command.

Blaming it on DB2 . . . or not?

DB2 may not be the source of your trouble. Ask yourself if any of the following can be the cause of problems:

- Hardware
- Operating system
- Network connectivity
- Communication software

If you think that it may be one of the preceding, check the Event Viewer for details. Start by looking at the Event Viewer System Log, as shown in Figure 16-1. To open the Event Viewer System Log on your NT/2000 desktop, click the Start button and choose Administrative Tools⇨Event Viewer.

The events in the log are sorted by date and time, with the most recent appearing at the top. Any hardware, operating system, or network connectivity errors appear here.

Next, check the Event Viewer Application Log by choosing Log⇨Application. Again, you see notifications sorted by date and time. This list contains events from applications only — you don't see adapter events, device events, or disk events, which all appear in the System Log. You can look through the DB2 notifications for clues on why you are having trouble.

Event Viewer - System Log on \\MELNYK

Log View Options Help

Date	Time	Source	Category	Event	User	Computer
6/19/00	5:32:43 PM	EventLog	None	6005	N/A	MELNYK
6/19/00	11:45:13 AM	Srv	None	2013	N/A	MELNYK
6/19/00	11:39:35 AM	EventLog	None	6005	N/A	MELNYK
6/12/00	12:57:30 PM	Srv	None	2013	N/A	MELNYK
6/12/00	12:51:49 PM	EventLog	None	6005	N/A	MELNYK
6/9/00	3:27:12 PM	Srv	None	2013	N/A	MELNYK
6/9/00	3:21:32 PM	EventLog	None	6005	N/A	MELNYK
6/8/00	12:50:33 PM	Srv	None	2013	N/A	MELNYK
6/8/00	12:50:33 PM	Srv	None	2013	N/A	MELNYK
6/8/00	12:44:57 PM	EventLog	None	6005	N/A	MELNYK
6/8/00	10:48:54 AM	Rdr	None	8006	N/A	MELNYK
6/2/00	9:03:37 AM	Srv	None	2013	N/A	MELNYK
5/25/00	9:03:25 AM	Rdr	None	3013	N/A	MELNYK
5/25/00	9:02:10 AM	Rdr	None	3013	N/A	MELNYK
5/25/00	9:00:55 AM	Rdr	None	3013	N/A	MELNYK
5/24/00	3:43:33 PM	Srv	None	2013	N/A	MELNYK
5/24/00	3:43:33 PM	Srv	None	2013	N/A	MELNYK
5/24/00	3:38:03 PM	EventLog	None	6005	N/A	MELNYK
5/24/00	9:00:34 AM	Srv	None	2013	N/A	MELNYK
5/23/00	3:00:26 PM	Srv	None	2013	N/A	MELNYK
5/12/00	10:30:34 AM	Srv	None	2013	N/A	MELNYK
5/12/00	10:24:55 AM	EventLog	None	6005	N/A	MELNYK
5/10/00	10:28:17 AM	Print	None	8	SYSTEM	MELNYK
5/10/00	10:25:06 AM	Print	None	8	SYSTEM	MELNYK
5/1/00	3:44:22 PM	Print	None	2	melnyk	MELNYK
5/1/00	3:29:16 PM	Print	None	2	melnyk	MELNYK
5/1/00	3:29:14 PM	Print	None	20	melnyk	MELNYK
5/1/00	1:47:48 PM	Srv	None	2013	N/A	MELNYK
5/1/00	1:42:13 PM	EventLog	None	6005	N/A	MELNYK

Figure 16-1: The Event Viewer System Log.

Making use of DB2 documentation

DB2 comes with all its documentation online in the Information Center. To bring up this wealth of geeky goodies, open the Control Center and choose Help⇨Information Center. The DB2 Information Center appears, as shown in Figure 16-2.

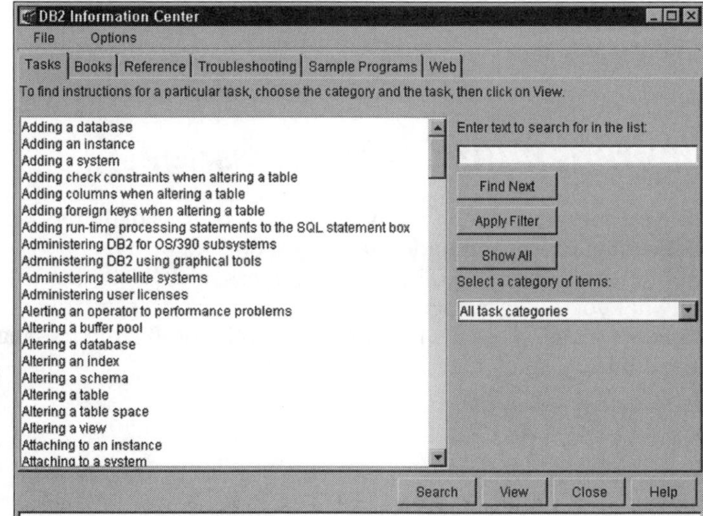

Figure 16-2: The DB2 Information Center.

You can access help files by clicking the different tabs in the Information Center. For example, you can

- Search for specific tasks, such as "connecting to a database"
- Open books in the DB2 Library
- Check the Reference tab for a specific command

If you want to search for a specific task or operation, such as adding an instance or importing data, click the Tasks tab and find the task in the sorted list. Double-clicking the task in the display brings up your browser with the online documentation for that particular task. The online documentation describes in detail how to perform the task and provides links to online documentation for other tasks.

If you don't have the hard-copy manuals for DB2 handy, you can also look through the online set of books available through the DB2 Information Center. To do so, click the Books tab and double-click any of the books in the listing. Your browser opens with the selected book loaded. You can read the documentation page-by-page, access different chapters from the table of contents, or retrieve specific information through the index.

Knowing the Different Types of Problems

You can categorize typical DB2 troubles into three types (which we describe in the next three sections):

- Error messages
- DB2 crashes
- A hang or a loop

Comprehending error messages

While error messages aren't really a problem, they're definitely indicative of a problem somewhere, and understanding them can be a real chore. Whenever you submit a command to DB2, you get a message back telling you whether or not what you did was successful. If it was not successful, the message explains why. Each message has three parts: the prefix, the message number, and the suffix.

An example of a warning message is:

```
SQL0100W No row was found for FETCH, UPDATE or DELETE; or the
         result of a query is an empty table.
```

In this case, the SQL is the prefix, 0100 is the message number, and W is the suffix.

The *prefix* of the message identifies the part of DB2 that is returning the message. Several prefixes exist, but the most important ones are:

Table 16-1: Error Message Prefixes

Prefix	*Which Message Use It*
ASN	Messages from Replication
CCA	Messages from the Client Configuration Assistant
DBA	Messages from the Control Center
DBI	Messages from installation and configuration components
DB2	Messages from the command line processor
SQL	Messages generated as a result of running SQL commands

The *message number* explains the results of the command.

You may hear DB2-geeks call the message number *SQL code.*

The easiest way to figure out what the message number means is to ask DB2. To do so, open the Command Center, type **? <*message number including prefix*>**, and then click the Execute button (the button with the picture of turning gears located in the upper-left corner). DB2 responds by telling you what the message means (Explanation) and what you can do about it (User Response). For example, `? sql1024` was the command typed to see the result shown in Figure 16-3.

You can also figure out what an error message means if you get a dialog box with the error message displayed, as shown in Figure 16-4. This is a simple dialog box that indicates that an operation was unsuccessful. The dialog box contains an error message explaining why the operation failed.

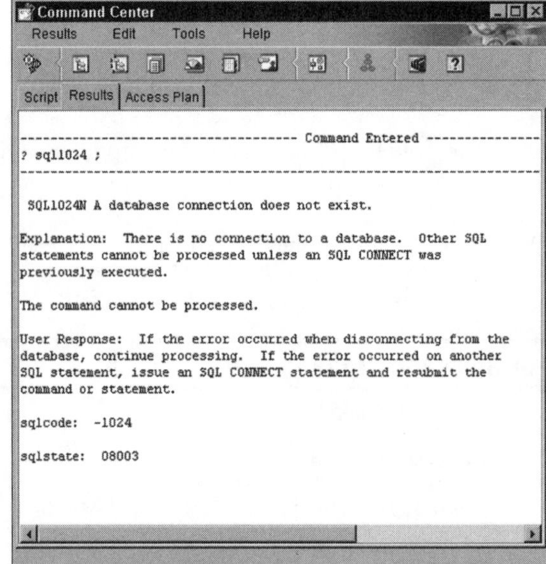

Figure 16-3: DB2 responds to the call for help.

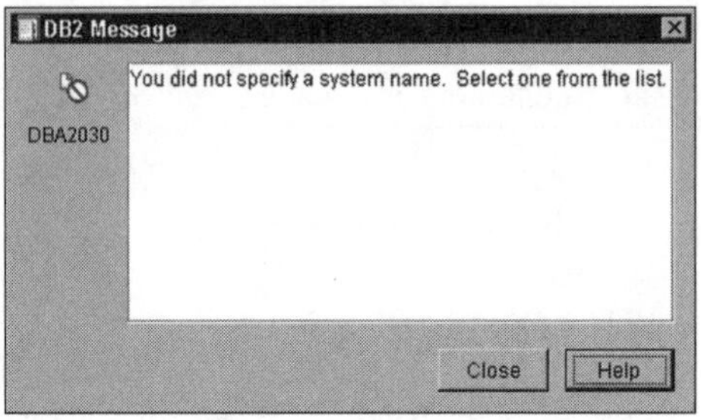

Figure 16-4: An SQL error message.

Click the Help button and a message explanation appears, as shown in Figure 16-5. Every time an operation doesn't succeed, you get a message and a Help button.

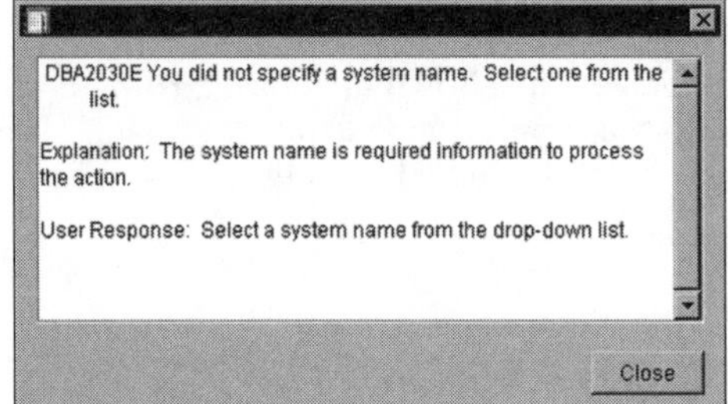

Figure 16-5: An SQL error message help explanation.

The *suffix* is meant to explain the severity of the error message. You can receive three types of suffixes: W is for Warning, N is for Notification and C is for Critical. See Table 16-2 for explanations of what each suffix means.

Table 16-2: Error Message Suffixes

Suffix	*What It Means*
W	Warning messages are just that — they indicate that the operation was successful, but that there may be something else you need to know about the operation. You see this error if you select rows from an empty table. It's just saying, "Hey, I did what you said. I successfully looked for rows in the table, but there's nothing there."
N	Notification errors are more serious. Receiving a notification error means that whatever you tried to do didn't succeed and you're going to have to figure out what went wrong and redo your operation.
C	Critical error messages are just nasty. This is usually when you end up calling support and begging for help!

Internal error codes

If you are going to get intimately familiar with the DB2 diagnostic log — `db2diag.log` (which we discuss later in this chapter) — then we also have to tell you about internal error codes. You see, every once in a while, you may be looking through the `db2diag.log` and see something like

```
An internal error occurred. Report the following error code:
         FFFF8139
```

or

```
ZRC=FFFFC11E
```

What's happening here is that some internal function in DB2 is printing out the hexadecimal error code. You can, luckily, translate the hexadecimal error code to an SQL error code easily. The key is that you must look it up in the product documentation. The *DB2 Troubleshooting Guide* in the DB2 Product Library has an Appendix titled DB2 Internal Return Codes, and this is what you want to check. This appendix neatly summarizes all the internal error codes and what SQL code they translate to. So, if you look up FFFF8139, you see that it translates to:

```
SQL0294N The Container is already in use
```

Unexpected errors

If you're getting an error message that you don't expect, make sure you look it up and thoroughly understand the explanation and proper user response.

Remember to check the prefix of the error message to see which component of DB2 the error is coming from. Is it the Control Center? Is it the command line processor, or maybe even DB2 Replication?

Look up the meaning of the error message by using the `? <error message number>` command.

The *DB2 Message Reference* is another good place for looking up error messages. You can also check the `db2diag.log` for any additional information, especially internal error codes that may be recorded there.

If none of the preceding solutions help, you can always reference the online DB2 support Web site at `www.ibm.com/software/data`, where you can search for the error message you have received and see if there is a Technote available for dealing with such a problem. You may even find a fix for the condition you are encountering.

If all else fails, contact DB2 support. Before you call, make sure that you can answer the following questions:

- What error code are you getting?
- What were you doing when you encountered this error?
- Can you reproduce the error?

Try to be as detailed as possible in your answers to the preceding questions. Two people may encounter the same problem, but both will often describe it in very different ways:

1. Every time I run my script it doesn't work.
2. Every time I select from a particular table, I receive an SQL1042C.

If you are specific as with the second option, your problem is sure to be isolated quicker and solved faster by the support team.

Here are some tips to make sure that your problem description is detailed enough. Ask yourself:

- What date and time did the error occur?
- What DB2 operation was I doing at the time?

- What was I doing just before the error occurred?
- Was I creating any objects, such as table spaces, tables, or indexes?
- Was I running any utilities, such as backup, reorg, load, or import?
- Did I change anything recently in my environment?

DB2 crashes

Although uncommon, DB2 can crash due to a GPF (General Protection Fault). In this case, check the `db2diag.log` and you see a message showing that DB2 has hit a GPF and that all DB2 operations have stopped. If DB2 crashes, check the online DB2 support Web site at `www.ibm.com/software/data` for any known problems and available fixes for the GPF that you are encountering. Search known problems for GPFs, or traps as the geeks call them, and check if the fixes are available. If such problems are known, download the necessary fixes and apply them. Otherwise, give DB2 support a call, and be ready to send them the `T<NNNNN>.000` files and `<NNNNN>.000` files along with the `db2diag.log` file. These files are located in the `C:\SQLLIB\DB2` directory. (We discuss these weird-looking `T<NNNNN>.000` and `<NNNNN>.000` files in the "Other Stuff In the Diagnostic Path" section later in this chapter.)

A hang or a loop

Sometimes, it may appear that DB2 is hanging. For example, you may be trying to look at some information in a table, but the information isn't being retrieved. Or, some rows come back, but before all the rows are returned, the query appears to hang.

In such a case, you can check a number of things. First, check the operating system. Is only DB2 hanging or are other applications hanging too? If other applications aren't responding, you're likely having an operating system problem and may need to reboot your machine.

CPU hogs

Use the Task Manager to see if you have applications running that are using up a lot of CPU time and not letting some of your DB2 operations proceed. Use your judgment to suspend any application that may be hogging the CPU, or let it complete before proceeding with your DB2 work.

Lock-wait

If only DB2 appears to be hanging, check what applications are connected to the database. Use the Connections folder in the Control Center to check the Status field in the output. If the Status indicates lock-wait, then the application may appear to be hung, but in fact it is just waiting for a lock on a row or table.

The likely cause of the hanging is that some other application is inserting or updating objects that the application in lock-wait wants to look at. In this case, it's not an actual hang or loop that has occurred. For the application in lock-wait to proceed, the other application has to commit its transaction.

If the problem is not a CPU hog or a lock-wait, check the `db2diag.log` for possible clues as to what is going on.

If the hang persists, check online DB2 support to see if hangs like the one you're experiencing are known.

Checking Out Some More Tools and Tricks

This section introduces you to more tricks of the trade; basically some ways to help you perform better problem determination and identification. First we cover the `db2diag.log`, where operations against the database and any errors encountered are recorded. You or DB2 support can use this log to isolate the cause of problems. We then talk about getting database definition statements so that a database can be reproduced. Finally, we discuss how to take a trace of a DB2 operation.

Hunting the DB2 Diagnostic Log

Every time that a database administrative event or error condition occurs, DB2 stores this information in a diagnostic log, or the `db2diag.log` file. The `db2diag.log` is a readable file that records any type of error that occurs, where the error is encountered, and maybe even why. Only the true geeks can decipher all that is in here.

Where is this thing?

The `db2diag.log` default location is in `C:\SQLLIB\DB2\DB2DIAG.LOG`. But, hold on, because DB2 lets you change this.

To move your db2diag.log to another location, all you have to do is modify the DIAGPATH parameter in the database manager configuration (see Chapter 7).

You can also configure the diagnostic level (DIAGLEVEL), which is how much information you want to gather in the db2diag.log. Five levels exist, as shown in Table 16-3.

Table 16-3: Diagnostic Levels

Level	*What It Means*
0	No logging
1	Logs only severe errors
2	Logs severe and nonsevere errors
3	Logs severe, nonsevere errors, and logging warnings
4	Logs severe and nonsevere errors; logging warnings, and information about all operations run in the instance.

The default DIAGLEVEL setting is 3. For most users, this is the best setting at which to have the DIAGLEVEL because there isn't too much information in the db2diag.log. But if there's a problem, you have enough information to diagnose the reason for the problem.

To change the DIAGPATH location or alter the DIAGLEVEL, you can use the DB2 command line processor or the Control Center. To change either one in the Control Center, follow these steps:

1. **Open the Control Center by clicking the Start button and choosing Programs⇨DB2 for Windows NT⇨Control Center.**
2. **Right-click the DB2 instance and choose Configure from the pop-up menu.**
3. **Click the Diagnostic Tab.**
4. **Click the Diagnostic Error Capture Level parameter and type the Diagnostic Data Directory Path.**
5. **Edit the location in the Value column by typing the location where you want the diagnostic file to go. In this example, type** D:\DIAGFILES, **as shown in Figure 16-6.**
6. **Click Diagnostic Error Capture Level, and then select a value (see Figure 16-7) from the list of options.**

7. **Click OK.**

   You have to restart your instance in order for the values to actually take effect.

8. **To restart your instance, from a command prompt type** db2stop **and press Enter, and then type** db2start **and press Enter.**

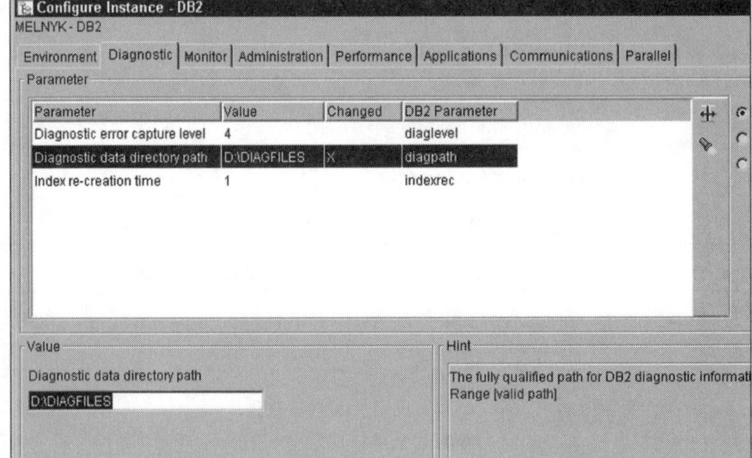

Figure 16-6: Changing the Diagnostic data directory path.

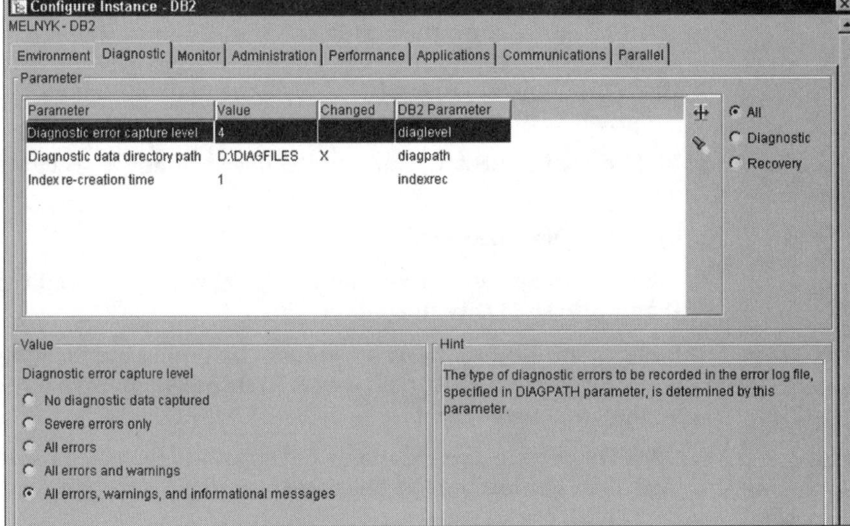

Figure 16-7: Changing the Diagnostic error capture level.

Increasing information levels

The default DIAGLEVEL is 3, but if you get really curious, you can set DIAGLEVEL to 4. Keep in mind that if DIAGLEVEL is 4, then more information is written to the `db2diag.log`. In turn, DB2 may run a little slower.

The `db2diag.log` is continuously appended to, so it's smart to back it up and clean it out every once in a while.

We recommend that you run with DIAGLEVEL set to 4 only if you are experiencing some kind of error condition and want to get more information about it. If you are having a problem and you call support, they may ask you to run with DIAGLEVEL set to 4 so that they can figure out what's going on in your instance.

Figuring out what's in db2diag.log

Warning! Technical details lie ahead. We're going to take you through a very simple `db2diag.log` entry so that you know what information is in your `db2diag.log` file.

You must first update DIAGLEVEL to 4 by following the instructions from the "Where is this thing?" section earlier in this chapter on changing DIAGLEVEL and DIAGPATH parameters. Next, in the Control Center, click the Tables folder for any database. You can then open the `db2diag.log` by using any text editor.

Here's an entry in the `db2diag.log` that appears after you select the Tables folder for a database:

```
2000-02-12-11.38.02.680000  Instance:DB2  Node:000
PID:203(db2syscs.exe)  TID:316  Appid:*LOCAL.DB2.000212163802
buffer_pool_services sqlbStartPools  Probe:0
          Database:DB2TEST
Starting the database.
```

A wealth of information is in here, including:

- **Date and time information**

  ```
  2000-02-12-11.38.02.680000
  ```

  This is pretty straightforward: It's just the date and time of when this particular event occurred

- **The name of the instance**

  ```
  Instance:DB2
  ```

- **The partition number**

```
Node:000
```

This is only important if you are running DB2 Enterprise Extended Edition (100-percent-proof geeks only!)

- **The process identifier**

```
PID:203(db2syscs.exe)  TID:316
```

This is another nerdy part of the information, but basically it tells you which process is reporting this event.

- **The application identifier**

```
Appid:*LOCAL.DB2.000212163802
```

This one is important. By clicking the Connections folder in the Control Center, you get the output shown in Figure 16-8.

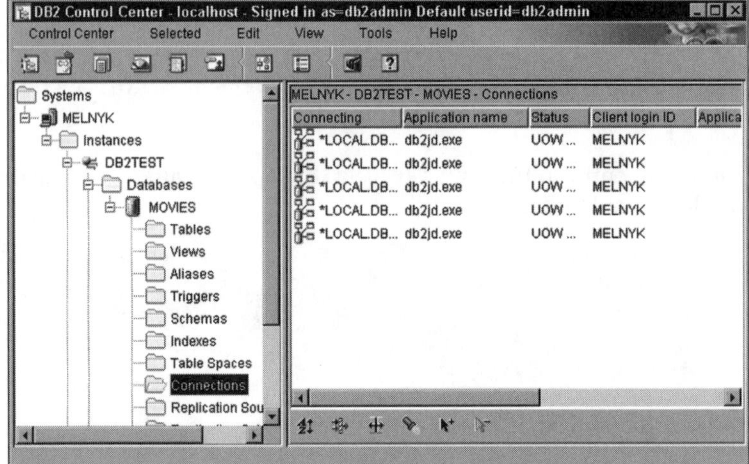

Figure 16-8: Connections to the database.

The Application ID in the Control Center output is the same as the Application ID in the `db2diag.log` entry. This piece of information is the unique way to identify an application, and it lets you associate a `db2diag.log` entry with the application that reported it.

- **The component identifier**

```
buffer_pool_services
```

This indicates the component of DB2 that is reporting the information. In this case, it is Buffer Pool Services.

- **The function identifier**

  ```
  SqlbStartPools
  ```

  This is the actual function that is printing out the error information.

- **The unique error identifier**

  ```
  Probe:0
  ```

  If you have the source code for DB2 at your fingertips, this tells you exactly what line of code is causing the output in the `db2diag.log`. But because you don't, this is something you can disregard.

- **The database name**

  ```
  Database:DB2TEST
  ```

  Here you have the name of the database, so that you know which one is reporting the information.

- **The error description and/or the error code**

  ```
  Starting the database.
  ```

  Finally! The actual text that explains what's going on!

The preceding example shows that someone has connected to the database and that Buffer Pool Services has responded by starting the database.

Other Stuff In the Diagnostic Path

You may occasionally look in the `\DIAGPATH` directory and see files with have names like:

```
T<NNNNN>.000
<NNNNN>.000
```

These are files DB2 dumps if a severe error or condition is encountered. The T prefix in `T<NNNNN>.000` stands for "trap" and the <NNNNN> is the number of the thread that encountered the trap.

If a filename is of the form `T<NNNNN>.000`, then DB2 encountered a segmentation violation, and this file contains information to help track why this problem occurred.

If the file is of the form `<NNNNN>.000`, then DB2 encountered any one of several severe error conditions , and DB2 has decided to dump out its memory structures and control blocks into this file.

Both of these types of files are used by IBM Support Analysts to determine why DB2 encountered such a condition.

The `T<NNNNNN>.000` file is a text file and the `<NNNNN>.000` file is a binary dump file.

If you have these files in your `\DIAGPATH` directory, investigate when they were generated and call IBM support. Don't delete them!

Definition statements

A couple of reasons exist for why you may need the definition statements to recreate your database. First, if you're having optimizer problems, you may need to supply the definition statements to DB2 support. Definition statements are a valuable troubleshooting tool. You may also want to create a second environment with a copy of your database. For example, you can create a test database so that you don't screw up a production database.

Again, the DB2 geeks had insight to provide a tool that extracts the definition statements for your database as well as all the SQL required to make a copy of the catalog statistics called `db2look`. This tool queries the system catalogs of a database, and outputs table space, table, index, and column information about each table in that database. You can also use this tool from the Windows command prompt.

To generate all the DB2 command line processor commands and SQL statements required to create a copy of the database, type the following at a Windows command prompt:

```
db2look -d <database name> -e -m -a -o db2look.out
```

When you run the `db2look` command, it creates a file that contains the necessary commands to recreate a database. To get more help on the different options of `db2look`, check the *DB2 Command Reference*, or just run `db2look` with no parameters. Figure 16-9 shows the help screen for the `db2look` command.

```
Command Prompt
C:\>db2look
db2look Version 6.0

Syntax: db2look -d DBname [-u Creator] [-s] [-g] [-a] [-t Tname1 Tname2...TnameN]
                          [-p] [-o Fname] [-i userID] [-w password]
        db2look -d DBname [-u Creator] [-a] [-e] [-t Tname1 Tname2...TnameN]
                          [-m] [-c] [-r] [-x] [-l] [-o Fname] [-i userID] [-w password]
        db2look [-h]

        -d: Database Name: This must be specified

        -a: Generate statistics for all creators
        -c: Do not generate COMMIT statements for mimic
        -e: Extract DDL file needed to duplicate database
        -g: Use graph to show page fetch pairs for indices
        -h: More detailed help message
        -m: Run the db2look utility in mimic mode
        -o: Redirects the output to the given file name
        -p: Use plain text format
        -r: Do not generate RUNSTATS statements for mimic
        -s: Generate a postscript file
        -t: Generate statistics for the specified tables
        -x: Generate Authorization statements DDL
        -l: Generate Datbase Layout: Nodegroups, Bufferpools and Tablespaces
        -u: Creator ID: If -u and -a are both not specified then $USER will be used
        -i: User ID to log on to the server where the database resides
        -w: Password to log on to the server where the database resides

C:\>
```

Figure 16-9: Getting help by using db2look.

Taking a trace

DB2 ships with a tool called `db2trc` that lets you trace all the DB2 events that occur in your instance. `db2trc` runs from the Windows command prompt and stores a running history of DB2 happenings in memory. `db2trc` then allows you to dump the trace to a file. `db2trc` isn't something you need every day, but if you are having problems, DB2 support folks may ask you for the output of `db2trc` so that they can see a running history of the steps that are causing problems. The following steps show you how to capture a trace, dump it to a file, and then send that file to DB2 support for further analysis.

1. **From a command prompt, start** `db2trc` **by typing** db2trc on –l 4000000 **and pressing Enter.**

   This turns on a trace with a buffer size of 4MB for collecting DB2 events. DB2 has a 4MB area of memory reserved for tracing any DB2 operation.

2. **Run whatever DB2 operation you want to trace.**

3. **Dump the db2trc by typing** db2trc dmp D:\db2.dmp **at the command prompt and pressing Enter.**

   This dumps the trace of events in memory into a binary file called `D:\db2.cmp`

4. **Turn the trace off by typing** db2trc off **at the prompt and pressing Enter.**

5. **Ship the binary dump file to DB2 support.**

Helping DB2 Support Help You Faster

Much as we try, there's no way this chapter can get you out of every possible situation that will arise with DB2. Sometimes you just have to bite the bullet and call DB2 support for help. Before you call DB2 support, make sure that you have a clear understanding of what kind of problem you are having and that you have spent some time collecting the proper information to diagnose it. The following list contains some helpful tips on dealing with DB2 support:

- **Make sure you can describe the problem clearly.** You must be able to explain what operation you are running, how many times you ran it, what sequence of events occurred, and the outcome.
- **Make sure you know what version of DB2 you are running and if you have installed any fixes or patches.** As with any software, DB2 has its own set of patches, fixes, and upgrades. In DB2-land we call this a FixPak. Although you installed DB2 at the beginning of this book, there are already FixPaks available for this version. You can download the FixPaks from the Web and install them by following the README file included. You can download FixPaks from the following URL:

  ```
  http://www-4.ibm.com/cgi-bin/db2www/data/db2/udb/
        winos2unix/support/download.d2w/db2ntv61
  ```

  Though we recommend you record any time you upgrade DB2, times arise in which you're going to forget. Fortunately, the DB2 geeks had insight into this and shipped a tool called `db2level` with the product to quickly let you know what version of DB2 and what FixPak you have installed on your machine.

  To run `db2level`, follow these steps:

  1. **From a command prompt, type** db2level **and press Enter.**
  2. **Collect everything and anything in the \DIAGPATH directory and compress the files using the WinZip utility that comes with Windows NT.**

     The DIAGPATH is specified in the database manager configuration.

     This ensures that you have all the information collected and in one place. (If you have problems with WinZip, see `www.winzip.com` for help.)

     The DIAGPATH is specified in the Database Manager Configuration (see Chapter 7).
  3. **From the Command Center, grab the database manager and database configuration files by clicking the Script option and typing the following in the space provided:**

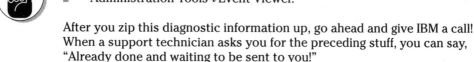

```
db2 get database manager configuration
db2 get database configuration for <database name>
```

4. **Click the Execute button.**

   The Execute button has a picture on it of turning gears, and is located in the upper-left corner of the Command Center.

   A dialog box appears with the results displayed.

5. **Store the script results in a file by choosing Results⇨Save As.**

   Save these results in the same directory as the DIAGPATH.

- **For problems with the Control Center, make sure you have access to the `db2cc.log` file in the `C:\SQLLIB` directory.** DB2 support may ask for this file if you call in problems with the Control Center. The Control Center keeps a log of all errors that it encounters in this file so that you can find the error type and the time when the error occurred in the directory. You can view the `db2cc.log` file with any text editor.

- **In the Event Viewer, select the Log pull-down menu and use the Save As option to save both the Event Viewer Application Log and the Event Viewer System Log in the same directory as the items from the DIAGPATH.**

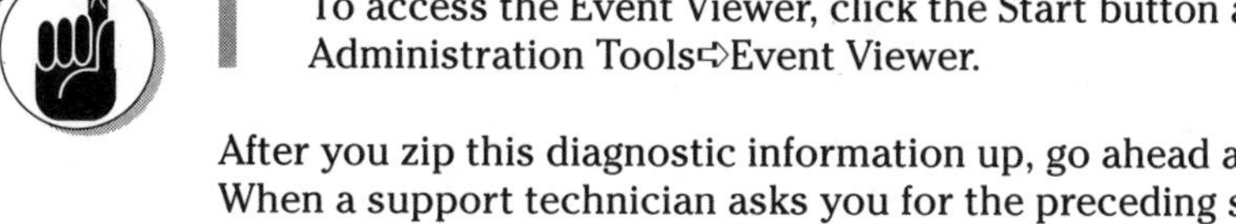

  To access the Event Viewer, click the Start button and choose Administration Tools⇨Event Viewer.

After you zip this diagnostic information up, go ahead and give IBM a call! When a support technician asks you for the preceding stuff, you can say, "Already done and waiting to be sent to you!"

Part V

The Part of Tens

"TELL THE BOSS HE'S GOT MORE FLAME MAIL FROM YOU-KNOW-WHO."

In this part . . .

In this part, you will be subjected to everything in tens! You won't find any of this information on David Letterman's top ten list, but you will be able to check out:

- Ten really important DB2 terms
- Ten cool things that DB2 can do that aren't discussed in this book
- Ten of the more common mistakes that people make in DB2
- Ten sources for DB2 information
- Ten cool tricks for running DB2

Did you notice that we use the word "ten" ten times on this page? Don't worry, we don't overuse the word "ten" in the rest of this part, we just give you lots of really useful information.

Chapter 17

Ten DB2 Things You Should Never Forget

In This Chapter

- Authentication
- Configuration
- Index
- Instance
- Normalization
- Primary key
- Referential integrity
- Relational database
- Roll-forward recovery
- View

To be a true database master, you have to understand and be able to use the terminology that other database masters use. Chapter 2 covers many database concepts and terms, but this chapter focuses on the terms at the DB2 core. Know these terms and you'll go far.

Many of the terms in this chapter are covered in more detail in Chapter 3. See that chapter for the lowdown on DB2 basics.

Authentication

Authentication is the process that DB2 uses to verify that you are who you say you are. This usually involves making you provide a valid user ID and password when you try to connect to a database. Authentication is checked at the instance level.

Authentication is not the same as authorization. *Authorization* is the process of verifying that you have proper database authorities and object privileges (we cover authorities in Chapter 2). Proper authorization enables you to do things such as create or alter databases, manipulate database objects, access user data, or perform routine administrative tasks.

Configuration

DB2 has a large variety of configuration parameters called *database manager configuration parameters* at the instance level and *database configuration parameters* at the database level. You can modify these parameters to customize your system. Most of these parameters affect the amount of system resources that are allocated to a single instance of the database manager or specify the amount of resources allocated to a particular database.

Index

An *index* is a set of pointers (called *record IDs,* or RIDs if you are really into DB2 lingo) that make it easy for DB2 to find data in a table. A table can have more than one index, and each index duplicates some of the data in the table. Indexes provide more efficient access to rows in a table by creating a direct path to the data through special pointers. DB2 generates *index key* values based on the index definition that you provide when you create the index (we describe this process in Chapter 11). While data records are stored in the database in no particular order, index key values are stored in the order specified by the index definition (for example, you can have an index in ascending or descending order). When creating an index, you must provide an index name, specify the table on which the index is to be created, and list the columns that will be part of the index key in the order that you want them to be processed.

If you run a particular query a lot, and if you have set up the query to return sorted data, consider defining an index by using the columns that are part of your query. Your query will run faster.

Instance

An *instance* is a unique and complete database manager environment. The instance controls what you can do to data and manages system resources assigned to it. Every instance has its own databases that other instances cannot access. Each instance that you define on your system must be started with a separate `db2start` command or by using the Start option in the Control Center. The default instance that you create when you install DB2 is called `DB2`. Working with a particular instance means that you are *attached* to it. You can create new instances by using the `db2icrt` command (but you cannot use the Control Center to create new instances). By defining different instances, you can keep multiple environments (for example, test and production environments) separate. (For more information on instances, see Chapter 7.)

Don't confuse being attached to an instance with being connected to a database.

Normalization

A part of database design, *normalization* is a defined process of restructuring database tables. The process can result in a table being divided (vertically) into two or more tables. After tables have been normalized, they are said to be in normal form. There are several *normal form* levels, the first three being the most common (these three are described in the bulleted list below). Normalization helps you to avoid data redundancies and inconsistencies, which is a huge advantage of using a relational database system, instead of just storing data in files.

- A table is in *first normal form* if there is only one value at the intersection of each row and column.
- A table is in *second normal form* if each column that is not part of the primary key (that is, a *non-key column*) is dependent upon the entire key (this really applies to tables that have a *composite key*, or a primary key that is made up of two or more columns). If a non-key column is dependent on only part of the primary key, awful things can happen. For example, values in the non-key column may get repeated in several rows. If those values get updated, then every occurrence must be updated. Otherwise, the table data becomes inconsistent.
- A table is in *third normal form* if each non-key column is independent of other non-key columns, and is dependent only on the primary key. You don't want one or more columns to be dependent on another column, which is not the primary key for the table. Again, values in the dependent non-key columns may get repeated in several rows. And if those values get updated, then every occurrence must be updated. Otherwise, the table data becomes inconsistent.

Primary Key

Each table can have only one *primary key*. A primary key is a column or a combination of columns that uniquely identifies a row in a table. DB2 creates a unique index on the primary key that enforces the uniqueness of primary key values. This index makes finding rows that match specific primary key values much faster. You can define primary keys, which are optional, when a table is created or altered.

Even though a primary key is optional, database tables cannot have duplicate rows.

Referential Integrity

DB2 uses rules, called *referential integrity constraints* (or *RI constraints* in DB2-speak), to ensure that there are no orphans in dependent tables. Without these rules, the links between two related tables may become broken, and the integrity of the data may be undermined. When a database has referential integrity, it means that all values in a column of some table (the child or dependent table) also exist in a column of another table (the parent table). You can use a foreign key — a column or a set of columns in a table that refer to a unique key or the primary key of another table — to establish a relationship with a unique key (usually the primary key) to enforce referential integrity among tables.

You cannot *insert* a row into a dependent table unless there is a row in the parent table with a primary key value equal to the foreign key value of the row that is being inserted. When you *delete* a row from a parent table, DB2 checks if there are any dependent rows in dependent tables with matching foreign key values. When you *update* a foreign key in a dependent table, the foreign key value must match some value of the primary key for the parent table of the relationship.

Relational Database

A *relational database* presents data as a collection of tables, which is a great way to store data when you want answers to complex questions pertaining to that data. Database tables are a representation of things (called *entities*) and their relationship to one another. For example, two tables comprising a relational database may be linked through a column that is identical in both tables; in one table, the column serves as the primary key column, and in the other table, it is a foreign key column.

Roll-Forward Recovery

Roll-forward recovery is the second part of what is essentially a two-part recovery process that you can perform when a disaster occurs. The first part is a database restore operation. If a database becomes unusable, the only way to recover what was lost is to restore the database from your most recent backup copy. After you restore the backup copy, you can use the database logs, which record all changes made to a database, to reapply (or roll forward through) the transactions that occurred between the time of the backup and the crash. For more information, see Chapter 13.

View

A *view* is a temporary table containing columns from one or more database tables. A view can include all or some of the columns or rows contained in the tables on which it is based. A view is an efficient way of representing data that requires no permanent storage. Views are particularly useful for restricting access to certain table columns or rows. A user can be authorized to access only those views that contain data the user is permitted to see. For more information, see Chapter 11.

Chapter 18

Ten Amazing DB2 (and DB2-related) Products

In This Chapter

- DataJoiner
- DB2 Enterprise ExtendedEdition
- DB2 Everyplace
- DB2 Extenders
- DB2 Satellite Edition
- Net.Data
- OLAP
- The Stored Procedure Builder
- Warehouse Manager
- WebSphere Application Server

This chapter briefly discusses add-ons to DB2 that you can use for different kinds of business applications. All products are manufactured by IBM, and we've included the URL to each product's home page.

DataJoiner

In today's world of different kinds of software, it's very likely that you have different relational databases installed on your computer or in your business. In DB2-speak, this is called a *heterogeneous environment.* For example, you may have DB2 and Microsoft SQL Server installed, but you need to perform a query that will access both databases and then return the results based on a certain condition. DataJoiner allows you to view data from different sources (and different vendors!) as if they were local to you. With a single SQL statement, you can access and join tables located across multiple sources of data. The best part about DataJoiner is that you only need to know DB2's SQL and APIs. The DB2 optimizer will migrate and optimize your SQL statement that runs against the other vendor's database. Now *that* is amazing!

For more information on DataJoiner, see the following Web site:

```
www-4.ibm.com/software/data/datajoiner/
```

DB2 Enterprise-Extended Edition

DB2 Enterprise-Extended Edition, which we briefly mention in Chapter 1, enables you to partition data on multiple machines. By partitioning, or splitting up, your database into parts and running operations such as selects, updates, imports, and loads simultaneously on each part, you are using the additional processing power and extra storage of multiple machines. For example, assume that you have partitioned your database on ten machines (or partitions) and you have 10,000,000 rows to load into a table. You can load 1,000,000 rows into each partition and have them all running simultaneously, which should be ten times faster than loading 10,000,000 rows on a single machine. Partitioning a database is a key component in business intelligence (sometimes referred to as BI) applications.

Business intelligence applications are programs that can look at large amounts of information about sales, customers, and so on, and determine how best to market a particular product in a particular region. DB2 Enterprise-Extended Edition lets you effectively build and manage these large amounts of information (large databases are often called *data warehouses* or *data marts*).

For information on getting DB2 Enterprise-Extended Edition, check out the following Web site:

```
www-4.ibm.com/software/data/db2/udb/devl_ed.html#db2eee
```

DB2 Everyplace

DB2 Everyplace is a tiny version of DB2 that lets you store relational data on a hand-held device. DB2 Everyplace can run on the Palm OS 3.0 or later, Windows CE 2.0, EPOC Operating System, and the QNX Neutrino-based hand-held devices. Just as you can synchronize your e-mail on these devices, you can also synchronize data from other DB2 sources, such as DB2 versions for Unix, OS/2, Windows NT/2000, OS/390, and DB2/400.

DB2 Everyplace is available for free download at the following Web site:

```
www-4.ibm.com/software/data/db2/everywhere/downloads.html
```

DB2 Extenders

DB2 Extenders enable DB2 to deliver images, video, audio, and text documents as if they were ordinary text-based data. For any multimedia data that you have, you can insert the data, query it, and manage it the same way that you manage any data in your DB2 database.

Because to DB2 multimedia data is just bits and bytes, DB2 Extenders are programs sitting on top of DB2 that know how to interpret the bits and bytes. For example, if an MP3 file is stored in a table, accessing the MP3 file through a DB2 Extender will invoke your MP3 player so that you can listen to the file.

You can bring any of these data types together in one SQL query and manipulate them with built-in functions. These functions include importing and exporting objects into and out of a database. DB2 Extenders enable you to browse or play objects retrieved from the database. You can also search for documents in a variety of ways, such as by a specific word, similar-sounding word, synonym, or variation of a word.

Other vendors write extenders for DB2. For example, ESRI created a Spatial Extender that you can use to model real world objects (rivers, parks, highways, etc.). This allows you to perform BI operations on spatial data types.

You can find more information about DB2 Extenders and the non-IBM Extenders from the following URL:

```
http://www-4.ibm.com/software/data/db2/extenders/
```

DB2 Satellite Edition

DB2 Satellite Edition, which we briefly mention in Chapter 1, enables mobile laptop users to connect to a main database. Mobile users can use DB2 Satellite Edition to connect to the database, get the information they need, and download it to their laptop computers.

DB2 Satellite Edition also offers a central location for keeping track of all satellite activity — who's connecting from where and what information they're gathering: a great plus for the people that have to administrate them!

For more information on Satellite DB2 Edition, check out the following URL:

```
http://www-4.ibm.com/software/data/db2/udb/devl_ed.html#db2se
```

Net.Data

Net.Data (which comes with DB2) can be an add-on to your DB2 installation. Net.Data helps you build applications that can access Internet and intranet data that is managed by DB2.

Net.Data provides full support for Java and XML. Because most Internet applications are built in Java, you can use Java applets to visually represent data, validate data entered by Web users, and do cool things, such as build an application that queries DB2 data and then represents it as a chart on a Web page.

For more information on Net.Data, including how to get it, check out the following Web page:

```
http://www-4.ibm.com/software/data/net.data/
```

OLAP

OLAP stands for *Online Analytical Processing*. OLAP is another branch of business intelligence in which large amounts of information are processed in different ways. The DB2 OLAP Server performs fast multidimensional analysis of large amounts of data. It works with a set of built-in financial, mathematical, and statistical functions to answer important business questions.

For more information on DB2 OLAP Server, check out the following Web site:

```
www-4.ibm.com/software/data/db2/db2olap
```

The Stored Procedure Builder

A *stored procedure* is a program or series of steps that is stored on a file system on the database server. When running a stored procedure, a client basically says, "run stored procedure" to the server. Because the steps of the stored procedure are stored in the database, no further communication is necessary between the client and server until the results of the stored procedure are returned to the client (for example, three rows from a table that satisfy certain conditions). This saves overhead costs of passing SQL requests back and forth between client and server that would occur in a regular application, such as a C program. So, when different clients are running applications to the server, all they have to do is say, "run stored procedure."

The Stored Procedure Builder (or SPB in DB2-speak), which is installed when you install DB2, is a graphical tool that enables you to quickly build stored procedures. You can build stored procedures on local and remote DB2 servers and test and debug already installed procedures.

For more information on this tool, refer to the *DB2 Application Development Guide*. This guide is part of the documentation that is installed with DB2.

Warehouse Manager

The process called *building a data warehouse* refers to the coordinated copying of data from sources both inside and outside a business into a location (such as DB2!) that is conducive to performing analysis on the data and to processing the data. Building a data warehouse (a large database) is a difficult, multi-step process.

You can use Warehouse Manager to build even the most complex data warehouse. Warehouse Manager helps you define relationships between your warehouse and data that is going to be stored. Warehouse Manager also deploys information over the Internet, works to transform or cleanse data extracted from other systems so that it can be properly loaded into the data warehouse, and implements a strategy to move data from many sources into the data warehouse.

For more information on Warehouse Manager, check out the following Web site:

```
www-4.ibm.com/software/data/vw
```

WebSphere Application Server

Because e-business is thriving, everyone is thinking of ways to expand their e-presence and succeed in the global marketplace. IBM WebSphere Application Server sits on top of DB2, or on its own, and provides tools to build an e-commerce site.

For more information on WebSphere Application Server, check out the following URL:

```
www-4.ibm.com/software/webservers/appserv
```

Chapter 19

Ten (Plus One) Sources of DB2 Information

In This Chapter

- *DB2 Answers!* by Richard
- *DB2 High Performance Design and Tuning*
- *DB2 Magazine*
- DB2 performance journal
- DB2 product documentation
- DB2 product family Web page
- DB2 support Web page
- DB2 technical conference
- The database you have in mind
- IDUG user group
- Internet newsgroups

Outlined below are some quick ways to get more information on DB2 Universal Database, with sources ranging from technical books and magazines to newsgroups and Web sites that give insight to other users' experiences with DB2.

DB2 Answers!

by Richard Yevich, Susan Lawson, Klass Brant, and Sheryl Larsen

This book is contains a whole bunch of DB2 answers regarding all kinds of service questions; it's a definite FAQ resource for the rest of us.

DB2 High Performance Design and Tuning

by Richard Yevich and Susan Lawson

This books teaches you more than you will ever need to know about tuning performance for an IBM DB2 database with expert tuning techniques. It's an all-in-one, start-to-finish guide to maximizing DB2 performance — definitely reserved for the governors of geekdom.

DB2 Magazine (CMP Media)

DB2 Magazine is a quarterly publication that contains user-driven articles written by DB2 experts. The material is always practical and the topics timely. *DB2 Magazine* targets database administrators, analysts, and programmers, and covers topics for all DB2 platforms.

Check out the Web site, `www.db2mag.com`, for a free subscription.

DB2 Performance Journal

Yevich, Lawson and Associates, Inc. (`www.ylassoc.com`) is a firm specializing in all areas of database performance. Its consultants are some of the most notable in the industry, in terms of experience and depth of knowledge. They have a performance journal that is read by thousands around the world.

DB2 Product Documentation

DB2 comes with extensive product documentation. DB2 UDB Workgroup Edition V6.1 for NT includes the following manuals in HTML format:

- *Universal Database for Windows NT Quick Beginnings*
- *Connectivity Supplement*
- *Installation and Configuration Supplement*
- *SQL Getting Started*
- *DB2 Administration Guide*
- *Replication Guide and Reference*

- *System Monitor Guide and Reference*
- *SQL Reference*
- *Command Reference*
- *Data Movement Utilities Guide and Reference*
- *Message Reference*
- *Troubleshooting Guide*
- *Glossary*
- *What's New*
- *APPC/CPIC/SNS Sense Codes*

We highly recommend the *DB2 Administration Guide*, but it does get quite technical. You can use the rest of the manuals for reference, or search online for specific information.

DB2 Product Family Web Page

The DB2 product Web site keeps you informed about new versions and FixPaks, offers free demo downloads, and describes how some companies are using DB2:

```
www.ibm.com/software/data/db2/
```

DB2 Support Web Page

The DB2 Support Web page details how to get DB2 support, including electronic support, and how to reference the online technical library:

```
www-4.ibm.com/software/data/db2/db2tech/indexhlp.html
```

DB2 Technical Conference

Every year IBM sponsors a DB2 technical conference for vendors and users. The conference boasts that it lets you "thoroughly examine advances across the entire family of DB2 products and discover faster, more efficient, and cost-effective ways to access data, manage it, and share it with anyone, anywhere in the world."

Check out www-3.ibm.com/services/learning/conf/db2/ for more information. IBM often makes the presentations available on the Web as well. Watch out, though, this stuff gets pretty technical!

The Database You Have in Mind

At www.ibm.com/software/data/inmind/ you find articles that explore different ways that DB2 can transform your business. The site includes articles on e-business success, using mission critical databases, and DB2 performance achievements.

IDUG User Group

IDUG is the International DB2 Users Group. IDUG defines itself as "an independent, not-for-profit, user-run organization whose mission is to support and strengthen the information systems community by providing the highest quality education and services designed to promote the effective utilization of the DB2 family of products."

IDUG's Web site, www.idug.org/, has a wealth of useful information, ranging from upcoming conferences and discussion forums to links to other DB2 resources. The site offers user group memberships and provides links to regional user groups and their activities.

You can also find local chapters of IDUG listed at:

```
http://dir.yahoo.com/computers_and_internet/software/databases/
          db2/user_groups/
```

Internet Newsgroups

Check out the following newsgroups, where DB2 users discuss their experiences with IBM DB2 products:

- bit.listserv.db2-l
- comp.databases.ibm-db2

Chapter 20

Ten Common Mistakes

In This Chapter

- What's going on with the install?
- Installing on a removable drive
- Getting clients to talk to servers
- Working with the Control Center
- Backing up using file system backups
- Migrating across platforms
- Specifying objects
- Full of it
- Don't touch that file!
- Creating a table not logged initially

This chapter covers common errors that users make when using DB2. Reading this chapter may help you to avoid making those same mistakes. We discuss errors encountered during installation or during setup of client server communications, as well as general database administration errors.

What's Going On with the Install?

You may find yourself running along, installing merrily, with the files being copied from CD to your hard drive . . . and then, all of a sudden, it stops, you receive an error, and can't seem to proceed. This is a common problem that usually happens if you are running an antivirus program. The best thing to do is to shut down all programs and any unnecessary services that are running, and then proceed with the install.

Installing on a Removable Drive

Laptop computers often include a removable drive. A common mistake that people make is to install DB2 on this removable drive. You will encounter an error if you attempt to install DB2 to a removable hard drive. DB2 cannot dynamically determine the location of installed code if the drive label is permitted to change. So, if today your removable drive is C:\ and you install DB2 on it, but tomorrow you play around with your hard drive and now the removable drive where you installed DB2 is D:\, you will no longer be able to use DB2. Remember to always install DB2 on a fixed drive on your computer.

Getting Clients to Talk to Servers

Yes, usually getting clients to talk to servers and vice versa is easy. You may, however, stumble upon a problem at some point and not know how to proceed. Here's the most common problem that we see: When working from a client and trying to connect to a remote server, you may get an SQL30081 message. SQL300081 is a communication error explaining that the client cannot communicate with the server.

A common problem is that the TCP/IP Service Name in the database manager configuration on the server is not set. Take a look at the database manager configuration through the Control Center and make sure that this value is set. Remember to do this on the server and not the client! Figure 20-1 shows that this value appears on the Communications tab in the Configure Instance dialog box.

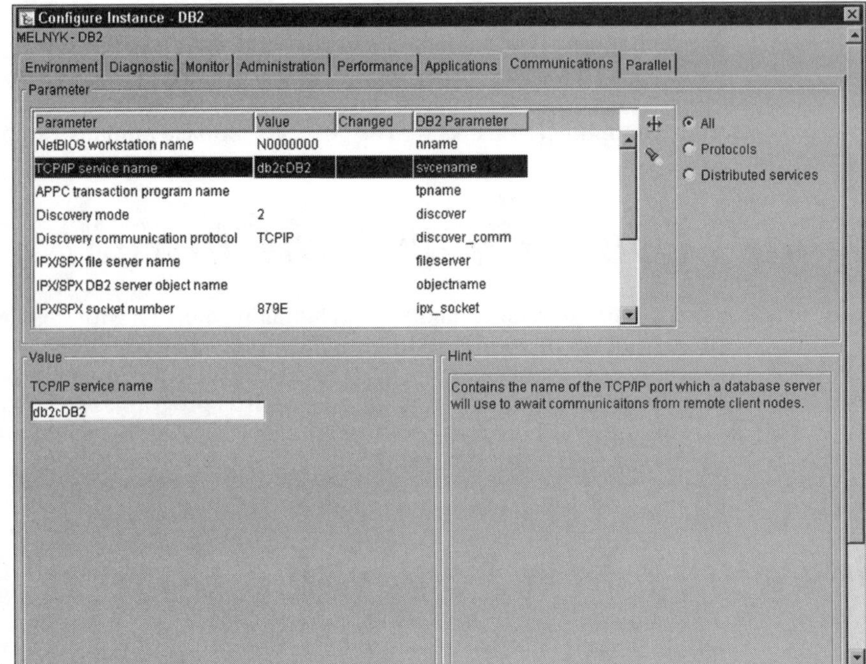

Figure 20-1: Checking that the TCP/IP service name is properly set.

So, as the Hint box in Figure 20-1 indicates, the parameter named TCP/IP Service Name must contain the name of the TCP/IP port that a database server uses to listen for communications from remote clients.

Working with the Control Center

You may see an error similar to the following when you bring up the Control Center:

```
CLI0618E: Userid and/or password invalid.
```

The problem is that as of DB2 Version 6.1, GA (GA means *general availability*), the Control Center does not run with IBM's JDBC 2.0 drivers, and those are the ones that are being loaded when the Control Center starts. To get around this problem, you must revert to JDBC 1.0 by running the following executable:

```
C:\sqllib\java12\usejdbc1
```

Backing Up Using File System Backups

A common misconception is that you can perform a file system backup of your database. Some users believe that if they back up all their table spaces and file systems where a DB2 database resides, then they have a valid database backup. Unfortunately, this is not true. You should never rely on being able to restore a file system backup and being able to use your database after that. Always use the DB2 `backup` and `restore` utilities to properly back up a DB2 database (see Chapter 13).

Migration across Platforms

Some people believe that they can back up a database on NT and then restore from that same backup image onto Linux, AIX, or any other operating system on which DB2 runs. This is often referred to as migrating a database across different operating system backups. DB2, however, does not permit this operation. You cannot take a database backup from one operating system and restore it on another. The proper way to migrate across platforms is to export all the data from the source platform, and then load the data on the target platform.

Specifying Objects

Sometimes, you create a table that includes both upper- and lowercase characters. For example:

```
db2 create table DB2ADMIN.NewMovies (Movie_ID integer,Title
          varchar(30), YearReleased integer)
DB20000I  The SQL command completed successfully.
```

In the Control Center listing of tables, however, you still see the NewMovies table in all uppercase letters.

The best way to create a table with mixed upper- and lowercase characters is through the Control Center, by wrapping your object name with quotation marks.

Full of It

You may run out of space in a table space that is defined as DMS, or in your file system (for table spaces that are SMS), as your database grows. If this happens, you will see either an SQL0289N error (table space full) or an SQL0964 error (file system full). These are very common problems, which is why it's important to plan ahead for database growth. But there is a way out if you do encounter these errors.

If you see a SQL0289N error pointing to a "table space full" problem, you can always add containers to your table space. (Tables spaces are covered in Chapter 9.)

If you want to check your table space, enter the `db2 list tablespaces` command from a DB2 command prompt. You receive output like:

```
Tablespace ID                          = 3
 Name                                   = DMS_TEST
 Type                                   = Database managed space
 Contents                               = Any data
 State                                  = 0x0000
   Detailed explanation:
     Normal
 Total pages                            = 32200
 Useable pages                          = 32000
 Used pages                             = 9600
 Free pages                             = 22400
 High water mark (pages)                = 9600
 Page size (bytes)                      = 4096
 Extent size (pages)                    = 32
 Prefetch size (pages)                  = 16
 Number of containers                   = 1
```

After you add a container to a full table space, DB2 starts a rebalancer that balances the data among all the containers. The most common mistake is when users invoke the `alter table space` command, and then look at the output of the `list tablespaces` command to see how many free pages they have. Well, the rebalancer is good, but not that good! It takes time for the rebalancer to shuffle data around containers. Wait a little a while, and then issue the `list tablespaces` command.

If your disk is full, you must find a way to extend your Windows partition or delete some unneeded files.

Don't Touch That File!

`sqltag.nam` is an important file that DB2 creates containing information about a particular SMS container. Never delete this file.

If you list the files in your database directory by issuing

```
dir C:\<instance_name>
```

where *<instance_name>* is the name of the instance where the database resides, you see more files that you should never delete, including:

- `sqlpcs.1` **and** `sqlpcs.2`**:** These two contain table space definitions and specifications.
- `sqlbp.1` **and** `sqlbp.2`**:** These contain buffer pool definitions and specifications.

Do not delete these files. Nor should you delete any files that you are unsure whether DB2 is using. End of story!

Creating a Table not Logged Initially

When you get into more advanced table creation, you can create a table with the option NOT LOGGED INITIALLY. This means that any initial inserts of data into the table aren't logged. Creating a table with the NOT LOGGED INITIALLY option is useful if you want to insert large amounts of data into a table after creating it, but do not want to log all those inserts.

People don't realize that if they issue the `commit` statement after creating a table, all subsequent actions are logged. The key is to create a table and not commit the transaction. If you are doing this from the DB2 command prompt, simply add `+c` to your command. For example:

```
db2 +c create table DVD_MOVIES (MOVIE_ID INTEGER, TITLE
          VARCHAR(30), YEAR_RELEASED INTEGER) NOT LOGGED
          INITIALLY
```

This command turns off auto_commit, which means that any subsequent inserts aren't logged in the transaction logs until a `commit` statement is issued.

Chapter 21

Ten Darned Nifty DB2 Tricks

In This Chapter

- Tricks in the Control Center
- Using short forms
- Doing fancy stuff with tables
- Doing fancy stuff with data
- Tricks for the road

Here are some tips and tricks so that you can impress the best DB2 whizzes in town! The tricks in this chapter show you how to quickly manipulate output in the Control Center and how to use short forms in DB2 commands. You also see how to quickly copy or rename a table and how to make sure that your queries are running swiftly.

Tricks in the Control Center

Sometimes, the output that you see in the Control Center isn't exactly what you were looking for. You may want to sort the output alphabetically, or perhaps filter out some values. The following tips can help you sort your output to suit your needs.

Sorting output

Control Center output, such as table listings and view listings, doesn't appear in alphabetical order, which can make finding a particular table difficult. But you can sort the output in alphabetical order by clicking a column in the Control Center. For example, an unsorted list of tables can appear in your database, similar to Figure 21-1.

Figure 21-1: An unsorted table listing as it appears in the Control Center.

If you want to sort that output by schema name, simply click the Schema column heading. You can also sort your output in multiple columns. Click the Sort button in the bottom-left corner of the Control Center (the one with the A and Z with two arrows).

Figure 21-2 shows where you can specify the columns in which you want to sort your output.

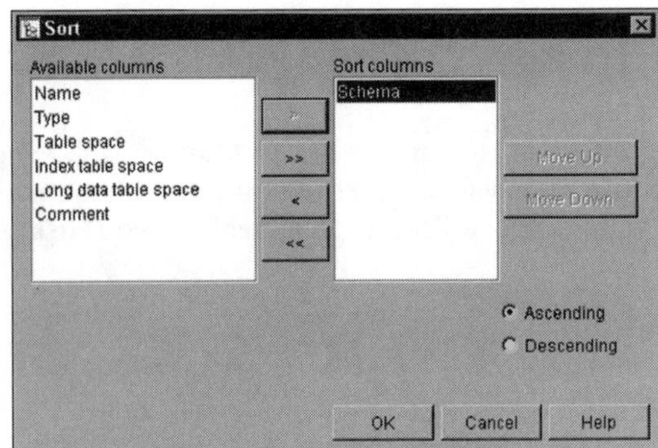

Figure 21-2: The Sort dialog box lets you specify multiple columns from which to sort.

Filtering outputs

You can also filter out things that you don't want the Control Center to show you. Click the Filter button at the bottom of the Control Center (beside the Sort button).

Figure 21-3 shows the Filter dialog box, which enables you to specify what information you want to appear in the Control Center.

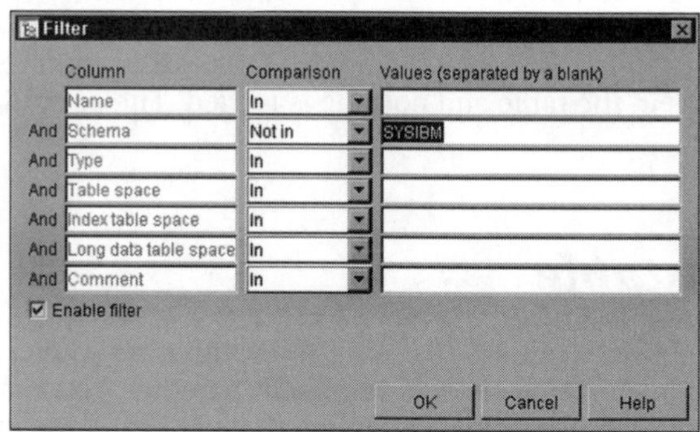

Figure 21-3: The Filter dialog box lets you select values that you want displayed in the Control Center output.

Using Short Forms

You can use short forms to run commands from the DB2 command prompt. For example: `database manager` is shortened to `dbm`; `database` is shortened to `db`; and `configuration` is shortened to `cfg`.

So, when you want to look at the database manager configuration, you don't have to type

```
db2 get database manager configuration
```

Instead, you can type

```
db2 get dbm cfg
```

Doing Fancy Stuff with Tables

You can quickly delete values from a table, copy a table, and rename a table. The tips below show you how to do these operations.

Deleting from a large table

You may one day decide to delete all the values in a table. But when you issue the SQL `delete` statement, the deletion of each row is logged in the transaction logs. This can take a long time for a big table. You can get around this by using the `load` utility. Simply load your table with an empty file. This deletes all the rows in the table and nothing is logged. The operation is instantaneous.

Copying a table

The easiest way to copy a table is to create a new table and then run an SQL `insert` statement and an SQL `select` statement together. You run the `insert` statement in the new table while selecting data from the old. Suppose that you want to copy the MOVIE table to an OLD_MOVIE table. Create the OLD_MOVIE table with the same column definitions as the MOVIE table, and at the DB2 command prompt, type:

```
db2 insert into DB2ADMIN.OLD_MOVIE select * from
         DB2ADMIN.MOVIE
```

This selects all the rows from the DB2ADMIN.MOVIE table and inserts them into DB2ADMIN.OLD_MOVIE.

Renaming a table

Renaming a table is simple. If you want to rename the table MOVIE to DVD, simply type the following in a DB2 command prompt:

```
db2 rename table DB2ADMIN.MOVIE to DB2ADMIN.DVD
```

After you rename a table, all the indexes are moved to point to the new table name.

Doing Fancy Stuff with Data

You may want to convert the data in a DB2 database into different forms. DB2 lets you do this by using functions. The next tip explains this in more detail. If you sometimes forget table definitions, the subsequent tip shows you how to quickly look them up.

Getting data in the correct form

Say you have a character column from which you want an integer, or a date column from which you only need the year. DB2 includes many built-in functions that let you select data in the form you need. For example, if you want to select only the year from a DATE type column, you can type the following in a DB2 command prompt:

```
db2 select year(birthdate)from birthdays where name='mom'
```

This statement selects only the year in which your mom was born from the BIRTHDAYS table. Check the *DB2 SQL Reference* for more functions that you can use.

Forgetting the columns in your table

If you forget what columns are in your table and you need to select from it, you can use the `describe` command. The following is an example using the MOVIE table:

```
C:\>db2 describe select * from db2admin.movie
SQLDA Information
 sqldaid : SQLDA     sqldabc: 896  sqln: 20  sqld: 3
 Column Information
 sqltype             sqllen  sqlname.data      sqlname.length
 ------------------- ------  ------------------------------
 497   INTEGER            4  MOVIE_ID                     8
 449   VARCHAR           30  TITLE                        5
 497   INTEGER            4  YR_RELEASED                 11
```

The `describe` command lets you see the column names, types, and lengths.

Tricks for the Road

Following are a couple of things that we think you should keep in mind as you journey down the long and winding DB2 road: Happy trails!

Running fast queries

We recommend that you schedule regular `runstats` and `reorg` operations on your big tables. This ensures that your queries always perform at their best.

Ensuring that your backups work

Test your backups at least once a month. You have no reason to create backups if you are unable to restore from them when needed. Suppose that you run into a disaster recovery scenario — you have to restore your database, but you discover that all the backups are written to bad tapes! All your data is lost. Remember to test the backup images occasionally to ensure that they work.

Appendix

About the CD

On the CD-ROM

- DB2 Universal Database Workgroup Edition, Version 6.1
- Administration Client
- Software Developer's Kit (SDK)
- Installation books in HTML format for online viewing directly from this CD-ROM
- Installation notes containing information that became available after the installation books were completed

The *DB2 For Windows For Dummies* CD contains a trial version of DB2 Universal Database Workgroup Edition, Version 6.1 for Windows NT/2000. The software is fully functional, but becomes disabled after 60 days. The CD also contains some sample files from the book that will make it easier for you to try some of the examples.

This appendix describes what's on the CD, how to install DB2, and what you need to run it.

System Requirements

Make sure your computer meets the minimum system requirements listed below. If your computer doesn't match up to most of these requirements, you may have problems in using the contents of the CD.

- A PC with an Intel-based 486 (or faster) processor.
- Microsoft Windows NT 4.0 with Service Pack 3 or later.
- At least 32MB of total RAM installed on your computer. For best performance, we recommend at least 64MB of RAM installed.

- At least 65MB of hard drive space available to install all the software from this CD. This amount of space will not be sufficient to install all the DB2 tools and to perform all the tasks that are referenced throughout this book. We recommend that you have at least 200MB of free disk space.
- A CD-ROM drive.

If you need more information on the basics, check out *PCs For Dummies,* 7th Edition, by Dan Gookin (published by IDG Books Worldwide, Inc.) .

Using the CD

To install DB2 Universal Database Workgroup Edition, Version 6.1 from the CD that comes with this book, insert the CD into your computer's CD-ROM drive and let the installation program walk you through the process of setting up your new software. When you insert the CD-ROM, the auto-run feature automatically starts the installation program for DB2 server. Even if the CD-ROM is in the drive, when you double-click on the icon for the CD-ROM drive, the CD should auto-run before looking at the drive's contents.

After you install DB2, you can eject the CD. Carefully place it back in the plastic jacket of the book for safekeeping.

If, after installing DB2, you want to copy the sample files, insert the CD into your computer's CD-ROM drive. After the installation program starts, a message window appears, telling you that DB2 is already installed on your system. Click Cancel. You can now copy the files to your hard drive.

What You Find

- **DB2 Universal Database Workgroup Edition, Version 6.1**, from International Business Machines Corporation. The CD that comes with this book offers a "try and buy" version of DB2 — it is fully functional, but becomes disabled after 60 days. You can find out more at the Web site, `www.ibm.com/software/data/db2/`.

  To install DB2 Universal Database Workgroup Edition, Version 6.1 for Windows NT/2000, insert the CD into your computer's CD-ROM drive and let the program's installer walk you through the process of setting up your new software.

- **Sample files from the book,** by the authors. These files contain sample code from the book. You can browse the files directly from the CD, or you can copy them to your hard drive and use them as the basis for your own projects. To find the files on the CD, open the `WorkDir` folder. To copy the files to your hard drive in Windows, drag the `WorkDir` folder and drop it on your drive icon. A file called `readme.txt` in the `WorkDir` folder describes the files and how to use them.

If You've Got Problems (Of the CD Kind)

We tried our best to create examples that work on most computers with the minimum system requirements. Alas, your computer may differ, and some programs may not work properly for some reason.

The two likeliest problems are that you don't have enough memory (RAM) for the programs you want to use, or you have other programs running that are affecting installation or running of a program. If you get error messages like `Not enough memory` or `Setup cannot continue`, try one or more of these methods and then try using the software again:

- **Turn off any antivirus software that you have on your computer.** Installers sometimes mimic virus activity and may make your computer incorrectly believe that it's being infected by a virus.
- **Close all running programs.** The more programs you're running, the less memory is available to other programs. Installers also typically update files and programs. So if you keep other programs running, installation may not work properly.
- **Have your local computer store add more RAM to your computer.** This is, admittedly, a drastic and somewhat expensive step. But adding more memory can really help the speed of your computer and allow more programs to run at the same time. If you add more RAM to your computer, you should ensure that the amount of 'paging space' is equal to the amount of RAM on your system. Paging space is virtual RAM that your computer uses instead of the physical RAM; it helps computers run faster. Contact your administrator for more information, or refer to *Windows NT 4 For Dummies* by Andy Rathbone and Sharon Crawford (published by IDG Books Worldwide).

If you still have trouble with installing the items from the CD, please call the IDG Books Worldwide Customer Service phone number: 800-762-2974 (outside the U.S.: 317-572-3342).

Index

• A •

• B •

• C •

• D •

• E •

• J •

• K •

• L •

• Q •

• R •

• S •

• T •

Notes

Notes

Notes

Notes

Notes

Notes

Notes

IDG Books Worldwide, Inc., End-User License Agreement

READ THIS. You should carefully read these terms and conditions before opening the software packet(s) included with this book ("Book"). This is a license agreement ("Agreement") between you and IDG Books Worldwide, Inc. ("IDGB"). By opening the accompanying software packet(s), you acknowledge that you have read and accept the following terms and conditions. If you do not agree and do not want to be bound by such terms and conditions, promptly return the Book and the unopened software packet(s) to the place you obtained them for a full refund.

1. **License Grant.** IDGB grants to you (either an individual or entity) a nonexclusive license to use one copy of the enclosed software program(s) (collectively, the "Software") solely for your own personal or business purposes on a single computer (whether a standard computer or a workstation component of a multiuser network). The Software is in use on a computer when it is loaded into temporary memory (RAM) or installed into permanent memory (hard disk, CD-ROM, or other storage device). IDGB reserves all rights not expressly granted herein.

2. **Ownership.** IDGB is the owner of all right, title, and interest, including copyright, in and to the compilation of the Software recorded on the disk(s) or CD-ROM ("Software Media"). Copyright to the individual programs recorded on the Software Media is owned by the author or other authorized copyright owner of each program. Ownership of the Software and all proprietary rights relating thereto remain with IDGB and its licensers.

3. **Restrictions on Use and Transfer.**

   (a) You may only (i) make one copy of the Software for backup or archival purposes, or (ii) transfer the Software to a single hard disk, provided that you keep the original for backup or archival purposes. You may not (i) rent or lease the Software, (ii) copy or reproduce the Software through a LAN or other network system or through any computer subscriber system or bulletin-board system, or (iii) modify, adapt, or create derivative works based on the Software.

   (b) You may not reverse engineer, decompile, or disassemble the Software. You may transfer the Software and user documentation on a permanent basis, provided that the transferee agrees to accept the terms and conditions of this Agreement and you retain no copies. If the Software is an update or has been updated, any transfer must include the most recent update and all prior versions.

4. **Restrictions on Use of Individual Programs.** You must follow the individual requirements and restrictions detailed for each individual program in About the CD appendix of this Book. These limitations are also contained in the individual license agreements recorded on the Software Media. These limitations may include a requirement that after using the program for a specified period of time, the user must pay a registration fee or discontinue use. By opening the Software packet(s), you will be agreeing to abide by the licenses and restrictions for these individual programs that are detailed in the About the CD appendix and on the Software Media. None of the material on this Software Media or listed in this Book may ever be redistributed, in original or modified form, for commercial purposes.

5. **Limited Warranty.**

   (a) IDGB warrants that the Software and Software Media are free from defects in materials and workmanship under normal use for a period of sixty (60) days from the date of purchase of this Book. If IDGB receives notification within the warranty period of defects in materials or workmanship, IDGB will replace the defective Software Media.

   (b) **IDGB AND THE AUTHOR OF THE BOOK DISCLAIM ALL OTHER WARRANTIES, EXPRESS OR IMPLIED, INCLUDING WITHOUT LIMITATION IMPLIED WARRANTIES OF MERCHANTABILITY AND FITNESS FOR A PARTICULAR PURPOSE, WITH RESPECT TO THE SOFTWARE, THE PROGRAMS, THE SOURCE CODE CONTAINED THEREIN, AND/OR THE TECHNIQUES DESCRIBED IN THIS BOOK. IDGB DOES NOT WARRANT THAT THE FUNCTIONS CONTAINED IN THE SOFTWARE WILL MEET YOUR REQUIREMENTS OR THAT THE OPERATION OF THE SOFTWARE WILL BE ERROR FREE.**

   (c) This limited warranty gives you specific legal rights, and you may have other rights that vary from jurisdiction to jurisdiction.

6. **Remedies.**

   (a) IDGB's entire liability and your exclusive remedy for defects in materials and workmanship shall be limited to replacement of the Software Media, which may be returned to IDGB with a copy of your receipt at the following address: Software Media Fulfillment Department, Attn.: *DB2 For Windows For Dummies*, IDG Books Worldwide, Inc., 10475 Crosspoint Blvd., Indianapolis, IN 46256, or call 800-762-2974. Please allow three to four weeks for delivery. This Limited Warranty is void if failure of the Software Media has resulted from accident, abuse, or misapplication. Any replacement Software Media will be warranted for the remainder of the original warranty period or thirty (30) days, whichever is longer.

   (b) In no event shall IDGB or the author be liable for any damages whatsoever (including without limitation damages for loss of business profits, business interruption, loss of business information, or any other pecuniary loss) arising from the use of or inability to use the Book or the Software, even if IDGB has been advised of the possibility of such damages.

   (c) Because some jurisdictions do not allow the exclusion or limitation of liability for consequential or incidental damages, the above limitation or exclusion may not apply to you.

7. **U.S. Government Restricted Rights.** Use, duplication, or disclosure of the Software by the U.S. Government is subject to restrictions stated in paragraph (c)(1)(ii) of the Rights in Technical Data and Computer Software clause of DFARS 252.227-7013, and in subparagraphs (a) through (d) of the Commercial Computer–Restricted Rights clause at FAR 52.227-19, and in similar clauses in the NASA FAR supplement, when applicable.

8. **General.** This Agreement constitutes the entire understanding of the parties and revokes and supersedes all prior agreements, oral or written, between them and may not be modified or amended except in a writing signed by both parties hereto that specifically refers to this Agreement. This Agreement shall take precedence over any other documents that may be in conflict herewith. If any one or more provisions contained in this Agreement are held by any court or tribunal to be invalid, illegal, or otherwise unenforceable, each and every other provision shall remain in full force and effect.

Installation Instructions

The *DB2 For Windows For Dummies* CD offers valuable information that you won't want to miss. To install the items from the CD to your hard drive, follow these steps.

To install DB2 Universal Database Workgroup Edition, Version 6.1 from the CD that comes with this book, insert the CD into your computer's CD-ROM drive and let the installation program walk you through the process of setting up your new software. When you insert the CD-ROM, the auto-run feature automatically starts the installation program for DB2 server. Even if the CD-ROM is in the drive, when you double-click on the icon for the CD-ROM drive, the CD should auto-run before looking at the drive's contents.

After you install DB2, you can eject the CD. Carefully place it back in the plastic jacket of the book for safekeeping.

If, after installing DB2, you want to copy the sample files, insert the CD into your computer's CD-ROM drive. After the installation program starts, a message window appears, telling you that DB2 is already installed on your system. Click Cancel. You can now copy the files to your hard drive.

For more information, see the "About the CD" appendix.

IDG BOOKS WORLDWIDE BOOK REGISTRATION